Managing for Excellence

Managing for Excellence

A Systematic and Holistic Analysis of the Process of Quality and Productivity Improvement

John Stitt

Quality Press
Milwaukee

Managing for Excellence

John Stitt

Library of Congress Cataloging-in-Publication Data

Stitt, John B.
   Managing for excellence / John B. Stitt.
      p.   cm.
   Includes bibliographical references (p.)
   ISBN 0-87389-064-7
   1. Organizational effectiveness.   2. Excellence.   3. Quality
control.   I. Title.
HD58.9.S75 1990   89-18019
658.4—dc20   CIP

Acquisitions Editor: Jeanine L. Lau
Production Editor: Tammy Griffin
Cover design by Walzak Design. Set in Century Schoolbook by
Carlisle Communications. Printed and bound by Edwards Brothers.

ISBN 0-87389-064-7

Printed in the United States of America

10 9 8 7 6 5 4 3 2 1

Quality Press

American Society for Quality Control

310 West Wisconsin Avenue

Milwaukee, Wisconsin 53203

This book is dedicated to

Bill, Marjorie, Susan, Georgia, Emily, Lee, and Hap.

Table of Contents

List of Figures, Tables, and Forms

Foreword

Quality. What a simple subject. We all know what it is.
After all, we set standards and measure quality almost
every minute of every day of our lives. We measure
quality when we make a phone call, when we talk to a
salesman, when we start our car, when we drive behind
another car, when we erase an error we made. We spend
most of our time measuring, evaluating, and setting
quality standards. We are the quality experts. I have
worked in industry for over 40 years, and I have never
heard a CEO tell his/her team to "go out and see how
much scrap you can make." Have you? So what's all this
talk about quality? The truth is, it's all a matter of
degree. You and I, the customers of the world, have, and
continue to, set high minimum acceptable standards for
the products and services we are supplied.

Simple quality systems run by quality assurance
were effective when the customer expected to bring back
his/her car to the dealer two weeks after it was
purchased to have a long list of problems fixed. This was
accepted by the dealer and the customer as just the first
step in the final inspection operation. A percent
defective mentality was acceptable under these
circumstances. This is no longer the case. Today, we are
faced with customers who think in the parts-per-million
range. In the 1990s, they will be thinking parts per
billion, and in the twenty-first century, customers will
be expecting perfection (error-free performance).

This new thinking pattern requires a major change
in the simple way we have looked at quality in the past.

It requires a radical change in the way we think, talk, act, and manage. No one person or organization can make the difference. This change must shake the very foundations of our business, government, and educational institutions. It will require every organization to have:

- A clear and common vision.

- Individual ownership of the organization's strategy.

- Total commitment to implementation.

- Continuous training and retraining.

- New measurement systems that measure efficiency and effectiveness.

- Reward systems that reinforce preventive behavior.

This is the model that John Stitt presents to the reader in his book, *Managing for Excellence*. It is not a simple model because quality today is not simple, and it will be even more complex in the twenty-first century. But it is a model we will all need to know and understand if our organizations are going to survive and prosper. John calls this model "Holistic Quality Management—HQM." It does not make a great acronym, but it does make a lot of sense.

We must have a holistic approach to quality management that combines the most effective ways of capturing the creativity of our people, the capability of our tools, and the full utilization of our resources, focusing them on providing output that exceeds customer expectations. The process that drives our business must be dynamic to meet today's business challenges. Only by placing a major portion of our effort on our critical business processes can we keep them in tune with our changing customer needs and expectations. Management's role is to work on improving the processes, not fighting the fires.

The time when we could let quality happen is long since gone. Today, we must manage quality with even more diligence than we manage our assets. A wise man once said, "Quality is best defined as your reputation." That's what this book is all about—managing your reputation. It systematically provides its reader with the new quality philosophy, its impact on people, how to communicate the need for change, how to organize for quality, and how to use some of the key improvement tools.

I like to define the difference between quality and perfection as:

Quality is doing things right every time.
Perfection is doing the right thing right every time.

In this book, John has set the stage for perfection. Mastering the concepts put forth in *Managing for Excellence* could do more to prepare you for doing business in the 1990s than obtaining an MBA from many universities.

H. James Harrington, PhD,
President
Harrington, Hurd & Rieker
July 1989

Acknowledgments

I want to acknowledge the mentoring, guidance, and contributions made by a number of people to the growth, insight, and direction that has ultimately led to this book. I cannot credit any one individual with providing a single great moment when I knew I had to write for others the concepts of Holistic Quality Management. Instead, the nurturing has been a constant pressure over many years. I list them in chronological order.

First, my grandfather, with whom I spent my childhood summers on an Iowa farm, who instilled in me the basic concepts of values. "Money is not as important as the quality of life." "Any job worth doing is worth full effort." And "People are more important than things."

Next, I thank Dr. Henry Webster, previously of Iowa State University, Department of Forestry, for introducing me to the works of Rensis Likert. This was my first exposure to formal works that directed my thoughts about the interaction between business organizations and the people of the organizations.

Third, I acknowledge the constant coaching of my wife, Susan, toward my recognition of my natural, but subdued, bent for excellence in relationship behavior. She also appreciated my skills in engineering and "thing" problem solving.

Next, I must acknowledge the influence of Dr. Gerald Bell of the University of North Carolina Graduate School of Business Administration. His two courses on management and organizational psychology stirred the pot of dissatisfaction within my scripting and extended my knowledge about the theories and techniques of relationship behavior.

The instructors of several seminars during my business career played key roles in my emerging dissatisfaction with the status quo both with myself and with the values and systems of the organization in which I participated. I then stopped expecting others to initiate change and realized that change was my responsibility. I still lacked the personal confidence and conviction to support my values and systems in controversial situations.

Mr. Christian Jensen, in a later seminar, again reinforced that the systems and values solidifying in my mind were worthy and supported my first shaky steps of self-actualization through presentations, writings, and mentoring higher management.

I cannot overstate the impact of meeting and participating in the four-day seminar with Dr. W. Edwards Deming. Again I found support for the direction of my thinking. Listening to Dr. Deming I heard more than statistics. He repeatedly spoke of learning to think through courses in the theory of knowledge. He talked about listening to great men not for the content of their discoveries but to discover how they think. Finally, I saw his love for development of the individual both in his red bead experiments and in the twinkle in his eye as he went into a tyrannical rage to promote dissatisfaction within the person who gives the pat answer to his questions.

I must mention the influence of Dr. Lee Sutter. Change is painful when an individual does not accept change as inevitable. Change and a deterioration of the basis of identity produce crisis. Thinking becomes irrational. My crisis occurred as my self-identity shifted from task orientation to abstract thought and behavior orientation. His guidance and nurturing are deeply appreciated.

Finally, every champion needs a sponsor. Mine was Mr. Gerald West. Jerry listened, critiqued, and endorsed new theories when few others understood. As a vision developed he provided opportunities for me to actualize the theories into applications. Without Jerry's assistance few of the new theories would have had a laboratory for verification.

To all of these people I extend a heartfelt thank you. They have helped write this book.

Introduction

This book is on the nature of excellence. It is not just about statistics. It is about methods of thinking, managing, problem solving, and organizational growth. It is targeted at managers who sense the need to move their organizations toward excellence. It develops and analyzes philosophy, policy, process, and technology. I attempt to explain the reasoning and the process of building an organization driven by comprehensive quality. This book does not focus on numbers or charts. It focuses on information, open minds, knowledge, constructive change, and action. It makes a statement founded on synthesis.

Looking objectively at global economics and accelerating societal change it is suicidal for organizations not to address the broad quality issues and act to maintain competitiveness. In 1932 Peter Drucker stated that the means for civilized man to achieve welfare and happiness focused during the Middle Ages on the development of the Spiritual Man, the Educated Man during the Renaissance, the Economic Man during the Industrial Revolution, and the Heroic Man during the early twentieth century. E. C. Tolman and A. H. Maslow agreed that these foci have failed. Maslow stated that emerging in the twentieth century will be a new focus on developing the Eupsychic (psychologically healthy) Man. The Eupsychic person seeks healthy growth through the hierarchy of basic human needs. He/she is highly and deeply satisfied with self and his/her role in society. This person is mentally healthy.

Evidence of the new focus is abundant to the open mind. *In Search of Excellence, Megatrends, Re-inventing the Corporation,* and *The One Minute Manager* confirm the shift. They state what is happening and what has worked for the new emphasis. The demand expressed through society for quality in the broad sense is a result of the shift of focus by global society.

Organizations can no longer think only of nationalistic and organizational economics. The free world is becoming a world-wide competitive market. Dynamic organizations concentrate on value, growth, health, information, productivity, and growth of the individual toward self-actualization.

Throughout history the great shifts in society have occurred through new thought in a mature society. The mature society would not accept the idea. Instead, a developing society incorporated the revolutionary concept. The old society withered. I believe there is another alternative to this pattern of change. It can be used in the current revolution. If existing organizations are to enter the new era they must break old patterns. They must acknowledge that if they do not flex the organization will slowly die.

Most of our American corporations operate as an established society. Without new knowledge and change at all levels America's slow demise as an economic and technological world leader is inevitable.

These shifts in organizational systems happen easily in crisis. Societies destroyed by war change. Developing organizations do not have to unlearn the old. Stable, ingrained, bureaucratic societies and organizations shift slower. The change is painful. Old institutions and thought patterns are tenacious.

Some American organizations have been forced into statistical process control (SPC), a system of process improvement based on sound statistics and charting that defines appropriate actions for process control. A crisis, decline in competitiveness and vitality in the global marketplace revived the technology developed in our society over 50 years ago. But it was not accepted.

Initial reaction to SPC usually is defensive. Later organizations realize the mandates of change have value. Typically when companies initially implement SPC they experience a burst of problem solving. In time they find making SPC a management and operating philosophy is not simple. Initial training does not last. Old methods are tenacious. Only in highly targeted projects does SPC become routine.

Because of the potential value of SPC, I sought to determine what factors prevented its acceptance and what action would cause acceptance. The non-acceptance of SPC was the tip of an iceberg. No single discipline could address the problem, and the problem is greater than just the acceptance of SPC. SPC alone is not the answer.

This search produced a new philosophy of management, a vision. It incorporates goals and a process for achieving competitiveness in a dynamic environment. I call the total program Holistic Quality Management (HQM). The management method synthesizes philosophy, psychology, organizational sociology, engineering, information systems, and problem-solving techniques. It is based in the thinking of such field experts as Kant, Bacon, Maslow, Berne, Likert, Shewhart, Deming, Juran, Ishikawa, Peck, Naisbitt, Aburdene, Drucker, Shainin, Haskell, Jensen, and others. Yet HQM stands alone. It is unique. This book is a presentation of the theory, the reasoning, the models, and the resulting operating policies that are HQM.

The truly excellent organization is not just concerned about product/service quality. Excellence is the result of concern and attention to quality of "people," "information," and "things." Although quality in people, information, and things, for the sake of simplicity and learning, must be studied independently, all are interrelated and intertwined in a holistic system.

Western man's desire to analyze complex entities produced the Aristotelian "A/not A" system of scientific analysis. To describe an entity we classify elements of the entity as either existing or not existing. To do this we separate the elements from the entity. Abraham Maslow broke with tradition. He posed that interactions between the elements and the environment prevent accurate description of the entity. Separated elements often cannot accurately define the entity. Outside the natural environment the traits of the elements change.

In defining the elements and process for achieving excellence I found a similar situation. The elements of excellence are highly interrelated in a system that can best be described by holistic analysis.

This book is divided into sections. HQM involves a synthesis of many aspects of the organization of corporations, interactions between and within people within and outside the organization, a quest for excellence in information, and a drive for state-of-the-art technology. As with any synthesis, this work amalgamates many different, often seemingly contradictory, ideas and disciplines to eventually arrive at a new unified system. The individual topics are developed separately and eventually synthesized.

First, we will examine a number of esoteric but essential philosophical topics. They are basic to a thorough understanding of the quality problems we now face. These topics are non-specific. A relationship exists between them and quality management, similar to the relationship between basic research, applied research, and manufacturing. Without the knowledge of basic research, applied research has no foundation. Manufacturing is not even conceivable. To fully understand and address the current quest for excellence requires knowledge of the basic concepts.

Second, we review models developed in different disciplines. Each model, incomplete as models must be, gives further insight into the nature of excellence.

A third section reviews the role of people in the process, both as individuals and corporately. *All non-entropic processes are ultimately controlled by people.* Understanding this concept is a prerequisite to an effective quality program. It is rare for hands-on managers to possess sufficient people skills. These are skills that make managers leaders. Yet in the new economy working effectively with people is essential.

Next we cover communications and information systems. Information often does not get to the right person at the right time. Organizations make wrong decisions because the right person did not have critical information. Organizations must promote actionable information for effective decision making.

The next section covers variation: definition of variation, the nature of variation, communication of variation, and appropriate action based on defined variation.

Now emphasis shifts to utilizing synthesized knowledge to develop organizational structure, policy, and procedures—systems that promote excellence. These policies and procedures are the foundation of the excellence-driven organization.

The final section focuses on the review of knowledge and the synthesis of thought. The emphasis here is perpetuated growth. I want the reader to continue the learning, thinking, and synthesis process.

I want managers to think about excellence in a new way. In the United States we are now playing a catch-up game; we must take a leap to again be the front runner.

I state what I believe to be a method, not the only method, but a method that works to drive change, promote excellence, and regain the lead.

The truth and change are sometimes painful. We have developed systems that historically were effective. These systems are no longer appropriate. That realization often hurts.

This book is an instrument outlining in an orderly manner, and, ideally with minimum pain, the changes necessary to enter a new era with a viable, responsible, and mutually beneficial organization.

The Macro Process for Achieving Quality

1

There is a definite, definable process an organization and the people of the organization go through as they strive to improve quality. Being aware of the process and the stage indicators of the process will help the organization and its individuals plan their actions to promote excellence. Different organizations and individuals become conscious of the process and enter the process at different stages, dependent on existing maturity, the level and nature of skills, and the attitude toward change. By defining the process an organization can determine what objectives have been accomplished, what the current pressing objectives are, and what the long-term objectives are. The current position of the organization and the individuals can be assessed by the behavioral traits as well as through fiscal analysis and the level of problem-solving sophistication.

Glenn E. Hayes, in a *Quality Progress* article, "Quality and Productivity: Five Challenges for Management" outlines five stages of the quality quest. These stages also correlate with the management and employee maturity of an organization and the stages of the individual learning process. Both subjects will be discussed later. The stages are as follows:

Stage 1   Quality: An Obstacle Course

- Coercive management
- Little understanding of quality and productivity
- Schedule and cost all-important
- High rework and scrap rates
- Low productivity
- Obsolete equipment

Stage 2   Quality: A State of Turmoil

- Strong use of downward communications
- Fear of error among employees

- Little commitment to quality
- Low workmanship quality
- Ambiguous directions
- High quality costs
- Declining market share

Stage 3   Quality: A Force in Transition

- *Initial development of an organizational value system**
- More knowledge of quality impact
- Stronger commitment to quality
- Efforts to achieve teamwork
- Use of consultants for direction
- Low productivity and high quality costs
- Low profit, but retaining market share

Stage 4   Quality: A Preventative Management Strategy

- *A solidifying organizational wide value system*
- Successful operation of productivity and quality teams
- Emphasis on up-front quality
- Reduction in quality costs
- Continuous improvement
- State of the art equipment and methods
- Strong emphasis on education and training

Stage 5   Quality: A Team Effort

- *A strong organizational value system*
- Open communications up and down the organization
- Gregarious involvement and teamwork
- Strong generic commitment to quality
- More leadership of people-less management of things (high maturity management)
- Long term strategies

---

*Italicized items were added by the author.

- High morale, stable employment
- Systems approach to quality
- Business stability

In the *Quality Progress* article, "The Seven Stages in Company-Wide Quality Control," L. P. Sullivan discusses the stages of the quality process as defined by Karou Ishikawa. These stages parallel Hayes' stages but Ishikawa's stages give more detail about the high end of the process. Perhaps because the Japanese have progressed further in the process they have defined the later stages in more detail. The most progressive Japanese companies have controlled their critical processes. They now search for refined techniques to improve competitiveness. Few American organizations have reached the higher levels. The American focus has not yet turned to the final stages. The seven stages are:

Stage 1 Product Orientation: Inspection after production.

Stage 2 Process Orientation: Quality control during production.

Stage 3 System Orientation: Quality assurance involving all departments.

Stage 4 Humanistic Orientation: To change the thinking of management and employees through education and training.

Stage 5 Society Orientation: Product and process design for more robust function.

Stage 6 Cost Orientation: Stressing minimization of the cost to *society* through use of the Taguchi loss function.

Stage 7 Customer Orientation: Quality function used to define the "voice of the customer" in operational terms.

There is no contradiction between these two attempts to define the process in stages. Both are useful. When examined both reflect the same growth in technology and behaviors. For the most part the U.S. struggle has not passed the third stage as defined by Ishikawa.

Each company, with direction from the highest levels, must analyze the current position of its organization, and develop a time and action plan specific for the organization's movement through the total process. Formalize the plan into a four to seven-year action plan. Be specific, yet flexible. Understand that the organization will change.

Figure 1

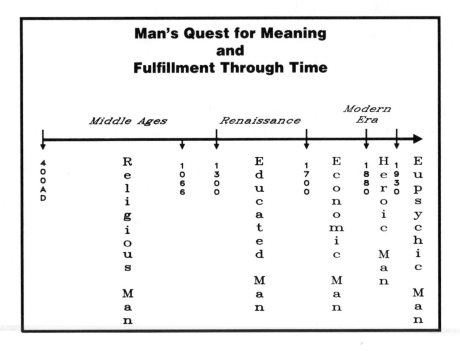

An Attitude of Change

One of the few certainties is change. Change is inevitable. Change is occurring at an accelerating rate. In fact, the rate of change in the twentieth century is so rapid that many individuals cannot function in the resulting environment of uncertainty. That an organization recognizes the need for a program to improve quality is de facto acknowledgment of the inevitability of change. Yet many individuals consider change to be necessary only in others. They don't comprehend the necessity of change in their own modus operandi. Change threatens the rubrics, or problem-handling patterns, each of us has established to simplify our lives. We establish methods of problem solving that we can use with minimal mental anguish. In general, we are all scared to death of change. Most of us are content to continue in our inappropriate rituals and routines instead of facing the uncertainties and admissions of "wrongness" that are inherent in change.

There is a story I am told is true about placing a bullfrog in a pot of water, placing the pot on the stove, and turning on the burner. As the water heats, the frog progressively sinks lower and lower into the water until the frog is cooked alive. The frog does not jump out of the pot. Instead it seeks the safety of a familiar wet environment. We too tend to sink into the water and cook when we decide, even by default, not to take action to address change. The world industrial environment is changing. We can either address and control the change or sink into the false safety of the pot and cook as the world changes.

Our old methods of managing and problem solving are based on outdated empirical information. Simply stated, our old methods of solving problems are often not appropriate for solving our current problems. The statement, "We've always done it this way!" is a key indicator that an individual and/or organization is frightened by change and locked into old patterns of behavior and problem solving.

One way of avoiding change is to attempt to limit one's perception of present reality and to deny the future. This involves keeping employees from comprehending changes in society, an action counter to overall development and growth.

By contrast, the way to *address* change is to increase the maturity of the individuals in the organization, acknowledge reality, and take action directed at taking advantage of change. The result of this strategy will be that threat and change will not block comprehension, growth, and action. The first way is centralized and autocratic. The second way shows high maturity and is Eupsychic. The second way mentors individuals who are scared of change to be self-sufficient. This way is in-line with the progress of society.

What Is Quality?

Undefined terms communicate very little information, cause great confusion, and cloud a vision of accomplishment. We all want "quality." But what *is* quality? What are the factors that determine the ultimate user's perception of quality? We cannot tell managers, employees and suppliers to make a quality product when we have no common understanding of the ambiguous term "quality." Do we mean conformance, engineered, or perceived quality? Is quality high production volume? Is quality high profitability? Conformance quality is the minimization of property variation. Engineered quality is the maximization of a desirable property. Perceived quality is providing maximum fulfillment of customer needs. When we talk about improving quality we must clarify and communicate the desired result.

Industrial customers respond favorably to an acceptable level of engineered quality and a high level of conformance quality. My experience verifies that industrial customers expect minimum variation while they often, but not always, can adjust their operations and engineering to the inherent engineered quality of a product or process.

Retail customers expect high conformance quality and a maximization of utility (cost/benefit ratio) in engineered quality. In each situation the ability to meet the customer requirements is a determinant of perceived quality. We now have more information about quality but still have not defined the single term "quality." As a first-pass definition, *quality is profitably, promptly and consistently providing the "customer" with the goods and/or services that meet his/her needs.*

Customers, Purchasers, and Suppliers

Throughout this book I will discuss customers, purchasers, and suppliers. A "customer" is any person who is affected by the actions of another person or process. Customers are both internal and external. Customers include any employee who is affected by the actions of another employee, manager, or process. They include individuals of a company purchasing goods and/or services, and individuals within the community affected by the organization.

A purchaser is any person or organization who has entered into a contract agreement with a supplier for goods and/or services in return for compensation. All purchasers are customers; not all customers are purchasers.

A supplier is any individual or organization who provides a product or service to another individual or organization, either contractual or not contractual. Not all goods or services from a contractual supplier are billed; yet the quality of both the contractual goods and/or services and the non-contractual goods and services determine the customer's perception of excellence.

The Search for the Source

When we experience a problem, what we first identify is the result or *effect* of a *direct cause,* and the *direct cause* is the result of a *root cause.* We cannot effectively take corrective action on an *effect.* For example, corporate management mandating that the cost of quality be reduced will not reduce the cost of quality no matter how authoritative the directive. In like manner, action on the *direct cause* may temporarily correct an *effect.* Almost always the *effect* will resurface. Effective long-term action can only be taken on a *root cause. The* root cause *is a glitch in the management system that allows the* direct cause *to occur.*

For example, if a customer complains of unacceptable thickness variation in a paper product, an *effect*–targeted directive may be "Control the thickness!" We may learn that variation in the ratio of fiber to water (stock consistency) going to the forming machine caused the thickness variation. If we act on the *direct cause,* the directive to the operator is "keep the consistency the same!" The real source of the problem, the *root cause,* may be due to improper management of pulper loading, improper specifications, ineffective communication of procedures to the operator, insufficient training, or improperly maintained or designed equipment. W. Edwards Deming has stated that approximately 85 percent of the *root causes* of *effects* are problems of the system. *The correction of the root cause is the responsibility of management.*

To make the progressive steps from *effect* to *direct cause,* then to *root cause,* one must have accurate information about what has happened in the "system." There are numerous techniques for obtaining this information. Some involve complex statistics. Some are as simple as asking open-ended questions of

Figure 2

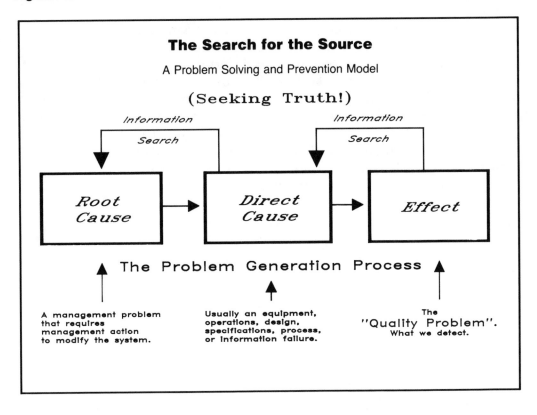

The Search for the Source

A Problem Solving and Prevention Model

(Seeking Truth!)

Information   *Information*

Search   *Search*

| *Root Cause* | → | *Direct Cause* | → | *Effect* |

The Problem Generation Process

A management problem that requires management action to modify the system.

Usually an equipment, operations, design, specifications, process, or information failure.

The "Quality Problem". What we detect.

others: *who, what, when, where,* and asking yourself *why.* All invoke the discipline of an open mind.

There are two steps in this model where assembly of information is necessary. The first progressive information search is from *effect* to *direct cause.* Information assembly in this step relies heavily on technical skills, process knowledge, statistical problem solving techniques and questioning. The second information assembly, from *direct cause* to *root cause,* relies heavily on people skills. Skill in motivational analysis, knowledge of the management process, understanding of the interaction between people, and philosophical skills in seeking the truth are utilized. The *root cause* problems are the 85 percent of the problems that are management's responsibility, which previously have not been adequately addressed.

If the *effect* is to be permanently eliminated, both scientific skills and humanitarian skills must be utilized in the information search. A synthesis of methods of thinking that many readers may initially believe contradictory is needed. The understanding of, and the solutions for, the *root cause* will only be as good as the quality of the information we gather as we make each search. An unquenchable thirst for truth and an open mind are absolutely necessary. If the information obtained is not true we will not formulate valid solutions.

Blind acceptance of a "belief" can ruin an otherwise procedurally correct *root cause* analysis.

I used a production problem as an example of the interrelatedness of *effect, direct cause,* and *root cause* but other effects are reduction in net income, decline in sales volume, unacceptable transportation or delivery of product, dissatisfaction with goods and/or services by a purchaser, or a person's ineffectiveness in carrying out assigned responsibilities. Throughout my quest for developing a quality management philosophy and system I used this procedure to gain understanding of the *root causes* and *direct causes* of *effects.* The common denominator of this procedure, of statistics, and all other problem-solving tools is a search for the truth and a recognition of responsibility for taking action to correct problems of the system.

Basic Concepts, Skills, and Philosophy

2

The Quest for Information, Knowledge, Wisdom, and Vision

Wisdom, a comprehension of that which is true and that which is not true (not necessarily through formal education), is the highest base of power (the ability to guide, direct, and control). Wisdom ultimately surpasses the power bases of position, persuasion, monetary worth, and fear. Wisdom is the basis for sound broad perspective decisions.

Wisdom is based upon the synthesis of multi-faceted accumulated knowledge. Once analyzed, understood, and stored in the mind, information becomes knowledge. Knowledge about human needs, knowledge about motivation, knowledge about planning, knowledge about equipment, knowledge about processes, knowledge about finance, knowledge about communicating, knowledge about data collection and analyses, knowledge about problem solving, and especially knowledge about how to think and how to learn, are all the building blocks of wisdom.

Wisdom is developed in others by facilitating a hunger for information, then providing access to a broad base of information. This process is a key factor in promoting increased management excellence and in the implementation of a comprehensive quality program. *People ultimately control all non-entropic processes,* even the most automated. Increased wisdom leads to better control of these processes.

Another aspect of an increase in wisdom is the parallel increase in open-mindedness. As knowledge increases an individual realizes how much is not known, not true, not absolute, and constantly changing. Knowledge allows us to acknowledge all that we do not know. Knowledge and an open mind modify the development of rubrics that lock us into our old patterns of action and behavior. Knowledge and an open mind allow us to analyze, experience, and take action on concepts and information that are new. Wisdom allows us to change without threat to our mode of existence.

Wisdom, knowledge, and information go hand-and-hand. Information can be collected through all the senses. But there is a catch-22. With minimal knowledge we tend not to have an open mind. We cling to familiar patterns of thought and action based only on what we know. Without an open mind we tend not to sense the information that will lead to increased knowledge. Often only an outside force can intervene and force the increased assimilation of information that will lead to increased knowledge.

In developing a comprehensive quality program, the mentors are behooved to promote and force the increased assimilation of information that will result in an increase in knowledge and then an increase in wisdom. Fortunately, as knowledge increases the hunger for more knowledge increases and eventually the mentoring is no longer needed for the quest for knowledge to continue. I call this level critical mass.

How does a mentor force the initial assimilation of knowledge? If an individual is to grow in knowledge, the knowledge must be *relevant to the needs of the individual.* Otherwise the individual will not consider the knowledge of benefit and worthy of remembering or utilizing. It thus behooves the mentors of quality to present new information in a manner that fulfills a perceived need of the individual. In practice this can be done by focusing problem-solving efforts on the significant problems of the learner. Help the learner address a problem he/she believes is significant, introducing new information and techniques to guide him/her in solving his/her problem. The mere presentation of a large amount of perceived insignificant information will not motivate the learner to remember or utilize the information.

Learning and implementation of knowledge are a definable continuous process. The process can be divided into steps or stages. The steps, feeling indicators, and coaching requirements are shown in Figure 3.

The first stage of learning is the unconscious incompetent. An individual is not aware that an idea or skill exists. The individual is oblivious to the knowledge. At this stage the mentor's objective is to make the individual aware that the idea or skill exists. Showing how the new information can help satisfy the learner's need is more important than detail at this point.

The next stage is the conscious incompetent. The individual is now aware of the existence of the information and the need to grow. Rules for applying the information are memorized. With the recognition comes fear, frustration, and a sensation of ignorance. These negative feelings can cause the student to turn back. Coaching and experience help the student move toward the next level.

In the conscious competent stage the learner starts to experience success with the new knowledge. Self-confidence begins to increase. The learner applies the knowledge according to strict rules without an intuitive sense of direction, probability estimation, and reaction. Feelings of awkwardness, unnaturalness, and excitement are normal. Coaching is still required to gain experience, gain breadth, and handle the unexpected.

The next stage is the unconscious competent. As the learner progresses through the conscious competent stage self-confidence increases and eventually he/she reaches unconscious competence. Experience increases. Breadth increases.

Figure 3

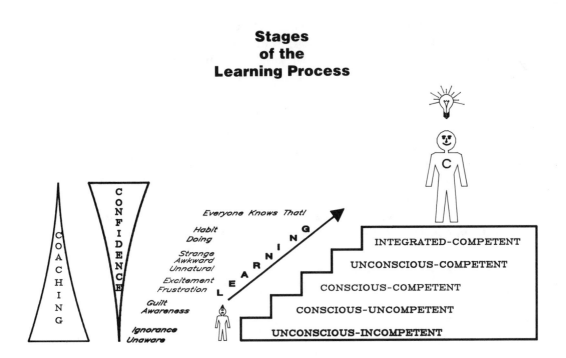

Stages of the Learning Process

The new knowledge is synthesized into the knowledge base of the individual. Coaching requirements diminish. As these changes terminate the knowledge becomes habit or routine. The individual is capable of applying the knowledge without coaching. He/she can easily handle deviations from the rules learned in the conscious incompetent stage. He/she is able to estimate probabilities of successful application given varying situatioms.

The final stage of learning is integrated competence. This state can be best described by an assumption of the learner that "I thought everyone knew that!" The information is truly part of the knowledge base of the individual.

For example, consider learning how to drive a car. First the learner decides he/she wants the mobility of driving. The learner determined that driving would be of greater benefit than walking or riding a bicycle. Next he/she learns the names and functions of the controls. He/she learns the standard procedures for driving. Then, with a parent, friend, or teacher beside him/her he/she takes the first hesitant drive. Many are close to a disaster. But initial fright or nervousness becomes excitement as learning progresses. The learner continues to oversteer, jackrabbit accelerate and stop, and maybe even run over a few curbs. He/she tries to follow the rules exactly. As he/she practices and gains skills and confidence he/she starts taking calculated risks. He/she will enter an intersection when another car approaches yet is considered far enough away and going slow enough not to be considered a danger.

Eventually routine driving becomes second nature. As the years go by even the reactions in crisis situations become second nature. The learner has gone through the learning process model.

The stages and feelings of the human learning process are universal. I have yet to find a learning situation where the process does not occur. Some individuals learn faster; some learn slower. How fast an individual learns depends on background, mental or manual capability, and the quality of coaching.

An individual may abort the process at an intermediate stage, falling immediately back to the conscious incompetent stage and later to the unconscious incompetent stage. Why do people fall back? Regression occurs when internal fear, disorientation and/or external pressure becomes greater than the drive to satisfy a need. Mental work in the form of "programming," reevaluation of conflicting old beliefs, and finally synthesis of thought are required to reach the unconscious competent stage. Some individuals are not willing to put forth the effort required. The benefits just don't fit their needs. Coaching is almost always required to move through the process. The amount of coaching is proportional to the negative feelings the individual experiences as he/she moves through the process. The coaching requirements taper until the individual reaches the unconscious competent level. The self-confidence of the individual grows as the individual progresses through the various steps of the learning process. The learning process will not reach a point of imminent completion until the top of the conscious competent stage.

When the unconscious competent stage is reached, the process for that unit of knowledge is essentially complete but the learning process continues. The unit of information learned becomes part of the knowledge base for the next related learning process. For example, in teaching process control with X-bar and R charts, operators often cannot plot points on a graph. The first learning unit to be addressed is plotting. When that process has reached the unconscious competent stage, the next unit, chart preparation, can begin. When unconscious competence has been achieved in chart preparation, the unit of learning on chart interpretation can begin. To forge ahead without the foundation renders the remainder of the teaching experience useless, destructive and alienating. Such action is counter-productive to development of a quality culture and a quality product.

The motivated individual is continuously involved in numerous learning processes. He or she is the person identified as open-minded, flexible, assertive, creative, and a leader. When an individual hardens and the thinking and learning processes decelerate, mental death begins. The person's ability to contribute in a changing environment starts to deteriorate. The individual loses a comprehension of reality. Business organizations have an obligation to keep managers and employees involved in learning processes. If the needs of the individual and the needs of the organization are synchronized, both the organization and the individual will thrive.

Selective Perception

One of the great contributions to the knowledge of man was made by the German philosopher Immanuel Kant. In Kant's essay, *Critique of Pure Reason,* he argues that humans tend to consciously process the signals from only one or two of the five senses at one time. We are selective in that which we sense. We quickly acknowledge that which fits into our current pattern of thinking, i.e., is in line with our present purpose. This selective perception is not a property of the senses. In fact, all our senses function continuously during our waking hours. The selective nature of perception is a property of the mind, of our method of thinking. Consider the person engrossed in a conversation who does not hear the surrounding conversations of others. Consider the mechanic who skins his knuckles but does not register pain until he sees blood on his hand. Consider the husband so engrossed in his newspaper or magazine he does not hear his wife's request to take out the garbage. Consider the car driver who, preoccupied in thought, drives right past the intended destination. The light rays enter our eyes, the sound vibrates our ear drums, the nerve endings send their electrical impulses toward the brain. Our selective perception is a mental process. *We* limit what we mentally perceive. We have the mental ability to control what we perceive.

If selective perception were not reality we would exist in a constant state of confusion. Imagine comprehending every sound, every smell, every touch, every sight, every taste at every waking moment. Each signal would override and confuse the others. We would short-circuit. We would cease to function.

But over-perception is not a common human problem. In fact, we most often limit our perception and thus limit our own knowledge, understanding, and capabilities. Through under-perception and locked thought and action patterns we also limit the potential productivity of others. We even endanger our own well being. We do not perceive nor comprehend much of what occurs around us. In fact, in many cases we choose to deny that which our senses detect. The quest for individuals today, if we are to grow and change with our changing culture, is not to limit perception but to expand perception and understanding. Without full consideration, we reject the thoughts and ideas that contradict and threaten that which we "already know to be true." We reject the very innovation that is necessary to grow and obtain competitive advantage. We only perceive that which is in line with our "purpose." Yet the "purpose" of our actions is unclear. "Our purpose" may be limiting or just plain wrong. We forge ahead without considering where we are.

Just as we limit our senses, we also limit our thought patterns to those that are familiar and provide a system for solving the problems of everyday life. The current situation is that our methods of solving problems are empirical and based on models and solutions that have worked in the past. But our society is changing so fast that the "same problem" seldom if ever occurs twice. If we trick ourselves into believing that the problems of today are the same as the problems of five years ago, then we are the victims of selective perception. We have not sensed, and have often blocked, the details of the current situation.

Consider a businessman driving an automobile setting out to drive from Atlanta to Memphis for an appointment. This is a trip he has not made before. He looks at a map then gets in the car to set out on the journey thinking intensely about his appointment in nine hours. After an hour of driving he passes a road sign that reads "Mobile 300 miles." The driver may not even see the sign because he is intent on getting to Memphis for the appointment; or he may glance at the sign and say "That can't be right." He says to himself "I'll go ahead and look for another sign." Next he sees Spanish moss on the trees and knowing that Spanish moss only grows in the Deep South says to himself, "Wow! That's strange that Spanish moss is growing this far north." All this time the morning sun (in the east) has been to the left of the car instead of behind the car. Perhaps when it is too late the businessman will acknowledge his unheeded perceptions, admit his error, and alter his actions to fit his purpose. His actions may be too late. At minimum he will have to speed to make up for lost time. At worst he will miss the appointment and lose the contract to a competitor. The quality of his sales performance was limited by *selective perception.*

Consultants have a great advantage when they come into a business from outside to make recommendations. Anyone from outside is not so involved in old thought and action patterns that he/she does not perceive the obvious. Most good consultants train themselves to have better perception and presentation skills. Their expert status is derived from a basic knowledge of a specialty along with expanded perception, and perception expansion of those within the organization due to the presence of the consultant. Often there are several people internal to the organization that have as good or better understanding of the consultant's specialty. After the consultant makes a "brilliant" recommendation there is often at least one person who will acknowledge with envy that the consultant didn't suggest or do anything the individual couldn't have done. The significant point is that the individual didn't suggest or do the same action, or if the individual had done so, the value of the suggestion or action was discounted within the organization due to the locked thought and action patterns of the organization.

Aristotle versus Taoism

Aristotle, the Greek philosopher and father of the Western method of scientific investigation, stated a basic procedure for analyzing and categorizing entities. The investigator determines whether a property exists or does not exist. By analyzing enough properties and determining whether each property exists or does not exist, the entity can be uniquely described. Aristotle's system permeates much of scientific investigation today. There are situations where such investigation is valid. And there are situations where this procedure falls short of a valid definition of holistic truth. Full reliance on Aristotle's methods in investigation and in thought patterns leads to a forced classification of variable information. Aristotle's system makes an attribute determination of property and an inference about the total.

Judeo and Eastern thought and analysis do not presume such absoluteness. They infer a continuum between "A" and "not A." Such an understanding of reality is more in line with the variability of nature that we attempt to define with statistics. Even more so, such an understanding of reality is more appropriate to understanding human nature and its variability.

In our heterogeneous culture we struggle between the two philosophies. We often try to simplify our problem solving with "A" and "not A" thinking. We deny the natural interrelatedness, variability, and continuum between extremes in nature.

The ability to analyze huge amounts of data rapidly with digital computing opens new vistas in the quest to define reality. Statistical analyses that just a few years ago took weeks can now be done in minutes. There are now workable procedures for accepting and then defining a dynamic and variable reality.

Rubrics

The behavioral psychologist, Abraham Maslow, whose theories of behavioral motivation will be discussed later, also wrote extensively about rubrics. Rubrics are patterns of thought and problem solving. We might call a rubric a road map we follow when we set out to think about or do a task. For example, most of us tend to follow the same route to work each morning. We often tend to read the same type of books. We analyze problems in "A" and "not A" style. We follow the same routine as we get ready for work in the morning. We are uncomfortable with the unfamiliarity of a change in the order of worship in our churches or synagogues, or the agenda at a club meeting. When we travel on business we tend to stay in the same motel or hotel each time we go to a distant city. We even mow our yards in the same pattern each time.

Rubrics are patterns of thought and behavior that simplify and systemize the routine problem solving of our lives. They are inherently neither good nor bad. We all must operate with rubrics. The alternatives for each decision are myriad. We cannot mentally make as many decisions as we would necessarily have to make in a life without rubrics. Even the most mentally mature individuals operate with rubrics.

Rubrics become problematic when we deny that we operate within a rubric and deny that there are alternative patterns of thought and action. Furthermore, we limit our perception of that which we do not know when we limit our world to our particular rubric. As the rate of change in our world accelerates we must continuously, individually and corporately, examine our rubrics, and determine if they provide more benefit than harm. Harm because, although the rubric is familiar and comfortable, it may be destructive to the welfare of the individual or the organization. If we drive to work by the same route each morning we may never see the new shopping center three blocks away. We may never realize that a parallel route has been improved and would reduce our travel time by 10 minutes.

In business, our destructive rubrics may be inflexible accounting systems that do not change as our product line, production systems, and organizational management change. Another destructive business rubric may be a sales force locked into "good-ole-boy" sales methodology while the industry is moving to high technology. A rubric may be denying the use of computers to employees because the information and systems may change the way an individual must run a department. It may be not considering advanced technology with the potential of increased productivity and quality because it would require retraining and change. Another may be a supervisor's insensitivity to statistical chart information either because he/she does not want to learn the new technology or because it may mean that he/she will have to change the way he/she operates the production facilities. He/she will have to admit that his/her old pattern of control is inadequate. Finally, another destructive rubric may be locking into one familiar methodology in problem solving.

Vision

Vision is a nebulous property of individual behavior and thinking that becomes more critical as the scope of responsibility and authority of the individual increases. It is difficult to quickly and concisely define vision, but its importance warrants an attempt. In defining vision I will limit my definition to *realistic* vision, not impractical illusion and nonsensical dreaming. There is a difference in the two concepts of vision but the line of differentiation is nebulous. To the person with limited knowledge and wisdom all vision may appear as impractical dreaming. To the highly visionary individual the ideas that to others appear irrational and dreamy are obviously practical and rational. Realistic vision is necessary for forward thinking and progress. The individual's base of knowledge and wisdom controls the realism of their vision. Vision without knowledge and wisdom of the path of implementation is simply daydreaming.

Prerequisite to realistic vision is broad-based wisdom—again, the ability to differentiate and define the probability of truth. But vision goes further. Vision includes the ability to critically examine the past, the present, and accurately project into the future. Vision incorporates a dissatisfaction with what currently exists and a willingness to risk for the development of a better organization, product, relationship, etc.

Vision is prerequisite to long-term planning. Long-term planning is basic to an organization operating through designed action instead of reaction. With vision we control the path of change. Without vision change happens *to us* and we are limited to reaction.

Maslow's Concept of the Holistic Organism

As mentioned, Abraham Maslow proposed numerous concepts about motivation and personality that are useful in understanding the effectiveness and behaviors of organizations.

He also presented the concept of the holistic organism. Maslow's holistic concept contrasts with classical Aristotelian thought, which says in order to understand a complex subject the subject can be broken into constitutive parts, studying each part in isolation, and reassembling the properties of the parts to understand the in-total entity. Maslow countered that because of the complexity and interdependence of the parts constituting the entity, the parts do not remain, nor respond to testing, the same when separated as when they constitute a part of the whole. Therefore, traits and properties of the constituent parts examined independently do not well represent the traits of the parts when assembled into the whole. If we are to understand the whole then we must study the properties of the parts *in situ*. Only then can we understand the parts that interrelate to form the whole.

Maslow's Hierarchy of Needs

Maslow also proposed a now classic model of motivation and personality relevant to new- and old-style organizations. When we understand the model we can understand how societal growth and change demand a shift to a new organization and management style. The model also sheds light on the current drive for quality in products and in the lifestyles of individuals.

According to Maslow, people act to fulfill basic needs, either perceived or real. Maslow defined a hierarchy of universal basic human needs. Individuals, and organizations, strive to fill needs beginning with the lowest need and move to the next need only when the lower need is relatively satisfied. When an individual moves to a higher need the lower needs diminish in significance for motivation. When gratifiers (actions that significantly satisfy a need and motivate) are designed to fulfill needs other than the current needs, the individual either erroneously assigns the gratifier to the current need or more appropriately discounts the gratifier as not significant. Every need of human existence is an element of one of the basic needs. When job challenges match the basic needs of the individual, both personal needs and organizational needs can be satisfied.

Each person establishes criteria for the satisfaction of a need. Actions will be viewed by the individual as either gratifying the current need or as unfulfilling (not gratifying) the current need. Often the matching of corporate needs and individual needs is more a problem of communications than of reestablishing priorities.

This priority of needs sounds abstract yet examples can be seen every day. In one plant, attempting to turn around their operation and profit situation, management tried to promote communications, a sense of mutual purpose for

Figure 4

A. H. Maslow's Hierarchy
of Human Needs

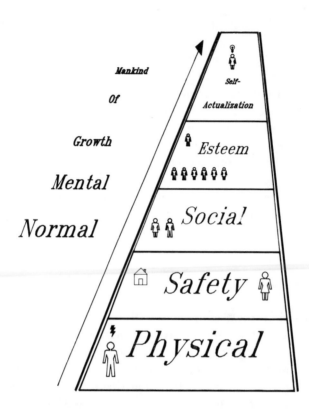

quality, an *esprit de corps*. Management's focus was on social belonging and esteem needs. All are worthy objectives. But the success was limited. Discussions with workers revealed that the workers concerns were short work weeks, death of the old standard product line, numerous firings, rampant management changes, and rumors of the plant closing. How would the workers make their house payments? Would they be able to buy groceries? Would they have to move to another town for work? A sense of *esprit de corps* was not one of their concerns. The workers were involved with physical and safety needs while management was promoting esteem and social belonging. The goals, as presented, and actions requested by management did not match the workers' needs. Later management addressed the workers' real concerns. Management emphasized that if feared actions were to be prevented, extra effort, a change in "business as usual" training, implementation of new procedures, and new products were necessary. Management's obligation was to provide the training, equipment, and environment for the changes. This course of action fulfilled the needs of the workers and the organization. The plant is now in the midst of a

Figure 5

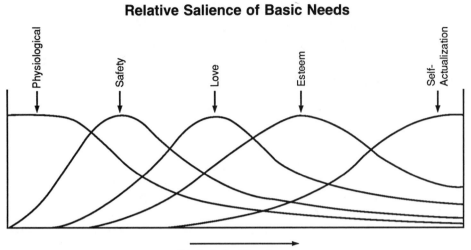

Relative Salience of Basic Needs

From *Elements of Psychology,* © 1958 by David Krech and Richard S. Crutchfield. Published by Alfred A. Knopf, New York.

financial and quality turnaround. Now most of the old fears of the workers are gone. The workers and the management have moved to higher need levels.

Examples at the top end of the need pyramid are just as, if not more, plentiful. Managers and executives often become bored with their work. The needs being fulfilled by past work were social belonging and esteem. Now the managers feel these needs have been fulfilled. They look for avenues of self-actualization, living and implementing their deep-down values, beliefs, and theories. If they do not find an open avenue to self-actualization they become bored and discontented. Often upper management tries to remotivate the stale manager with more money, sometimes as salary, sometimes as stock options or other fringe benefits. The actions of upper management do not match the needs of the manager. Money and fringe benefits fulfill needs lower than self-actualization. The stale manager already perceives these needs as satisfied. Most managers, bored and seeking self-actualization, when offered lower-level motivation but not opportunity for self-actualization eventually leave the organization. Money sometimes can be a good motivator with high-level managers. The manager motivated by money has established high, and sometimes unrealistic, internal requirements for need satisfaction. The reasons for these higher-than-normal need requirements are extremely interesting but beyond the scope of this book. Beware. Peoples' requirements for need satisfaction can change as they grow and mature. What worked once may not work the next time. Management must continually tune to the needs of others.

From a quality training perspective, if people are to buy into the objectives of the organization the organization's needs must be presented as meeting the needs of the individual as well. If the needs of the organization do not match the individual's needs, the individual will seek satisfaction outside of the organization. If we are to stress excellence in production processes and management, then managers and trainers must express the need for excellence as satisfying the needs of the individual at the individual's current need level.

Needs of the individual and the organization are dynamic. People normally seek to grow and move up the need structure. Downward movement of the individual or organization to a lower need, usually due to a threat to the established base of need gratification, is viewed as a crisis. Individuals facing the loss of job and income, or the loss of a support community used to maintain gratification of lower needs feel severely threatened. Companies lose their profitability due to threats from innovative technology, foreign competition, or other reasons. A crisis often leads to reevaluation and action to maintain stability. But crisis decisions are often not sound decisions. It is preferable that decisions be made with full understanding of the *causes*, required actions, and long-term ramifications of the actions. Foreign competition, innovative technology, and the demand for quality are a real threat to many individuals and many American business organizations. Understanding the nature of the threat will help subdue panic reactions and promote purposeful action.

Societies also mature and grow through the same need structure as do individuals. The early emigrants worked hard at jobs that fulfilled low-level basic needs. By current standards the hours were long and the working conditions were detestable, but workers trying to gratify low-level needs did not complain. Once these low-level needs were gratified, workers concentrated on the next level of needs—social belonging and esteem. Business organizations were slow to change to meet those needs and labor unrest developed. Workers sought gratification either through unions, lodges, community, church, or outside activities such as sports or other hobbies. The focus on need gratification through "the job" diminished. Today, with a few exceptions, only a small portion of our working society is concerned primarily with the two lower-level needs. The current focus of American society is on social, esteem, and self-actualization gratification, especially individuals in management. American business has been painfully slow to recognize this shift of society to higher-level needs. Only in the last few years have a few organizations recognized this shift, and reinvented the corporation to operate in the changing society. These organizations are perceived as the best places to work. Because they facilitate the fulfillment of the needs of the individual in conjunction with the fulfillment of the needs of the organization, the members of these companies are highly motivated. They are creative, conscientious, and their productivity is fantastic. These individuals are self-actualized achievers with opportunity and support. And these companies are competitive in the best sense of the word. They play win/win games.

In summary, the need base of the work force, from the lowest level to upper management, has shifted during our country's history. Business organizations have not sought to understand the needs of the individuals constituting the organization and change their management styles to effectively motivate and fulfill these needs. When such needs are not fulfilled, individuals lose interest in their work (since they lose a sense of ownership) and part of the justification for the organization is diminished. The organization drops in effectiveness and quality dwindles. Thus, an organizational structure designed to promote excellence must motivate the individuals of the organization. This can best be done through understanding and action based on a synthesis of the needs of both the business organization and the individuals.

Static and Dynamic Decisions

I view and advocate classifying decisions on a continuous spectrum ranging from static to dynamic. Purely static decisions, once made, are final. Only if the factors affecting that decision change do we then decide differently. For example, consider the choices of what size motor is proper for a pump or what office furniture to buy. Once made, these decisions are over. Dynamic decisions, however, are made over and over again with almost continuous input of data and an almost continuous output of action, including the action of consciously taking no action. As long as the process continues we continue to make decisions. When we drive a car we continuously make decisions about speed and direction. These are dynamic decisions.

The quest for excellence is not a static decision in either the macro or the micro sense. Quality improvement is a continuous, never-ending dynamic process. The ultimate goal of perfection is never fully reachable. The mark of success is continuous progress toward that goal. In every decision that managers make each factor of holistic quality must be weighed.

Power, Power Bases, and Leadership

3

This chapter will discuss concepts of leadership and the power bases for leadership. I draw heavily on the work of Hersey, Blanchard, and Natemeyer as presented in the article, "Situational Leadership, Perception, and the Impact of Power." (Copyright © 1988 Leadership Studies. All rights reserved.) I highly recommend that the serious mentor of organizational growth and quality study this article. I also again rely heavily on the works of A. H. Maslow. I have blended the leadership system of Hersey etal with the motivation system of Maslow. I now see little, if any, conflict between these definitive systems. Both systems are presented so that the reader will thoroughly understand power and leadership. In moving toward holistic and dynamic quality management, effective leadership and efficient use of power are primary elements of success. As Hersey, Blanchard, and Natemeyer state,

> ". . . leadership is the process of attempting to influence the behavior of others, and power is the means by which the leader actually gains the compliance of the follower(s); the two are inseparable."

In their article the authors review significant power bases. These are coercive, connection, reward, legitimate, referent, informational, and expert. I have taken the liberty of melding the authors' definitions with Maslow's definitions of basic needs.

Fear and threat are the primary tools of coercive power. A leader strong in coercive power uses fear of punishment or withdrawal of basic needs to gain compliance with desire. Often such power is used to motivate individuals to do otherwise unthinkable tasks, such as blindly charge a machine gun nest in battle. Or threatening to remove a previously satisfied gratifier of a basic need can produce a crisis and otherwise irrational behavior.

Connection power is based on knowing, or giving the perception of knowing, the "right" people, other people with the power to remove gratifiers of basic needs. Again, fear is inherent in connection power. Threat is not necessarily from the actions of the person exerting connective power. The statements "I'll report you to the plant manager" or "I'll send a note home to your parents if you don't behave!" are examples of connection power.

Reward power is effective because the subject perceives the bearer can gratify a significant need. This is the first power base which *pulls* the subject toward the desired behavior. The previous two power bases pushed the subject toward a behavior by fear. Fear and threats are not factors of reward power. The subject of reward power makes a rational decision about behavior, assuming the subject is not neurotic in seeking gratifiers to basic needs. Regardless of whether the reward believed bestowable actually gratifies an appropriate need, if the subject believes the user can provide it, the user can effectively exert power over the subject.

Legitimate, or position power, is solely a property of position in an organization. The appropriateness of the power directive is not a determinant of position power. The higher the rank of the user in an organization the more position power the user possesses. Position power often plays heavily on neurotic behavior of individuals with low self-esteem.

Referent power is based on the personal traits, the admiration and likeability, of an individual. Referent power is based in the social and esteem basic needs. Because the subject likes, admires, and seeks to be identified with the user, referent power is effective.

Information power is effective when the subject views the user as having information that is or can be useful to the subject. Such power is not necessarily organization-dependent. The user of information power does not have to be even geographically adjacent to the user. Again, such power can be based on a broad range of Maslow's basic needs.

Expert power, the final category, is effective when the subject perceives that the user has expertise in areas that can lead to basic need gratification. I believe such power differs from information power in generality, quantity, and synthesis. I perceive information as specific bits of data that the subject can use while the expert provides not only an abundance of information but the mental ability to synthesize the abundance of information into systems. Experts are experts because they understand and can communicate the ramifications of broad, diversified, yet interrelated information. I see no conflict between the concept of *wisdom* being the highest base of power, as presented previously, and the belief that *expert* power is the highest base of power.

I have listed these power bases in what Hersey, Blanchard, and Natemeyer state to be ascending order when referenced to the "maturity" of the subjects. In the next chapter I will describe a model defining the relationship between the power bases as stated here and maturity.

When we appropriately use these power bases we first assess the maturity level of the individual upon which we will exert power. The authors state that the "fear and greed" power bases are coercive and connection power. I submit that any power base below the maturity level of the subject will be construed as a threat, and as "fear and greed" power. Only when the power base exerted is directed at the subject's current or a higher maturity level will the power base be viewed as appropriate.

For example, to highly self-actualized persons such as Abraham Lincoln, Thomas Edison, Albert Schweitzer, Albert Einstein, and Dietrich Bonhoeffer, the only effective leadership power for leading them was expert, or wisdom power. Any attempt to exert lower-level power over such individuals would be viewed as a threat to the established gratifiers of lower needs. The user of such power may obtain compliance, and resentment, if the threats and fear are great enough. The conformance is not certain. Bonhoeffer, a Lutheran, died in a World War II concentration camp ministering to other prisoners because he would not modify his professed theology to the official theology of Hitler's Germany. Remember that as a person grows in psychological maturity the gratification levels of the lower needs are reduced. In a few individuals the need for self-actualization will overshadow the most severe threats to physical and safety needs.

Individuals seeking to gratify lower needs, such as physical and safety, view the use of a lower power base as leadership. The military "leader" who takes his soldiers into battle with pure task (dictating) behavior leads because he is gratifying the basic need for safety. When bullets are flying the soldier is not highly concerned with relationships or psychological growth.

The power base used to *lead* an individual must be equal to or higher than the maturity of the individual to be led. This means, as Hersey et al state, that the effective leader must be competent in using *all* the leadership power bases and must know when a specific power base is appropriate.

Before leaving the subject of power, power bases, and leadership, I want to return to Maslow's order of basic needs and investigate another system of defining power and leadership based specifically on his system of motivation and basic needs.

Again, the healthy individual seeks to fulfill basic needs in a specific order with gratifiers. The individual seeks to gratify each need to a level the individual has determined as sufficient. But there is overlap. The gratifiers sought are distributed around the currently dominant basic need.

I propose that realized power and leadership are affected through the ability to guide, direct, and empower one or more individuals toward *more effective gratification* of the dominant and/or near-dominant basic needs, and through prevention of threat to the individual's gratifiers of these lower needs. The use of fear, therefore, can only be a *negative* factor in true leadership. The privilege and burden of leadership is only granted by those who are led. The individuals are only led, long-term, to perceived greater gratification of significant needs.

The talents of leaders may vary. Some may have expertise in gaining gratifiers and preventing threats to lower needs. Others may be effective in gaining gratifiers and preventing threats to higher needs. There may be a very few people who have the talents to lead toward gratification and prevent threats to *all* the basic needs. Such a person is truly the wise leader.

History supports this assessment. Expert military leaders such as Ulysses S. Grant led admirably in overcoming a threat to safety, yet he failed miserably as president of the United States after the Civil War. Socrates and

Plato could serve as mentors for the higher needs of their students, but could not manage the perceived threat their inspired thoughts posed to the safety of the Greek republic.

The greatest leader is the person who can meet the varied needs of the organization. A leader is someone who can address the safety and physical needs of some members of the organization without posing a threat to the esteem of a self-actualized individual, and vice-versa. My hope for leadership by such individuals may not be fully in tune with reality. I believe there are a few such leaders, and I believe as society and organizations grow there will be more.

If an organization is to function in the current reality, leaders must be chosen who come closest to the concept of the ideal leader. Even the best individuals will not be totally able to address needs at both ends of the structure, but they certainly will do better than the person who cannot accurately assess the current basic need levels of the members of the organization at any level.

Organizations must also be cognizant of the talent limitations of leaders, and of the followers within the organization. The organization may have to select a level of the need structure within which they wish to operate and structure the organizational culture in an appropriate manner. Some high maturity leaders may not be effective with individuals seeking gratification of lower needs. Leaders talented in gratifying lower needs may not be effective in leading individuals seeking gratification of the higher basic needs.

It seems obvious to me that an organization could be developed utilizing individuals at the highest need levels to lead individuals seeking gratification at the same or one-step lower level. Individuals talented in leadership based on fulfillment of the middle needs would be utilized as middle leaders and, finally, those individuals able to lead based on gratification of the lower needs would lead at the lower levels.

Not all organizations require leadership spanning the full range of basic needs. The missions of various organizations require different levels of complexity and require different levels of skills, knowledge, and wisdom.

Such a system, therefore, satisfies both the tasks of maintaining a growing society and the proper distribution of leadership talents within the populace.

Today, almost without exception, we do not choose our leaders on such a behavioral basis. We promote based on connections, referent, legitimate power, and based on performance of lower tasks requiring lower level skills. The wisdom necessary to systematically organize leadership is sorely missing.

Quality growth in an organization is strongly dependent on leadership. The leadership must be appropriate. It must effectively meet the dominant basic needs of the lead individuals charged with the tasks of producing the goods and services that justify its existence. In the chapter on organization I will specifically define an organizational structure utilizing this rationale.

Models for Quality

Models help us understand authority, responsibility, communication patterns, effective approaches to conflict, needs and motivation, personalities, and business management styles. Models do not explain all situations. They are necessarily simplistic. But they do help us to learn and understand. We have already looked at several models. In this chapter we will review more models to increase the reader's background knowledge. Each model incorporates significant information on individual motivation, group dynamics, and organizational structure and focus that broadens the knowledge base necessary for developing holistic excellence.

Chapter 18 describes an organizational structure optimal for maturity and quality. The models in this chapter are part of the basis for this later model. The development here leads up to a team matrix organization charged with specialized implementation of a vision. Each team member shares the vision and utilizes skills and behaviors to reward both the individual and the organization.

Likert's Four Styles of Communications

Rensis Likert defined four patterns of organizational management, interaction, and communications. He analyzed both vertical (superior-subordinate) and horizontal (peer-peer) patterns. The behaviors are determined by the management style.

In the first style, the Exploitative Authoritative, communication flows only from the manager to each subordinate. The communication is one way. The manager does not listen to or tolerate the ideas and opinions of subordinates. Horizontal information transfer between subordinates is strongly discouraged. The Exploitative Authoritative style is the purest form of autocratic, dictatorial management.

Figure 6

Likert's Description of Management Systems

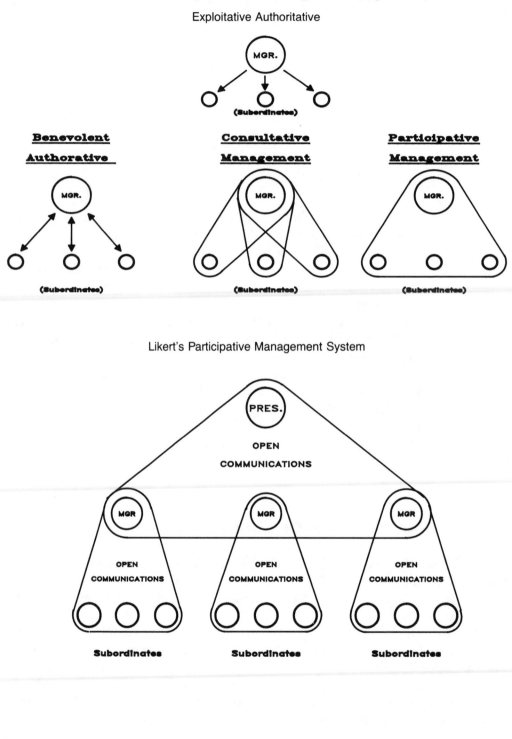

Exploitative Authoritative

Benevolent Authorative

Consultative Management

Participative Management

Likert's Participative Management System

In the second style, Benevolent Authoritative management, information flows downward and from subordinates to the manager at the manager's discretion. Downward communication prevails. Horizontal communication is discouraged. Each subordinate speaks only when requested. The manager will ask for responses but listens only to responses to direct inquiries.

The third style, Consultative Management, allows for open communication between the manager and individual subordinates. The manager consults with individual subordinates and actively seeks their ideas and opinions. Yet in this style open communications between subordinates is frowned upon. The manager does not trust subordinates to openly discuss issues among themselves.

In Likert's final style, Participative Management, the manager and all subordinates communicate openly and freely. The manager is a facilitator, coordinator, and leader for a team effort. Control is executed by the group. Responsibility and authority are distributed throughout the group.

In the final drawing of the model, the relationship between numerous teams is shown. Each manager is a member of a higher authority team. The team concept continues all the way through to the board of directors of the corporation, the highest authority team.

Likert's styles of communication and interaction require increasing levels of maturity in both managers and employees. Only relatively mature, self-motivated individuals would have the self-confidence for a team-based organization.

Again, note that in the participative management system communication flows freely horizontally *and* vertically. For effective delegation of authority and sound decision-making, the managers and other team members must have broad and accurate information.

People, Data, and Things

Richard Bolles, author of *What Color Is Your Parachute?* cites a model developed for the U.S. government publication *Dictionary of Occupational Titles*. The model defines the component skills of three major skill categories, Data, People, and Things. The model is shown in Figure 7.

I find this model effectively defines generic skills. Effectively using the model to evaluate people and position requirements benefits both the individual and the organization. I believe in the new business era, managing will require high-level people and data behaviors. I prefer to call the data category of skills information behavior. I will do so throughout the rest of this book.

Take another look at the three major skill categories and the elements of each category. These skills will be used later to discuss staffing, position requirements, individual skill levels, and to further define the growth process for individuals. The skills are listed in order of decreasing maturity. We will discuss maturity in much more depth as we progress.

Figure 7

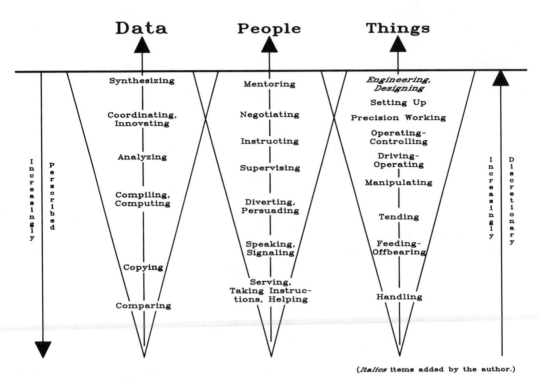

(*Italics* items added by the author.)

From *What Color Is Your Parachute?* © 1988 by Richard Nelson Bolles. Published by Ten Speed Press, Berkeley, Calif.

McGregor's Theory X and Theory Y Management

An early, often-used model describing manager and management behavior was developed by Douglas McGregor. McGregor's model quantifies two determinant factors of management style, task and relationship behavior. Pure theory X management emphasizes task and autocracy as the effective management style. Theory Y management focuses on relationships for effective management. McGregor supported theory Y management in reaction to the prevalent autocratic task-oriented style of the day.

The model is often shown graphically with an X-Y graph. The level of task orientation is plotted on a horizontal axis. Relationship orientation is plotted vertically. Thus the names, theory X and theory Y for the two styles.

The Managerial Grid ®

A parallel, yet significantly different, approach to defining management style is described in *The Managerial Grid* by Robert Blake and Jane Mouton. In this model levels of two attitudes or mind-sets—concern for people and concern for

Figure 8

The Managerial Grid®

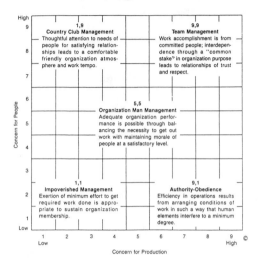

The Managerial Grid figure from *The Managerial Grid III: The Key to Leadership Excellence,* by Robert R. Blake and Jane Srygley Mouton. Houston: Gulf Publishing Company, copyright © 1985, page 12. Reproduced by permission.

production—are assigned ranges from 1 to 9. A maximized level of merged concern for people and concern for production is presented as the ideal management style.

Dr. Blake's model differs significantly from the models discussed earlier, and several models to be discussed later. The emphasis in this model is on attitude instead of behavior. Various synthesized management attitudes are characteristically defined by plotting the two attitude levels on the grid. Each grid segment defines a management style.

I believe Dr. Blake's 9,9 position is analogous to the self-actualized manager or the "Achiever" manager that will be discussed later.

It is worth noting that no parallel to Richard Bolles' information skills, or a "concern for information" has been made directly in the grid, although the descriptions in the literature of the 9,9 manager reflect high information concern. As I will develop as we proceed, management behavior, the actions actually observed by others, involve the internal factors of possessing necessary skills and appropriate concern and then result in an appropriate behavior.

Dr. Bell's Model

The next model to be discussed I learned from Dr. Gerald Bell of the University of North Carolina Graduate School of Business Administration and is presented in his book, *The Achievers*. In his model Dr. Bell first defines six styles

Figure 9

Dr. Bell's Management Styles
and Relative Percent Effectiveness

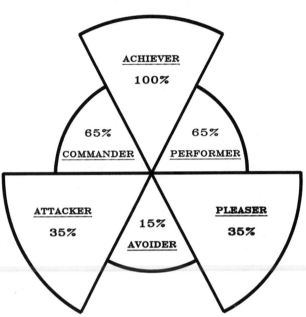

From *The Achievers*, © 1973 by Dr. Gerald Bell. Published by Preston Hill, Inc., Chapel Hill, NC.

of management, then describes communication style, motivators, how each style develops, and relative mental health for each style.

The first style is the highly self-disciplined "Commander." The primary emphases of the Commander are authority, obedience, and control. Communications by the Commander is one-way downward. The self-concept of the commander is awkward; internally his/her beliefs are contradictory yet he/she sees each solution as black and white. The Commander keeps a safe social distance. The Commander often is raised in a family where one individual, usually the father, "rules the roost" and the other individual, usually the mother, is passive and timid. The Commander learns that through autocratic power an individual can get what he/she wants. This pattern carries on into adult life. The basic flaw of the Commander in high maturity management is that the pattern does not value other individuals as having anything worthwhile to contribute to the organization. The Commander believes he/she is fully and solely responsible for all actions at or below his/her level of the organization. He/she tries to do it all. Others are not allowed to contribute. The Commander is considered to be 65 percent psychologically healthy.

The next style is the "Attacker." The Attacker has many of the same patterns as the Commander but has more contradictions in his/her value system. The early childhood environment usually is one of conflict and conflicting values. The second parent is not necessarily timid and passive and does not possess the same value system as the dominant parent. The attacker hates and rebels against authority. The Attacker seeks to prove his/her independence. The Attacker often cannot determine what he/she wants. He/she will spouse and job hop, always hunting for something better. The Attacker often works well independently. The Attacker is considered to be 35 percent psychologically healthy.

The third style is the "Avoider." The Avoider is the least healthy management style of this model. The Avoider usually is raised in an environment of Avoiders and over-protection. The self-image of the Avoider is extremely low. The Avoider will have numerous nervous habits, including psychosomatic illnesses, and often mumbles in conversation. The Avoider is extremely sensitive to criticism. The Avoider's goal is to hide from the criticism of the rest of the world. The Avoider's low self-image motivates him/her to behave in a manner that avoids criticism. The Avoider's attitude toward risk is to accept challenges with either 100 percent or 0 percent chance of success. Simple tasks with little risk or the impossible tasks are viewed by the Avoider as similar. In both situations the Avoider will not be criticized. He/she will be successful at the simple task, and other people will know that the impossible task could not have been done by anyone and will therefore not criticize the Avoider's failure. The Avoider is only 10 to 15 percent psychologically healthy.

The fourth style, the "Pleaser," has an overwhelming desire and drive to make others happy. The Pleaser usually is highly over-protected during childhood. The basis of self-image for the Pleaser is the positive strokes he/she gets by pleasing others. He/she views positive strokes only as pleasant interaction with other people. It is often hard to define other personality traits of the Pleaser other than the general perception of a "nice guy." The Pleaser often hates the Attacker and the Attacker hates the Pleaser. The Pleaser is considered 35 percent mentally healthy.

Forty-five percent of the general population generally fit into the next category, the "Performer." The parents of the Performer push the child for accomplishment, but do not reward the child appropriately for achievements. The parents push the child to do what they think is best. The Performer is not taught to think for him/herself nor to recognize self-value other than through recognition by others. The Performer is driven for "success" and "prestige" according to what others tell the Performer success and prestige are. The Performer must always strive to prove himself/herself, sometimes in a way that can be considered obsession. The Performer has little concept of his/her own value system but is driven by the desire for the acceptance and prestige he/she seldom experienced as a child. The Performer is *externally* driven instead of internally driven. The Performer is results-oriented and often deals only with the "relevant." Relationships are defined as payoffs. Performers tend to be experts at norm analysis. Others may consider the Performer as "foxy." Because they are externally driven, Performers are extremely conscious of status and prestige. Perhaps Maslow would state that the driving force behind the Performer is esteem. Again, the self-image of the Performer is determined by others. Performers have four times more heart attacks than do Achievers. Performers are considered 65 percent mentally healthy.

The last style, the "Achiever," in pure form approaches 100 percent mental health. The Achiever is Maslow's Eupsychic, self-actualized man/woman. Achievers constitute 10 percent of the general population and only 8 percent of the business population. Yet the current of Western society is now toward development of the individual as a self-actualized achiever.

Achievers are raised in an environment of love, acceptance, positive reinforcement, and self-reliance. Both parents often are Achievers. Achievers are honest and readily accept change. They are willing to take risks and state opinions. They accept failure as part of taking risks, and as normal. They conform with trends in fashion, clothes, hairstyle, etc., but are not driven by them. Such things are not of great significance to the self-actualized achiever. They are not cocky; they are natural, spontaneous, and laugh easily. People like and respect the Achiever. The Achiever is creative, innovative, and problem-centered instead of self-centered and has realistic perceptions. The Achiever is internally driven by a well-defined value system and lives his/her life according to that value system. At times the achiever may appear separated or aloof. He/she does what is his/her "bag" yet is not self-centered. Along with the self-actualization also comes the altruism of the self-actualized individual.

It is rare for an individual to purely fit any one of the six styles. In different situations or at different times different styles may dominate. It may be helpful to think of most individuals as possessing the traits included in a region of the drawing smaller than the drawing but larger than any single area. Achievers may possess traits of Performers or Commanders; Pleasers exhibit many of the traits of Performers and Avoiders.

In my mind, the styles of the model taught by Dr. Bell do not contradict the models of McGregor, Blake, and Maslow, or Berne's model, which will be presented in Chapter 5. Each of these models broadens the understanding of human nature, motivation, and the assembly and interaction of unique individuals into the structures we call "organizations." Thus far, I believe that no one has been able to make understanding people and organizations an exact science. Seeing this is critical to understanding the process for building an excellence driven organization.

Formal, Informal, and Achievement Management and Organization

The next model was presented to me and endorsed by Christian Jensen of The Dan Group. Jensen breaks management and organizational styles into three categories: Formal, Informal, and Achievement.

Formal management and organizations exhibit the traits of centralized authority, inflexible procedure, and fixed role definitions. Management tends to be autocratic and highly task-oriented. Dominant and subordinate roles are well-defined and inflexible. Procedures often become more important than achievement and contribution. Tremendous energy is used in maintenance of

Figure 10

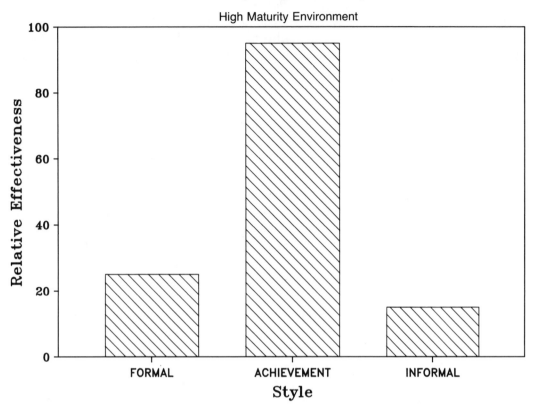

Three Management Styles

High Maturity Environment

the organization and in keeping everyone in line. Creativity and innovation are unofficially frowned upon because they tend to upset the order. The organization only changes as a reaction to crisis, and is usually heavy in Commanders, Performers, and Avoiders. The traits of Achievers and Pleasers are not welcome. The Pleaser is viewed as weak and the Achiever is viewed as a rebel or malcontent. Organizational units are large with many tiers of management. A key emphasis is on adherence to procedure. Traditionally such organizations are financially driven, and view success only in terms of profitability. There is little rational problem analysis. Problems are addressed through delegation of responsibility without authority, according to procedure. Many tasks "fall through the cracks." Much effort is directed at *effects* with little understanding of the relationship between *root cause, direct cause,* and *effect*.

By contrast, an informal organization can be described as "one big happy family" where no one wants to hurt the feelings of another person. Management and the organization are highly relationship driven. Everyone has authority but no one has responsibility. Inappropriate actions and behavior are not confronted. Little conflicts tend to fester, never get resolved, and seldom come out in the open. Problem solving is through panic reaction without order or role definition. Pleasers, Avoiders, and sometimes Attackers tend to migrate to the informal organization. Achievers, Performers, Commanders, and Attackers usually are not welcome in the organization because they tend to promote change, innovation, responsibility, order, role definition, task behavior, and/or just upset the big happy family. Informal organizations tend to be either marginally profitable or not at all. They also are usually not very productive.

The third management style and organization category is achievement-driven. Achievers determine the organizational culture and are highly visible at all levels of the organization. Many of the other personality categories of the model taught by Dr. Bell are also members of the achievement-driven organization. They function in well-defined, yet flexible roles suited to their motivation. Operating units operate as teams with open, honest, direct, and specific multidirectional communications. The organizational value system is well-defined and broadly communicated, while defined and calculated risk is promoted. A reasonable amount of failure is accepted as one of the possible results of risk-taking. Initiative, creativity, and innovation are rewarded. Individuals are valued for their positive traits and contributions. Self-esteem of the individuals and the organization as a whole is high. The organization successfully integrates task, information, and relationship behaviors. High achievement organizations tend to be highly productive, innovative, and profitable.

In his seminars, Jensen demonstrates the dynamics and productivity of the three organizational styles by dividing the group into three smaller groups. Each smaller group is given the objective and general directions for making as many paper airplanes as possible in ten minutes. Prior to the project Jensen chooses one person as a leader for each group. Each leader chosen naturally exhibits traits of one of the three categories. He/she is directed to manage the group in that style.

The informally managed group exhibits great confusion. A few individuals make a few innovative design airplanes on their own. There tends to be an abundance of test flights. There is lots of laughter. The end result is a limited number of unique design airplanes.

In the formally managed group, autocratic instructions are given for design and production. The leader defines the role of each person in an assembly line. No suggestions or innovations are allowed from the production workers. In the two times I participated in the seminar, the formal group once produced a few more planes than the informal group and once dissolved in revolt against the manager without producing a single paper airplane.

In the achievement-managed group, the objectives and directions are stated by the leader and group participation is sought in developing a system of production. Roles are defined by the group, as is the final design of the product. A team effort at production then usually produces five to ten times more airplanes than either of the other two groups.

In this model, of course, the most effective style of management is Achievement. In achievement management, energy is concentrated on solving problems, not in maintaining unproductive relationships or in establishing and maintaining an unproductive bureaucracy.

Again, there is no conflict between the various models I have discussed. The informal group is similar to McGregor's relationship behavior group; the formal group is the task behavior group; the achievement group is similar to Blake's merged concerns for people and production groups. These groups utilize motivation through the basic needs. The appropriateness of the motivation is the key to success.

Foxholes

There is one more model I want to discuss. John Haskell uses the analogy of a "foxhole war" to describe the dynamic interactions and politics of organizations. The analogy is excellent. The basic premise: A tremendous amount of energy is used shooting at, and defending against, other individuals and organizations. In fact, in some cases most of the energy is used in fighting this war. In the past all has not been lost because the "customer" was consumed in his/her own war and the competition had their own wars to sap their energy.

Figure 11

Foxhole Wars

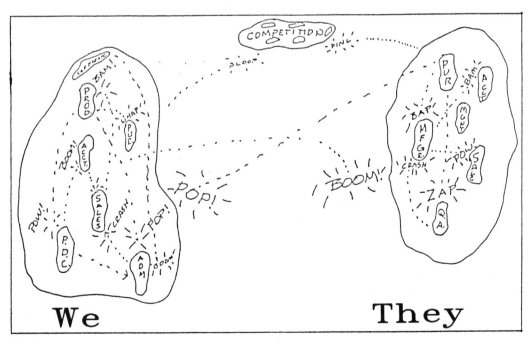

Once in awhile a shot is fired at the competition but most of the "external shots" are fired at customers and/or suppliers.

When we analyze actual organizational behavior it is evident that very little energy goes to meet the needs of the final consumer. There must be a *direct cause* and a *root cause* for the foxhole wars. Part of the quest for quality is to identify the *root cause* and take action to eliminate behaviors leading to foxhole wars. One of the first steps in the excellence process is to fill the internal foxholes. Next, the greater foxholes between supplier and customer must be filled. When this occurs, the total energies of all organizations are then directed at meeting the needs of the final consumer.

It takes a lot of guts, assertiveness, and self-confidence to call a truce in the foxhole wars, stand up on high ground, face potshots, and be vulnerable. Such action is part of the excellence process.

The current situation in American industry has demonstrated that if we don't resolve our conflicts, competitors will, and their energy will be better used to meet the needs of the consumer. Foxhole wars lead to slow but certain death.

A New Model

I believe there are three dimensions in determining management style and employee role. This factor is the ability to handle information or data. I have developed a new model incorporating this third dimension. The model is a synthesis of the concepts of the models previously discussed. In graphic form the third dimension, plotted in Z direction, scales information behavior. Ideal behavior and maturity becomes the highest level of each behavior, 9:9:9.

Next, I propose that to quantify the impact of an individual a summary scale can be developed using the product of the evaluations on the three axes. Thus, the highest maturity possible would be $9 \times 9 \times 9 = 729$. Mid-range maturity would be $5 \times 5 \times 5 = 125$. The purely autocratic, purely informational, or purely relationship oriented person would be $9 \times 1 \times 1 = 9$.

I believe that the synthesis of the three behaviors is highly dependent upon the self-esteem of the individual. Self-esteem is a nebulous property of the personality that I will address here and further as we progress. Briefly though, high self-esteem is the result of the individual's ability to unify as the same the individual's perceived image of self, as forced by values and the environment, and the individual's internal ideal of self, the ego image. Assuming this definition is correct, then the development of self-esteem and behaviors goes hand-in-hand. Excellence is a high maturity trait and requires high self-esteem. To obtain excellence values and behaviors must either be developed in the individuals and/or the roles must be aligned with the self ideal.

For excellence to be the driving force in an organization each individual should strive for the appropriate synthesis of relationship, task, and informa-

Figure 12

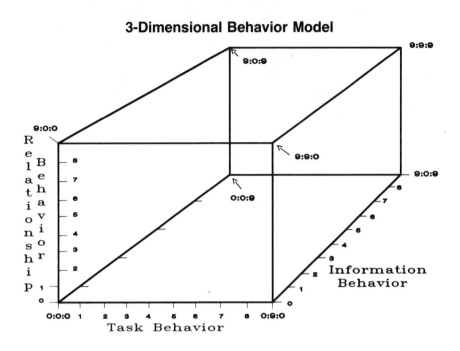

3-Dimensional Behavior Model

tion behaviors. Roles must be aligned with behaviors. Furthermore, flexibility is an attribute to be developed and rewarded.

My experience indicates that people exhibit varying levels of ability to integrate the behaviors. In Western society people traditionally tend to migrate to occupations and life styles that strongly emphasize one category of behaviors. The "A"/"not A" orientation of our Greek ancestry permeates our actions. The integration of the behaviors requires first, a recognition that the behaviors can be integrated in a continuum, then a conscious decision to do so.

Summary

We have looked at several models of management, management styles, and communications, and I have begun the development of an expanded model of behavior synthesis for excellence. Traits common to each model of the effective manager and effective leadership are a high level of self-confidence, a broad range of behaviors, an open mind, a defined value system, and a sense of direction. Effective individuals and organizations are able to understand the need gratification of others and themselves, accept deficiencies in themselves and others, and build on assets. The effective managers and organizations are working toward self-actualization.

The quest in structuring a quality driven organization is to facilitate growth and utilization of highly effective employees and managers. In the current terminology these individuals are "champions." The organizational task is to utilize these highly motivated people, in their highest productivity role, to meet both the needs of the individuals and the needs of the corporation, and to nurture these individuals to grow into even more productive roles. When a company can follow this course of action it fulfills the organization's responsibility to customer, employee, and stockholder.

For the achieving individual to make a maximum contribution to both self and organization he/she must be in the right position, have resources, be mentored, and have opportunity. Not stopping the opportunity for maximum productivity in a system that benefits both the individual and the organization is basic to the development of an excellence-driven organization.

Quality Responsibility

5

The history of American industry has been to establish a quality department and delegate the responsibility for quality to that department. The action taken by the quality department was primarily to inspect the produced goods and recommend their acceptability for shipment to a purchaser. This function is generally known as "lot acceptance." The department policed the production process. The costs associated with unacceptable goods were born by the customers, the stockholders, and the employees. The determination made by the quality department was after the fact. The quality department made little effort to determine the *direct causes* and *root causes* for materials not meeting the acceptance criteria. That function, when done, was considered the responsibility of others. Production was volume driven, purchasing and accounting were cost driven, while upper management was profit driven. Each department had a myopia for the factors driving that department.

HQM refutes this definition and delegation of quality control and other functions. Quality is everyone's responsibility, as is fiscal responsibility. In HQM, the quality improvement and control functions are broadly delegated to all individuals who impact the quality of the good and/or service. If ultimately, after the elimination of lot acceptance procedures, there is to be a quality department, the focus will be on providing information and mentors for sound decisions and changes in the systems of providing goods and services to better meet the needs of customers.

Quality is a significant portion of the focus of each individual touched by the organization and the organization's products. By each individual I include every employee and principal of the organization—from the CEO to the janitor, every employee of all supplier organizations, and every purchaser and employee of customer organizations. The quality function cannot be delegated; it must be distributed. The actions of one individual can undermine the good intentions and quality-oriented actions of other individuals. Every reader of this book has a significant responsibility for quality. In HQM philosophy it is not acceptable to consider how the quality responsibility can be delegated but to seriously and constantly ask yourself "What am I doing to improve quality?"

"Am I acting to solve *root cause* problems?" "Am I influencing others to be driven by a quest for excellence?"

Management Responsibility

To whom is a corporation responsible? To whom is management responsible? Historically management and the corporation managed have been viewed as synonymous. In the new corporations this limited concept is no longer completely true. In view of the current societal changes emphasizing the role of the individual, the responsibility is now extended to include all employees. Employees certainly can affect the overall perception of a corporation by those outside but touched by the corporation.

In sales there is an axiom that the territorial salesperson *is* the company to his/her customers. The actions of the representative determine the customer's perception of the company. To the manufacturing employee, the company is the

Figure 13

Management's Responsibility

(Disregard of One Will Lead to Long–Term Decline)

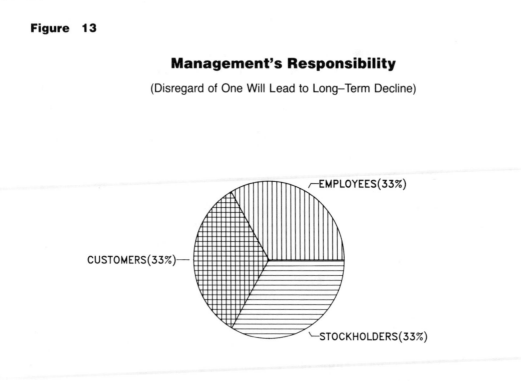

Balance Is Essential To Quality Growth

people the employee sees routinely. Management, other employees, and even the suppliers are the corporation. Together they share corporate responsibility.

The original question remains unanswered. To whom is a corporation responsible? *A corporation is equally responsible to its customers, its employees, and its stockholders.* Responsibility, therefore, extends to every person associated with the organization. Neglect of responsibility due any category will, in the long run, undermine ability to serve the other categories. This responsibility requires a concerted conscious effort and multiple leadership behaviors to maintain balance. If the effectiveness of fulfilling these responsibilities could be objectively quantified, the categories would be: product/service quality, fiscal quality, and human resources quality.

Returning to the proposed definition of quality, we can now state that corporate responsibility is to provide the "customers" profitably, promptly, and consistently with the goods and/or services that meet their needs. Excellence is *exceeding* the needs of the "customers."

Management Maturity

Digging a ditch does not require high-level management or employee maturity. Task behavior is usually appropriate. The tasks, although strenuous, are not complex. The information requirements are minimal and the minimum behavioral requirement is autocratic. On the other hand, the revealed management policies leading to the space shuttle Challenger tragedy indicate that a high-level mix of all three behaviors is required to launch space shuttles. This goal demands high management maturity. But the levels of task, relationship, and information behavior differ for each objective. For maximum effectiveness the maturity level of objective, management, and employees should all be matched.

Hersey and Blanchard, in *Management of Organizational Behavior: Utilizing Human Resources,* propose that the interrelationship of task behavior and relationship behavior in a manager can and should be varied for each individual and each task. In many ways this model is similar to McGregor's model discussed earlier, but Hersey and Blanchard go further. They divide the task and relationship behavior into four quadrants (Figure 14). Starting at the lower right-hand quadrant and moving counterclockwise, the four quadrants are "Telling," "Selling," "Participating," and "Delegating." Hersey and Blanchard state that there is an optimum complementary behavioral mix between manager and employee and task. There is no correct management behavior, but given a task to be accomplished, the behaviors and the motivation of the employee, there is a most effective management and employee interaction style. An employee experienced in a specific task may require little direct instruction and only minimal psychological reinforcement. The appropriate management style is delegating. With the same manager and employee and another task, perhaps one the employee has never done before but is eager

Figure 14

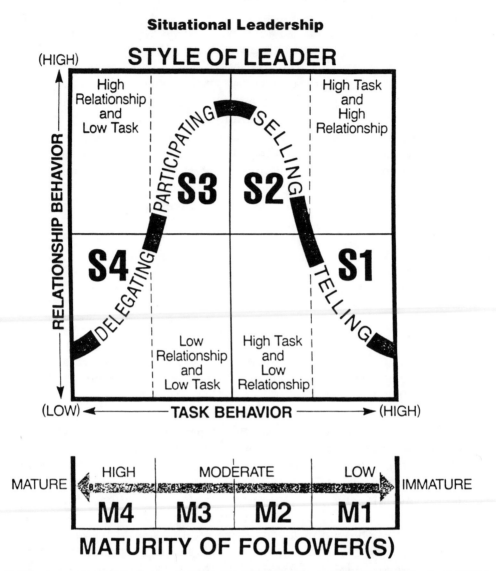

Situational Leadership

STYLE OF LEADER

(HIGH)

RELATIONSHIP BEHAVIOR

High Relationship and Low Task

PARTICIPATING

S3

High Task and High Relationship

SELLING

S2

DELEGATING

S4

Low Relationship and Low Task

S1

TELLING

High Task and Low Relationship

(LOW) ◄——— **TASK BEHAVIOR** ———► (HIGH)

MATURE ◄ | HIGH | MODERATE | LOW | ► IMMATURE

| **M4** | **M3** | **M2** | **M1** |

MATURITY OF FOLLOWER(S)

From Management of Organizational Behavior: Utilizing Human Resources, 3rd ed., © 1977 by Paul Hersey and Kenneth Blanchard. Published by Prentice-Hall, Englewood Cliffs, NJ.

to learn, the appropriate management behavior may involve much telling and little psychological reinforcement. Different behaviors are required in different situations. It is up to the manager to determine and assume the appropriate behavior for each task assigned to an employee.

Hersey and Blanchard make a maturity assessment of the four styles, ranging from "Telling" at the low end of the scale, to "Selling," "Participating," and "Delegating" at the high end. Such a maturity evaluation appears to coincide with other models of behaviors and Maslow's order of basic needs.

Delegating is appropriate for individuals with high-level behaviors. They don't have to be told the specific steps of a task. The individual is self-motivated enough to accomplish the project.

Although I find this model highly descriptive and helpful in teaching desired interactions of manager and employee, I question how the chief delegator, the CEO, cannot exhibit task or relationship behavior. These talented individuals are different from the "no personality" individuals. The highest level executives utilize predominantly information behavior, backed up with high level people and task skills, while the top executive surrounds himself/herself with highly qualified people and makes decisions based on the information provided.

The flexibility of style advocated by Hersey and Blanchard is rare, though desirable. Under pressure to perform most managers react like the frog in the heating pot. They revert to their natural behavior. Many have not found the confidence to jump out of the pot and develop the broad skill base necessary to function in line with this model. That doesn't mean that some won't; some few will, and they will be far greater managers by modifying their style to fit the situation.

The implementation of a comprehensive quality program is an objective requiring a high level of maturity in both management and employees. To accomplish the objective of continually moving to higher and higher quality, the maturity of managers and employees must also continually increase. There is a high correlation between the five stages of the quality process discussed earlier and the levels of management maturity defined by Hersey and Blanchard.

In moving toward an excellence-driven organization, *the early actions of upper management toward implementation of a quality culture may often have to be autocratic.* The truly mature manager will recognize that the organizational culture has been historically of lower maturity. Therefore, starting the movement and growth toward higher maturity may require a command toward excellence, a command to consensus. People do not change quickly. They must first be commanded into the growth process and then led constantly toward higher and higher levels of organizational maturity.

Historically, many attempts to shift the culture of existing organizations have failed because upper management expected individuals to jump at the opportunity for a better organization. They expected the change to be instantaneous. In an earlier chapter I discussed the psychological concept of the rubric-ingrained patterns of thought and behavior. Older organizations often are locked into rubrics of historic behavior. A tremendous amount of effort by upper management is necessary to break the rubrics and concurrently provide an alternative behavior pattern.

Breaking the rubric patterns is a growth process for the individuals of the organization. Each individual will go through the stages of learning and growth discussed earlier. But again, a tremendous amount of coaching is necessary in the early stages of growth.

In the initial stages of benevolent and wise autocracy, individuals will need to sense a discomfort, a dissatisfaction, with the old rubric behavior. This discomfort is short of crisis and is coupled with an intellectual desire to reduce the discomfort. Again, this dissatisfaction must be promoted by upper management. The errors of the old system must be pointed out at every opportunity without belittling the individuals. Individuals must not remain comfortable with the old behaviors. They must be motivated to change and at the same time they must be coached toward an improved behavior pattern. Such coaching requires flexibility of style by top management to match the exhibited maturity of those being managed. I will discuss many of these techniques further in the next chapter.

With an understanding that continual growth in quality requires a continual increase in the maturity level of all parties, the questions arise, "What are the specific characteristics inherent in high maturity management?" and "What actions lead to growth in maturity?" We have started this investigation. Finding answers to these two questions and coaching increased maturity are prerequisites to achieving a comprehensive quality program.

Delegation and Values

An essential element of high maturity management is delegation. Delegation increases capacity for taking action and solving problems. Delegation is effective only when authority for decision making is also passed on to others. Passing on responsibility without authority is not delegation. When only responsibility is delegated, the decision-making process is not moved to a lower level. The person to whom responsibility is assigned without authority continually "upward delegates" the final decision to the higher level where the authority exists. The expected capacity and productivity improvements are not realized. The person to whom decision-making is delegated must have the authority to make the decision, right or wrong.

Responsibility for decisions cannot be delegated. The person passing on authority is always responsible for passing on the authority. This non-transference of responsibility does not relieve the subordinate of responsibility for the quality of his/her decisions. Both parties share the responsibility.

Since management shares responsibility with those to whom they delegate authority, there must exist a high level of trust between the delegator and the delegatee. Without this trust, the authority for decisions will never be delegated.

Trust is developed through a mutual understanding of the value system of each party. The two value systems do not necessarily need to be identical but must be understood and appreciated by the parties participating in the delegation. The delegator wisely decides when and where sufficient trust exists for sound decisions by the delegatee.

Most individuals are not conscious of their own value system much less the value system of others in the organization. Most of our value systems are not solidified sufficiently. To others our values often appear to change with the situation. The apparent flux inhibits development of trust, initiative in managing and problem solving, and delegation of authority. Individual value systems will be discussed further in Chapter 6.

If a corporation is to endorse high maturity management, it behooves the highest authority policy setters of the corporation to determine the value system of the organization and communicate these values to all parties affected by the corporation. Few other actions can do more to further the development of trust, communications, delegation, high maturity management, and quality. Those individuals who severely disagree with and do not respect the value system of the corporation, or their fellow workers, will not be productive. Their undefined or contrary value system severely limits effectiveness. Both the organization and the individuals will ultimately be better off if such individuals join another organization with complementary values.

Clear Definition of Roles

When change is initiated, management is, in fact, asking that the role of each individual change. The role played previously is no longer desirable nor acceptable. Individuals will be asked to take on new responsibilities and execute newly delegated authority. Therefore, in the overall vision of the new organization must be included the specific vision of the roles of each position in accomplishing the mission of the organization. Because of historic low maturity and the resistance to change, each individual will need to be told and understand, in detail, what will be expected and the specific role the individual will have in accomplishing the mission.

This change in role definition does not limit the focus of the individual. The difference may appear non-distinct. Role definition can be envisioned as directing the focus and defining the responsibilities of the individual. With a focus there is a peripheral vision to other needs and roles. The total view encompasses the total organizational vision. Once again, accomplishing this goal requires high management maturity and the flexibility to direct, control and empower at the maturity level of the managed individuals.

Facilitating

John Naisbitt and Patricia Aburdene point out in *Megatrends* and *Reinventing the Corporation* that the effective manager of the new corporation is a facilitator. The new corporations are the companies that constitute the basis of our future economy. They are the corporations that will be viable as we pass into the twenty-first century.

A facilitator is a self-actualized person with the highest development of internal and external people behavior. The facilitator brings out the best in people. He/she mentors others to be all that they are capable of being. The techniques of facilitating are: listening, valuing, counseling, motivating, assembling information, and analyzing information. The predominant visible trait is wisdom. The best employees recently and currently entering the job market are highly intelligent, independent, and to a large extent, self-motivated. They resent an autocratic, task-oriented management style. They quickly leave or do not join autocratic organizations. These employees are the most creative, most self-actualized, and most productive. They handle and welcome a dynamic environment. These are the people we want in excellence-driven organizations. We certainly don't want them in the offices of our competitors. The power of the facilitator is derived from people. The facilitator's power is based on his/her ability to empower other people. The facilitator is a "Hi-touch" individual that adds balance to the new "Hi-tech" environment. The organization managed by facilitators is perceived by the best employees and customers as one of excellence.

The facilitator is not a "soft" individual. His/her objective is growth of the individual being mentored. The facilitator recognizes that the objective of mentoring is not to "please" the employee, but to nurture the employee toward achievement and psychological health. The mentor desires each individual to stretch to be all that he/she can be. Through this action, total corporate responsibility will be fulfilled.

The facilitator/mentor must often force the "frog to jump out of the pot." Such action is not emotionally comfortable. Because a mentor promotes growth in an individual without destroying the self-esteem of the individual, it is considered the highest form of people-skills behavior.

Understanding and Guiding People Behavior

6

The more we can understand people the more effectively managers and employees can work toward the mutual goals of both the individual and the organization. It is sad, but often we as people are our own worst enemies. We not only intentionally and unintentionally undermine the efforts of others but also of ourselves. We continue to behave in ways that do not get us the results we seek. We become locked in conflict with others and with ourselves. We hinder the development, confidence, and behaviors that are necessary if excellence is to be achieved. We forget that for long-term goals of the organization to be achieved, the short and long-term goals of the individuals that constitute the organization must also be achieved.

I am not a professional psychologist, but psychology is as much a part of the job of managing as is the ability to read a financial statement, interpret a control chart, or engineer a machinery modification. In fact, I believe it is one of the prerequisites of managing. In managing, we seek to accomplish tasks indirectly through guiding, directing, empowering, and acting as mentor to other people. A manager does not manage machines; a manager manages the people who design, set up, and tend machines. Managers do not directly produce the communications and reports that are the information system of an organization. They manage the people who do these tasks. People ultimately control all non-entropic processes and managers coordinate and control the activities of people who struggle against the entropy of nature. The main focus of true management is people and to attempt to manage without the skills and understanding of people is analogous to an average-grade school student setting out to design and build a skyscraper. This chapter is devoted to increasing some of the basic skills for understanding people.

The Three States of Personality

Dr. Eric Berne first proposed a system of psychology called Transactional Analysis (TA). Berne was seeking to develop a system explaining the actions of the individual and the interactions of individuals without the massive jargon of classical psychology, and in a manner understandable and teachable to laymen. TA certainly does not explain all the situations of psychology, especially abnormal psychology, yet with an understanding of its limitations it is an effective system. TA is useful in defining, understanding, and acting upon one of the major problems the American corporation faces today as it attempts to address the quality issue: the quality of life and motivation of the people who ultimately are responsible for quality. Managers, or anyone else who is interacting with people, must know how to understand, guide, direct, and motivate the people touched by an organization.

First, in TA, Berne states that the personality of each individual consists of three distinct sub-personalities: the Parent, the Adult, and the Child. The interaction of these three sub-personalities determines the internal and external personality of the individual.

From the time we are born, and there is some evidence that it is actually from the time we are conceived, our brains start recording information. These recordings are much like tape recorders running constantly. All of our senses feed data into these recordings, even the data of which we are not necessarily mentally conscious. Berne cites the work of Dr. Wilder Penfield, who found that by touching an electrical probe to parts of the human brain, the recordings could be replayed through the conscious mind. The replaying is not just remembering, but actually takes the conscious mind through the situation recorded, just as if the event were being relived by the subject.

There is not one, but two recorders going in the brain, in unison. One is recording perceived facts while the other is recording the emotions that go along with the facts. Each recording can be played through electrical stimulation of the brain. The recordings of the perceived facts Berne calls the Parent. The recordings of emotions he calls the Child. Berne makes a clear distinction between the Parent and parent-like behavior and the Child and child-like behavior. The nature of an observed behavior is a judgment call on the part of the observer. The judgment call does not necessarily reflect the original mental recordings of the subject.

These recordings of the Parent and Child in the subconscious brain can also be stimulated by the signals of the nervous system. Current situations that are similar, and the resulting sensory signals, may recall the emotions of recorded childhood situations. An individual who was frightened, hurt, or made to feel guilty by authority figures during youth—a Child recording—may sense the same fright or guilt in the presence of someone who now has authority over the individual.

The situation does not need to justify the emotion, i.e., the authority figure is not now necessarily adversely exercising authority to control the actions of the person. The emotions are not rational, but to the person the feelings are real.

Dogma of the Parent can be recalled similarly. Most prejudices are Parent dogma. It is not rational nor true to believe that all people of a race, creed, or

Figure 15

Transactional Analysis

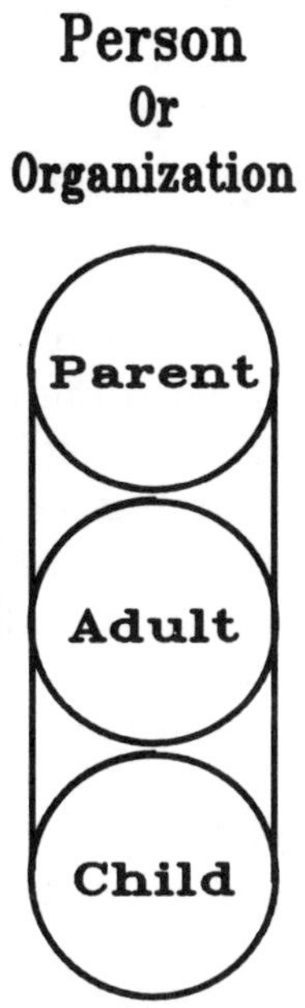

Person
Or
Organization

Parent

Adult

Child

The personalities of people and organizations can be thought of as being composed of three personalities, ego states, the *Parent*, the *Adult*, and the *Child*.

Stored in the Parent are beliefs and values recorded, like tape recordings, very early in life. These recordings are accepted as unquestioned truth. They are the beliefs of our parents and perhaps their parents. The information stored in the Parent can be helpful or distructive. We can tell when the Parent is in *executive control* when we hear "should", "never", "shouldn't", "must not", "do", "Don't", etc.

The Adult in a personality is the rational, thinking, state of mind. The Adult obtains information from the Parent, the Child, and the outside environment. The Adult processes this information for rationality, and formulates and evaluates forward thinking. The Adult asks the questions "who", "what", "when", "where", "how", and "why." These key words are easily identified indicators that the Adult is in executive control.

The Child is the emotional, inquisitive, fun-loving part of a personality. As with the Parent, the Child is recorded early in life like a tape recording. These tape recordings can be started by stemuli and played back in various situations. We laugh, love, play, get emotionally hurt, get angry, feel guilty, get excited, are inquisitive, and are creative when our Child is in executive control.

Sometimes the Parent and/or Child contaminate the Adult. When this happens the actions and/or thought processes are inappropriate for the situation.

There is no "right" executive control. There are times when each personality is appropriate. In high maturity management the Adult is in control for planning, problem solving, and evaluating alternatives.

---

color possess a negative trait. The Parent of the person was taught the prejudice as truth. It is recorded as such in the mind.

Only the rational Adult of a personality can effectively counteract and show to be incorrect the recording of prejudice or fear that reside in the Parent and Child.

The Parent holds recordings of "facts and values." These beliefs are unquestioned dogma. They are the beliefs of our parents and perhaps their parents, etc. We can detect when we or others are operating in our Parent when we hear ourselves or others use *should, must, always, never, shouldn't, must not,* etc. Unless we discipline ourselves through the Adult, we accept these commands from the Parent as truth. Some of our Parent recordings are helpful and useful, and some are destructive.

A child is taught the dogma of "Don't play in the street" or "Don't run out in front of cars" usually by parents as soon as he/she begins to walk and play outside. The impact is recorded in the Parent of the brain. Such a recording is almost always valid throughout life. There are few situations where playing in the street will be beneficial to health and welfare. Yet, such dogma might be detrimental to the health and welfare of the individual if he/she refused to attend a street dance or block party under controlled conditions because such action is literally "playing in the street." Only when the Parent dogma is filtered through the Adult is a rational decision made about the reality of the dogma.

The Child is the emotional part of our personality. As with the Parent, the Child is developed early in our life. We laugh, love, get angry, feel hurt, feel guilty, feel elated, and are creative when we are acting in our Child.

The Adult in each of us is the rational, thinking part of us. The Adult develops later than the Parent and Child. The Adult is the state of mind where we truly *think*. The Adult seeks data and information. The Adult asks the questions who, what, when, where, how, and sometimes *why*. The Adult is the processor of information that leads to reasoned decisions.

Along with the previously mentioned actions, the Adult processes information from the Parent and Child to determine the validity of that information. The Adult is the area of reason within our personalities.

Quite often, within an individual, the Parent and Child interact with each other without the evaluative and reasoning influence of the Adult. When this happens it can often lead to a feeling that "I am bad" or "I am not pleased with myself" or "I am not okay." Also, in some individuals, one aspect, the Parent, Adult, and/or Child may be deficient, contaminated, or not exist at all. These situations are defined as such "mental illnesses" as neurotic, psychotic, manic-depressive, and schizophrenic.

The basic unit of interaction, according to Berne, is the "Transaction." In interactions with other people, and with the three sub-personalities of an individual, we interact in either a complementary or a "crossed" manner. The diagram shows complementary transactions, and crossed transactions. Two people are involved in each external transaction.

Figure 16

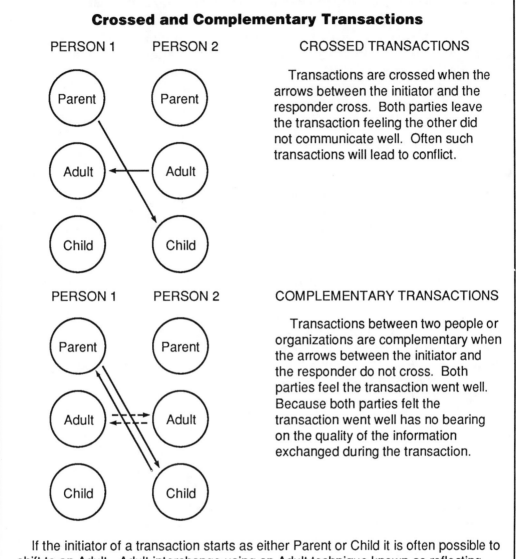

Crossed and Complementary Transactions

PERSON 1   PERSON 2   CROSSED TRANSACTIONS

Parent   Parent

Adult   Adult

Child   Child

Transactions are crossed when the arrows between the initiator and the responder cross. Both parties leave the transaction feeling the other did not communicate well. Often such transactions will lead to conflict.

PERSON 1   PERSON 2   COMPLEMENTARY TRANSACTIONS

Parent   Parent

Adult   Adult

Child   Child

Transactions between two people or organizations are complementary when the arrows between the initiator and the responder do not cross. Both parties feel the transaction went well. Because both parties felt the transaction went well has no bearing on the quality of the information exchanged during the transaction.

If the initiator of a transaction starts as either Parent or Child it is often possible to shift to an Adult - Adult interchange using an Adult technique known as reflecting. Once the shift has occured the conversation can continue on an Adult - Adult basis.

Each person can choose to act out of their Parent, Child, or Adult. The party initiating the transaction not only chooses his/her own state but usually has an expected response state in mind for the second party. For example, an initiator may open the transaction from the Parent, with the expectation that the second party will respond from the Child. As long as the second party *does* respond from the Child, the transaction is not crossed. The situation is not tense and outwardly the transaction appears friendly. There are situations where such a transaction is perfectly all right.

There are non-crossed transactions between Parent and Parent as there are between Child and Child. A typical Parent to Parent transaction would be a conversation about politics that is actually a "game" of "Ain't it awful!" Kidding, humor, and flirting are usually Child-Child transactions. Again, there is no "always right" type of transaction. There are only transaction styles that are appropriate for the occasion and objective.

The Adult is the only state of personality in which we truly think, i.e., we listen, we evaluate, we make probability estimations, and we arrive at weighed conclusions. When we seek to make sound decisions in a changing environment, the dogmatic Parent and the emotional Child must be filtered through the Adult. It is the area of personality where we have the highest probability of determining the truth of a situation.

The Adult is the preferred area of operation for the high maturity manager. The high maturity manager does not act directly out of unconscious rubrics from the Parent or the Child. The Adult-Adult transaction is the transaction style for business decisions.

Because the high maturity manager operates out of the Adult does not mean he/she is not at times fun-loving nor, when necessary, stern. Just the contrary. The Adult manager filters the Parent and the Child of his/her personality through the Adult, analyzes the situation, and determines when Parent or Child behavior is appropriate.

Often in tense situations what is needed is relief from the tension. The Adult-filtered Child may return perspective to the situation. In like manner, when individuals are not cognizant of the seriousness of a situation and levity is excessive and not appropriate, Adult-filtered Parent behavior may be appropriate.

Before an individual can effectively analyze and control the transactions between others, the individual must first understand his/her own internal transactions. Without such understanding, the contamination of the individual's personality will be transferred to the parties of the external transaction being analyzed. For example, the individual who does not comprehend through Adult filtration that authority irrationally produces anxiety in himself/herself will most likely view all uses of power/authority with anxiety. That individual will presume a similar reaction in other people. That individual will not recognize that there are appropriate and inappropriate uses of authority or that other people may not have the same reaction to authority.

In many states professional psychologists are required to undergo extensive psychological analysis before being considered qualified to assist others with psychological problems. In like manner, managers who seek to analyze motivations and behaviors need to first understand themselves. Without such a basis, transference becomes common and is extremely confusing to the people being managed.

In seeking to understand the composition of one's own personality, a technique called tracking is advocated by Dr. Thomas Harris and his wife Amy.

Figure 17

Internal Dialogue

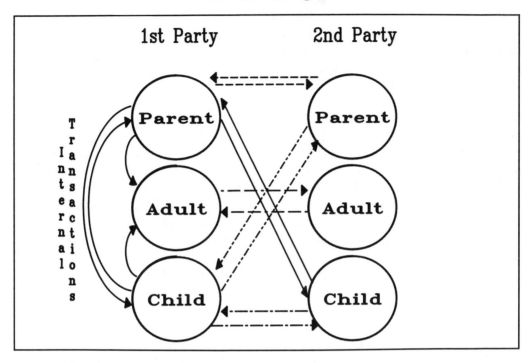

Internal dialogue is the source of our level of self confidence, assertiveness, sense of well-being, and passive aggressive behavior. The internal messages in the Parent and the Child, the "rule" and the feeling, can agree or they may conflict with each other. As long as the two messages agree we perceive a sense of "self." We outwardly are self-confident and have few problems with being assertive, expressing our thoughts, and being open through the Adult to the thoughts and ideas of others. When the Parent and Child develop in conflict, through mixed messages, wars are waged within our personality. We are internally confused and often act impulsively based on which personality segment is winning the current battle.

To resolve these wars we activate the rational, thinking, probability estimating Adult. Through the adult we consider each side of the conflict and develop a new programming for the Parent and/or Child. The reconciliation of these battles leads to the generation and solidification of our own personal value system. We become true to our "self," open to learning, self confident, and truly assertive.

In tracking, an individual first becomes cognizant of the Parent or Child reactions of his/her personality. It may be helpful to make a written list of Parent reactions. Next make a list of Child reactions. Addressing each reaction and using Adult analysis, ask yourself the questions who, what, why, when, how, and where. *Why* do I feel anxious in the presence of authority? *What* in my recordings produces this reaction? *When* and *where* as a child did I repeatedly experience a similar reaction? Do I *like* the reaction? Is such a reaction gaining me the need gratification I seek? Do I really want to change the reaction?

Through such a tracking process an individual cannot only gain insight into the makeup of his/her own personality but can also assume, if desired, the necessary responsibility for his/her own actions that is necessary if change is desired. Is this self-psychoanalysis? *Yes*.

When a person has an understanding of, not necessarily a change in, the makeup of his/her own personality, the person can begin to effectively analyze the transactions of others. Now the person can effectively analyze what sector of the personality is acting in a transaction.

Transactions can occur between two or more people. Ideally, at least one of the parties of the transaction will be trained to determine what part of the personality is talking. If more than one party is familiar with the theories and techniques of TA it becomes quite simple to shift the type of transaction to an appropriate style when necessary. Often the simple query "Who is speaking— your Parent, Adult, or Child?" is enough to change the transaction. Other times a statement of observed behavior and a request for a shift in behavior may be necessary to bring a transaction to the appropriate level.

For example, arguments over business matters often tend to become either Parent-Parent "Ain't it awful," or Child-Child tantrums, or Parent-Child complementary transactions. None are appropriate when the resolution of a problem requires a rational Adult-Adult transaction.

The declaration that follows usually will bring the improper transaction to an Adult-Adult basis, if not on the first try then on the second or third restatement. "I recognize that we both have gotten angry about this situation. You feel that it is important that we adjust for maximum output. Let's cool down and see if we can find a way to maximize output and quality at the same time. That will work for both of us." Such Adult statements addressed at the Parent will eventually force the mentally healthy person to respond from the Adult.

Similar situations are common when a father and/or mother addresses the hurt Child of a child. "Will you please tell me what happened? I can see you are angry," or, "Please tell me what made you so angry?" Again, these questions bring the conversation to an appropriate Adult-Adult basis.

In almost all situations the proper transaction for doing business is Adult-Adult. How else can rational decisions be made?

Other People Skills

Active Listening

Effective listening is an active, not passive, task. Good listening requires tremendous energy. After an extended listening session the listener will feel physically tired.

Listening involves the ears, the eyes, and sometimes touch. We communicate with our bodies through gestures, facial expressions, tone of voice, touch, and with words. In fact, the majority of communication in an effective transaction is by means other than the actual words.

In communicating we attempt to transfer to another person both content and feelings. Many people are not conscious of the transfer of feelings, although they respond readily to the communicated feeling. Think about the sentence "Oh yeah, I'll do that." It can be stated with excitement, anger, despair, nonchalance, or other feelings. The listener makes a judgmental assessment of feeling based on tone-of-voice, expression, gesture, eye contact, or other non-vocal communication. Without an assessment of feeling in communication we only assume the communication accurately reflects the intended transference of information.

In organizations, memos play a valid role in providing a hard record or broadly disseminating thought and transaction. But they all too frequently are used to avoid effective communication. How can a person effectively listen to a memo? Less than half of the communication is contained. Individuals short in relationship skills and behavior often resort to writing memos for transactions when personal or telephone transaction would be much more effective. If a permanent record is required, there are other means of providing that record.

Listening involves complete attention. The active listener should not expect to be able to listen effectively and address other tasks or thoughts at the same time. There is a natural problem here. We think faster than a person talks. The natural response is for the listener to fill the voids between statements with thought directed at other activities or problems. This mixed thinking process is deadly to effective listening. During the time mental activity drifts elsewhere, an effective listener will repeat the statement of the speaker or make an evaluation of the feeling communicated along with the words. This is much of the work of active listening.

Another natural response to the difference in the speed of thinking and the speed of talking is for the listener to start to formulate a response to the talker. Again, this activity is deadly to effective communication. The listener that pre-formulates a response does not hear or sense most of the communication of the speaker.

There are many good books and courses on active listening. I believe active listening to be one of the basic behaviors of effective management. Listening behavior is an area of vast need between the current behavior of managers and the desired behavior necessary for the excellence-motivated organization.

An individual seeking to improve active listening skills will go through the stages of learning discussed in Chapter 2. The awkward and inadequate feelings are normal. But perseverance through the learning process will be well-rewarded.

Questioning

Effective questioning is one of the prime tools of controlling transactions and bringing them to an appropriate level for the resolution of problems and goal accomplishment. The question words *who, what, where, when,* and *how* start open-ended sentences that require the respondent to give more than a simple yes/no answer. Such questions force a rational Adult response. Such questions are usually not judgmental, but if used improperly can be construed as controlling.

Note that I did not include the word "why." "Why" is a word that is tied to our childhood. Usually it is tied with situations that were not pleasant. Parents use the word excessively. "Why did you break the vase?" "Why did you get in a fight with your sister?" The word "why" hooks the guilty Child in us and automatically puts most people on the defensive. The response is often "because" or "I don't know." Direct, rational answers often do not come when the word "why" is used in a question. The appropriate use of the word "why" is in a discussion with yourself.

Reflecting

Reflecting is another procedure for controlling a transaction and modifying it to an Adult-Adult basis. Active listening is prerequisite to reflecting. Reflection is the restatement of first the feeling and then the content of the previous communication by the other party of the transaction. Reflecting is an Adult procedure which values the feeling and content expressed.

There are numerous levels of skill in reflecting. In the first level the second party repeats the statement of the first party exactly. For example, an employee may state with wild gestures, "None of the mechanics know what they are doing!" The level one reflection response would be "None of the mechanics know what they are doing." Such a statement acknowledges to the first party in an Adult manner that you listened to the statement. The normal response to a properly made level 1 reflection is more detail about the problem with the mechanics.

The level 2 reflection changes an "I . . ." statement to a "You . . ." statement. For example, the level 2 reflection of the statement "I can't believe the mechanics took three hours to fix the machine!" would be "You can't believe the mechanics took three hours to fix the machine."

At the third level, the "you" is incorporated but only part of the statement is restated. The reflection of "I wish we had good mechanics. They didn't have their tools when the machine went down and it took three hours to get it back up!" would be "You wish we had good mechanics." The lower level reflections sometimes are perceived as "phony" to a speaker if used inappropriately. Level three through level five are the main tools of the business active listener.

In the fourth level of reflection, the person reflecting summarizes in his/her own words the example statement, "You had troubles with the mechanics and the machine was down longer than you expected."

At the fifth level, the reflector restates the first speaker's feeling and summarizes the content. The example would be reflected as, "You're frustrated with maintenance because it took three hours to get the machine running."

The sixth level is the most advanced form of reflection. It is best used by professionally trained listeners, for example, analysts, therapists, and ministers. The reader should be aware of the sixth level but in a business environment the non-professional reflector risks alienating the speaker by misinterpretation of the actual feeling being expressed and can actually do more harm than good. At the sixth level an assessment is made of feelings and/or content expressed by the original speaker, but of which he/she may not be aware. "I'm worried about getting the project done on time!" might be reflected as "Sounds like you're anxious because you fear the late project will affect your performance review."

In the higher levels the appropriateness of the reflection is based on much more of the communication than the actual words. Body language, tone-of-voice, and eye movement may communicate much of the feeling and content that is stated in the reflection.

In reflecting, the tone-of-voice is important. Reflecting is a statement of understanding, not a question. It is important that a reflection statement be ended in a lower tone of voice than the tone of voice of the rest of the statement. Most questions end with a higher tone of voice. The voice drops at the end of a statement. Control of the tone of voice is part of effectively communicating.

Reflecting is a skill and a behavior. It can be learned like most other skills. The learning process will be as described in Chapter 2. By reading this section the reader who has never used reflection has moved from the unconscious incompetent to the conscious incompetent stage of learning. Conscious practicing will initially produce awkward, anxious, and inadequate feelings in the novice. Persistence will build skill to the conscious competent level and the feelings will change to excitement and a sense of accomplishment. Continued use will continue behavior growth to the integrated competent stage. Reflecting will be the natural reaction.

Fortunately, as an individual learns the skill of reflecting he/she does not have to start with the sixth level. Routine use of lower levels will produce dramatic results during interactions. Over a number of years the reflector can progress to competence with higher level reflection.

Expected Behavior Is Fulfilled

There is a now classic and widely known experiment with a teacher and a class of school children. The children of the class were divided into two groups. Each group contained children of low measured intelligence, average intelligence, and high intelligence. The teacher was told privately that one group was slow learners and the other group was high achievers. Of course, this statement was not true. At the end of the school year the children were tested. In the "slow learner" group even the highly intelligent children had dropped in measured intelligence. The same drop was noted in the children of lesser actual intelligence within the "slow" group. In the "high achiever" group all the children, even the slow learners, made remarkable progress.

The point is that people, individuals, and groups perform toward a level of expectation. An expectation of excellence and quality will lead even the low-skilled individual to growth. Likewise, a preconceived notion of slothfulness, inattention, and lack of ability by a manager toward an employee or employees, or by employees toward fellow employees, will promote the expected behavior.

The essence of this principle is actualized through "CAN DO!" programs. People are accomplishing tasks that others would have thought impossible. Those who say it can't be done had better step aside and get out of the way of those who are doing it.

Understanding Value Systems

As with organizations only a few individuals are cognizant of their own value systems. The people who do not know their own values have never struggled with the basic concepts of what is actually important to them. They usually do have a value system buried deep in their subconscious mind. We might say it is part of their Parent. They have little basic understanding of the criteria upon which routine decisions are founded. They believe a decision can be made based on the significant factors and their merit. Perhaps they can. What establishes the relative merit of the factors of a decision? A value system.

The decisions made by people without clearly understood values reflect a lack of comprehension of their values. Their decisions appear to be inconsistent and contradictory. These individuals are unable to weigh the relative merits and disadvantages of taking a certain course of action. Instead of their controlling life, life happens to them. They make a decision and then cannot live with the consequences of the decision. They become angry, a Parent-Child internal transaction, because the effect of their decision is counter to the subconscious value system.

Such effects may be initiated by the individuals or they may be the default effects of allowing someone else to make a decision contrary to the value system of the individual.

Becoming consciously aware of one's own value system is part of the maturation process. It is part of taking responsibility for one's own actions and life.

Once an individual's value system is consciously understood then the implications of forced choices become more evident. The individual realizes that the *effects* are the result of a forced choice and the individual made a calculated trade-off. This is an *Adult* decision.

The actualizations of a value system, once the value system is understood, may be quite dynamic, but the value system usually does not change except through conscious Adult decision. There may be great changes in the activities of life but these changes are now in agreement with the value system.

For example, an employee who is not happy with the system of management of his/her organization might feel dissatisfaction with the situation. The employee has three choices: accept the system, change the system, or separate himself/herself from the organization and find another position that better fits the expectation of a work environment. This decision is the employee's—no one else's. It is probably not an easy decision. The decision is much easier if the employee understands what aspects of the decision are truly important to him/her, and what basic values each alternative impacts. By taking no action the employee defaults the decision to someone else or accepts the null-set decision—keep the situation the same. The employee was already conscious of dissatisfaction—usually a conflict of values. Continued dissatisfaction with the null-set decision probably will block need gratification, promote either apathy or belligerence, and may eventually lead to termination. Who made that decision? The *employee*.

If individuals are to address their dissatisfactions effectively, then a value system gives a solid basis for taking some action to correct the dissatisfaction. Without the action, individuals either take inappropriate action or simmer in the heating pot of dissatisfaction.

To bring the subconscious value system into the conscious is a relatively easy task but may be psychologically straining. Simply sit down with a pencil and paper and start to write out "These are my values. I believe in: . . ." It's not a quick process. It may require many revisions and resolution of numerous conflicts. The numerous conflicts are part of the psychological strain. The history of one's life may show numerous actions that were not in agreement with the basic values. Guilt and internal conflict will have to be resolved before the value system can be fully functional in future decision making. This process is similar to the tracking process for understanding internal transactions. Both processes are part of maturing the Adult in a personality so that it is in effective control.

Valuing

Valuing is the full appreciation of another individual for all his/her capabilities, talents, values, and basic needs. Effective valuing facilitates a positive self-image, maximum motivation and productivity. When people are not valued they can become despondent, uninterested, unmotivated, uncreative, poor thinkers, and do not believe in their own abilities. In high maturity management there is a great appreciation for the value of each individual of the organization. Every individual has skills that can be contributed positively, if not in the present organization then in another. Valuing behavior is directed at both self and toward others.

An individual cannot effectively value another individual if he/she does not first value himself/herself. Learning to value self is prerequisite to effectively valuing others. Chris Jensen of The Dan Group prepared the following rules for acknowledging self-worth:

Rules for Acknowledging Self-Worth

1. Give yourself permission not to be perfect. Unless you can walk on water, you are not; so don't require impossible standards of perfection from yourself.

2. Trust and value yourself. Don't compare yourself unfavorably to "perfect people." In reality, they are not perfect either.

3. As an adult, you are entitled to live your life without seeking everyone else's approval. You do not have to make excuses, justify your actions, or say "I'm sorry" when you are acting in line with your own values. No matter what you do, someone is not going to like or "approve" of it. In reality, you often risk being disliked and may even have to end relationships in order to live your life with your own best interests at heart.

4. Refuse to let other people manipulate you into doing what's best only for them because of their anger, helplessness, or greed. Don't allow them to make you feel guilty through their use of the term "you should."

5. Feel okay about saying "no." Say "no" when you really want to say "no" and you mean "no." Recognize that any lurking feelings of guilt or fear of rejection are probably carryovers from childhood.

6. Examine and throw out your old, useless "shoulds." The "shoulds" we learned in childhood, usually imposed upon us by well-meaning parents or parent figures, may have helped us develop values but now, as adults, they may not be reality.

7. Acknowledge the fact that feelings of guilt, inadequacy, and low self-worth are also carryovers from the past and are not reality. Throw those feelings in the garbage and love yourself.

8. Don't be threatened, manipulated, or intimidated by people's questions. If you don't want to answer, don't and feel okay about it. There is no stone tablet that says you must.

9. Acknowledge the fact that you only control 50 percent of a relationship, your half. If you don't understand what the other person is saying or what he/she wants, say so, and feel okay about it. There

are limits to your power, you can't get inside someone else's head to know what he/she is thinking.

10. Stop blaming others or the world for your problems. Every human being on the planet has problems and you have the ability to deal with them and solve them. However, if your behavior is directed toward making you feel better instead of dealing with them, you are defending instead of coping.

Rules for Respecting the Self-Worth of Others

1. Listen carefully and attentively to the content and feelings others express.

2. Since you can't get inside other people's heads, don't make assumptions about how they think, feel, or act.

3. Give others permission to have their own feelings. Never tell others how they should feel or shouldn't feel and don't correct their statements when they express their feelings. Don't judge another's expression of their feelings, especially about whether the feelings are real, important, right or wrong.

4. Give others permission to have values and beliefs that are different than yours and don't impose your values and beliefs on others.

5. Avoid labeling others—as stupid, lazy, childish.

6. Recognize that joking, sarcasm or kidding is dirty fighting. What may seem harmless fun to you may hurt others. Thinking or saying they shouldn't feel that way violates rule #3.

7. Confront unrealistic or manipulative behavior and disagree with opinions, but don't attack the self-esteem of others. The other person is not stupid, they may simply be acting stupid at some point in time.

8. Be *open, honest, specific,* and *direct* with others. Avoid pseudo-communication and avoid playing manipulative games.

9. Avoid sending mixed messages that will confuse people. "Walk where you talk."

10. Give others the opportunity to be responsible for themselves. Avoid giving unsolicited advice or being destructively generous.

11. Give others permission to have an opinion different than yours. Don't state your opinions as facts. Try to be tentative and avoid preaching. Give others space to move.

12. Avoid putting others on the spot through the use of questions. Questions can be a demanding, controlling form of communication.

13. When you have differences with others, be willing to work them out.

Self-Confidence

With the information discussed so far in this book we can now make some observations and statements about the nature and role of self-confidence/self-esteem in the determination of the excellence of the actions of individuals and the excellence consciousness of an organization.

Individuals and organizations that do not believe in themselves do not believe, at the most basic levels, that they deserve excellence. They do not have basic values that allow them to make the forced choices necessary for nurturing an excellence-driven organization. The Adult is not in control of either the individuals of the organization nor the units of people that make up the organization. The actions of both the individuals and the units are in conflict with the subconscious value systems. These internal conflicts prevent the development of self-esteem and block true self-confidence.

When these internal conflicts are being acknowledged and addressed, and the realization that each individual is ultimately responsible for his/her own actions occurs, self-esteem starts to develop. Effectively directing actions toward fulfillment of healthy dominant basic needs produces self-confidence. Every healthy individual, at some level, wants to grow. This is a basic property of the healthy human species. The *effect* of realization of that desire is self-confidence.

The highest level of fulfilling this drive is self-actualization. Once self-actualization is addressed effectively, the self-actualized individual wants nothing more than for other individuals to experience the same quality of life. The energies of the highly self-confident individual are devoted altruistically toward the growth process of society to self-actualization.

Risk

Healthy risk-taking is highly correlated with psychological health, as are management styles. People take risks to achieve healthy psychological growth through the fulfillment of the dominant basic needs or to alleviate a threat to fulfilled basic needs.

Some risk-taking, excessive and/or minimum, is related to neurotic behavior. By neurotic behavior I mean that the action or lack of action of the individual is not moving the individual toward healthy psychological growth. Healthy risk is calculated risk taken by the Adult. The probability of benefit of a proper risk, based on Adult appraisal by the risk taker, is less than 100 percent and greater than 0 percent. Rational risk taking has a probability of benefit gain greater than 50 percent. Actions approaching 100 percent probability of benefit are not risks. They are the routine activities of everyday life.

Risk can be thought of as an equation:

$$\text{Probable Benefit} = (P_g \times \text{Gain}_{max}) - (P_p \times \text{Price})$$
where P_g = the weighted mean probability of gain
and P_p = the weighted mean probability of price.

We take healthy risks for gain, whether tangible or intangible. Many of the risks we take are for gain that is extremely hard to quantify. The activity with which a risk is associated is either an action, or it may be not taking an action when an action is appropriate. I term both as actions. We take or do not take the action because we want something more than that which we have or we want to prevent the loss of something we already have. The gains of risk can just as easily be called gratifiers of basic needs.

For every risky gain there is an uncertain price. The price may not be financial. It may be time away from family. It may be effort devoted toward learning. It may be pulling up roots and moving to an unfamiliar part of the world. It may be psychological, i.e., the scenario of failure may involve a threat to one's existence, humiliation, loss of prestige, loss of financial security, termination from a job, rejection by peers, or the realization that one's ideals are not practical in the real world. The impact the risky action has on these factors is the price of taking a risk. Again, we call an action risky because the gain of the action is not certain. There is also a possibility of loss of previously realized gain. I call the loss of previously realized gain "price."

As with most events of the future, we do not know the outcome so we make a calculated estimate of what we believe the possible outcomes could be. The probable benefit of an action can be determined by estimating the mean probable gain minus the mean probable price.

The business world offers classic cases where quantifications of the equation are used. The XYZ Company makes widgets. Let's consider an investment in a new widget machine. Our board of directors has told us that any investment we make must have a two-year payback. We already make widgets and sell them for a one dollar profit each. Our current machine will make 100 widgets per day. The salesperson tells us that with the new machine we can make 125 widgets per day at the same cost. We all know that salespeople are always right! Right! We also have looked at the design of the new machine. We think the salesperson might be right but we are not sure. Two other plants with the new machines operate at 110 widgets/day, five are at 125, and four are at 130. The engineers think there is a 10 percent chance they can make modifications for a 140 unit/day production rate. Already there is a degree of uncertainty evident.

The same salesperson has told us that the cost of the new machine is $10,000. That price is F.O.B. his/her plant. Our engineers tell us the new equipment can be installed in seven days but we will have to take the old machine out at the same time and will not be able to produce widgets with it during that time. Also, the engineers say the cost of installing the new machine based on total labor and other materials will be $6,000. Okay! Again, an estimate.

Don't we wish it was that simple. In considering the future there are few, if any, absolutes. There are just probabilities. With additional information we can close in on the reality of the statements made about the new widget machine. We can estimate the probability of each factor affecting the probable benefit of buying the new widget machine. We can also estimate the probability of a production rate of the widget machine, and the total price of the machine.

Estimated Cost (first look)

Machine	$	10,000
Shipping		850
Installation (7 days)		6,000
Productivity Loss (7 days)		700
	$	17,550

Stated Gain

25 Units/Day @ $1 Profit	$	25/Day
for 350 day/yr operation	$	8,750 profit

Payback Period = 17,550/8,750 = 2.01 yrs.

The result is above the two years, but the estimates may be off a little. Using more of the information given including the estimations of the probability distribution of the other factors, a second estimate can be made. Let's consider the probability distribution of two significant variables, production rate and installation time.

Probable Production Rate

Units/Day	Probability	Profit/Yr	Probable Product
110	.1818	3,500	636.36
125	.4545	8,750	3,977.27
130	.3636	10,500	3,818.11
140	.10*	14,000	1,400.00
Probable Profit			**9,831.74**

*10 percent probability by engineers of system change is an additional 10 percent factor. Total is 110 percent.

The knowledge that has been added to the decision has altered the risk. The probable gain is over $1,000 higher.

Now let's look at the probable price. The engineers estimated that installation would take seven days at $6,000. We asked and learned that the labor for each day is $400. The installation is a fixed $3,200 for materials and the rest of the estimate is labor. We can pay $600 for an extra shift of laborers on overtime if we want to speed up the installation but because of fatigue and diminishing returns on effort, only so much speed-up can be done.

Probable Installation Costs (Including production loss)

Time	Labor	Production Loss	Total	Estimated Probability	Probable Product
5 DAYS	$3,800	$500	$4,300	.10	$ 430
6 DAYS	3,800	600	4,400	.30	1,320
7 DAYS	2,800	700	3,500	.50	1,750
8 DAYS	3,200	800	4,000	.15	600
9 DAYS	3,600	900	4,500	.05	225
Probable Installation Labor Cost					$4,325

Probable Installation Cost Total ($3,200 + $4,325) = $7,525

This compares unfavorably with the estimate of $6,000 given previously. What is the difference? We have a better understanding of reality because we have received more information. Now the estimate of profitability becomes:

Estimated Cost (second look)

Machine	$10,000
Shipping	850
Installation (7 days)	7,525
	$18,375
Expected Gain for 350 day/yr operation	$ 9,832 profit

Payback Period = 18,375/9,832 = 1.87 yrs.

Would the smart manager take the risk and install the widget machine? That depends on his/her willingness to risk.

The example used is highly quantified. It is not as easy to quantify decisions concerning less tangible gains and prices. What is the psychological benefit of changing jobs, marriage, divorce, taking control of one's self instead of being controlled by others, or of shutting out people who have a value system that conflicts with yours? The probable benefit is equal to the probable gain minus the probable price. The more information we have about the real gain and the real price the better our assessment of probable benefit will be. Only a psychologically healthy person with a reasonably well solidified value system can weigh the significant factors of intangible gain and price and decide to take or not take such a risk.

A Propensity for Action

Given that an individual has the understanding of risk necessary to make an Adult decision, there are several other factors that determine an individual's willingness to take an action that incorporates healthy risks. In the previous section's example of the widget machine we still do not know if the manager bought the widget machine. Was he/she willing to take the calculated risk? The risk was less after more information was obtained. The probable benefit was greater.

Again we return to a philosophical and psychological analysis. In the example what is the risk? What would happen if the estimates were negatively wrong and the payback period was three years? The manager might take a verbal tongue lashing. The manager might be fired. He/she might go on unemployment, lose his/her home, be divorced by his/her spouse, be alienated from his/her children, become a skid row bum, catch pneumonia and die. Such thinking is called catastrophic. The probability of such a scenario is minute.

On the other hand, the engineers might be conservative in their estimates and the machine payback might be less than a year. The manager would become a hero, gain the eye of the chairman of the board, and eventually become a member of the board. This is wishful thinking. Again the probability is remote.

Outside influences are not the main factors determining the propensity to take action. Wisdom, knowledge, and true self-esteem are the primary factors that determine the willingness to assess risk and take action. None of these factors are properties that can be forced on a person. The individual must develop them internally. The old adage "you can lead a horse to water but you can't make him drink" applies. We can only *facilitate* the growth of knowledge, wisdom and self-esteem in our organizations. We cannot make them happen. Therefore we cannot force an individual to take appropriate action containing risk.

I have previously discussed knowledge and wisdom. Self-esteem means that a person likes himself/herself. The individual believes in himself/herself and is happy with what the self is. The self is okay. This feeling is very strong.

It cannot easily be shaken by the actions of others or the events of the world. Self-esteem is not haughty or conceited.

Self-esteem is present in an individual when the individual is actively and in good health seeking to gratify a dominant basic need. It is not present in the neurotic quest for gratification. Something inside us tells us we are in conflict with our own value system in neurotic behavior. We do not like the behavior even though we persist in it. Our neurotic behavior destroys any esteem we may have for self.

When self-esteem is present, an individual has a firm grip on reality. The individual is willing to act on calculated risks because negative results do not threaten a system of esteem which is not held up through the actions, praise, and respect of others. The esteem and the willingness to act on calculated risk comes from within.

To facilitate the development of self-esteem in others an organization can only provide the environment and resources for self-development of esteem. Valuing, trust, reflection, positive motivation, positive expectation, listening, and Adult behavior all provide the environment. Parent behavior, Child behavior, negative expectations, unrealistic expectations, poor communication, lack of valuing behavior, and especially fear are negative factors that inhibit the development of self-esteem and inhibit people from taking appropriate action in risky situations.

People Engineering

People engineering is a form of valuing and is often overlooked as we plan for change, growth and excellence in our operations. Yet guiding, directing, motivating, and empowering the actions of people are all part of management. People engineering is more than industrial engineering, although industrial engineering can be part of people engineering. In many organizations we fail to understand and implement the full implications of managing. We try to maximize task behavior without establishing a maximized balance with relationship and information behavior. People engineering is the inclusion in the overall planning process of the abilities, skills, capabilities, convenience, and productivity of the people who design, manage, control, operate, purchase, sell, and use the products and services of our organizations.

Absurd examples of a lack of people engineering would be the placement of the gas pedal on the right side in a car with the steering wheel on the left side because it was close to the carburetor linkage, or placement of all telephones in an office complex next to the switching equipment because this required less wire. It is no less absurd when instrumentation and controls are placed at a location close to the signal and/or equipment but far away from the operator's main center of activity, or when key operating information reports are kept confidential to management due to lack of trust of some individuals. It is no wonder an operator does not get information, properly control the equipment, and fulfill assigned responsibilities. People engineering is not only the maximization of output by an operator, à la Fredrick Taylor, the founder of time-motion studies and the father of industrial engineering. People engineering is a form of valuing the individual and seeking a sense of involvement and relevance that is of value to both the employee and the company. It behooves every member of an organization to take into consideration the abilities of fellow workers, the members of the supplier organizations and the customer organizations. Consider the information needed to properly execute a task, and consider what the maximum production potential is when information, motivation, and tasks are incorporated.

Approaches to Conflict

Change causes conflict. Conflict arises from threat. As we learned earlier, each person and organization has a defined set of hierarchical basic needs they are consciously or unconsciously attempting to gratify. The actions of the individual or organization are intended to protect both the current dominant need, and, to a lesser extent, the previously gratified needs. When we sense that the structure of gratifiers we are seeking or have established is not stable we feel threatened. We become anxious, frightened, and/or angry. Our actions to counteract the threat may be either appropriate or inappropriate in view of our total structure of need gratification and our environment. We can tolerate far more threat to previously gratified needs and unperceived needs than we can tolerate threat to the need we are currently seeking to gratify.

A method for teaching rational approaches to conflict resolution is through training in and an understanding of Transaction Analysis along with an understanding of valuing. Transactional Analysis, or TA, has already been covered in detail. The basic objective of TA training is to facilitate Adult to Adult rational problem-solving behavior. One of the objectives of HQM is to accept the inevitability of change and appropriately resolve the resulting conflict to the benefit of all parties. This is not always an easy task but it is essential in a unified effort to achieve excellence.

One aspect of compromise is that no one wins! Winning could be defined as gratifying the needs of the party. In compromise, each party in the conflict gives up part of what is perceived as important, granted that the attributes which have been given up may be of lesser importance to the party than the attributes which were accepted. We call this political expedience. In a compromise, each party continues to sense threat and harbor anxiety or anger. The next time a conflict arises each party recalls that anxiety and/or anger and enters discussions with increased defensiveness.

In conflict we fear no action or losing more than we fear the sacrifice of lesser attributes. Because of fear we fail to acknowledge that there may exist not-thought-of new solutions to a problem that will fully or far better satisfy the needs of both parties. There may be a "Third Way."

To seek a Third Way, each party must seek to understand as fully as possible the conscious and unconscious objectives of the other party. The means to an end are far more open to modification than are the ends. This understanding of another person's objectives can only occur through open-minded and honest communication.

People and organizations vary greatly in their perception of threat. Reactions to threat vary from subtle agitation to visible panic and shock. Some individuals inappropriately redirect their threat reaction into neurotic and self-destructive behavior. Some always feel threatened and others almost never feel threatened. Both situations can be destructive to the health of the individual or organization because the reaction and behavior do not facilitate a mutually beneficial solution to the threat.

The individual's assessment of threat is directly linked to the psychological health of the individual and the individual's level of maturity. In attempting to resolve conflict, at least one party must be consciously sensitive to his/her own and the other person's perception and reaction to threat. Someone must control the atmosphere of interaction to promote open and honest communication and a consensus agreement.

The Resolution of Conflict

Conflict is inevitable and healthy when well-handled. Unresolved conflict leads to anger, resentment, alienation, disenfranchisement, and ultimately to disassociation. Out of the healthy resolution of conflict comes growth.

When a problem develops either internally or between an organization and a supplier or customer, seek to resolve the problem quickly and to the mutual benefit of both parties. Unresponsiveness to problems festers to ruin otherwise mutually beneficial relationships. Key to the resolution of problems is open, candid, and frank communication of the views and desires of all of the involved parties. Try to keep all individuals party to a problem acting in an Adult manner with the ultimate goal being a mutually beneficial solution. Following are guidelines for the resolution of problems:

1. Problems should be addressed as quickly as possible with the other individual(s) party to the problem. Contact the responsible person as soon as possible. If an individual does not feel he/she can effectively confront the other individual(s) party to a problem then quickly bring the problem to the attention of someone of higher leadership who can mediate the resolution. For problems between supplier or customer, be sure to address the person who can effectively take action to resolve the problem.

2. Acknowledge anger and frustration for what they are, childish responses that will be detrimental to arriving at a solution to the problem.

3. Determine and state as many facts as possible. Work to develop an understanding by the other person(s) of the nature and significance of the problem.

4. Listen to the other person's point of view. Try to understand the needs of the other person while being conscious of your own needs. There may be aspects of the situation that you have not considered.

5. Be willing to frankly state your true opinion of possible solutions. Inform the other party of your objections to a potential but not satisfactory solution. Don't end the discussion without a mutually beneficial solution.

6. Confirm the understanding of the details of a solution. A solution is a form of contracting and both parties must be fully aware of the details and obligations of the solution. Confirm the expected actions for a solution by each party in writing. This action will provide clarity; it can't hurt if you truly agree with the solution.

7. Follow through on the actions to which you obligated yourself through acceptance of the solution. Notify the other party(ies) of the completion of your obligation.

8. Finally, verify the satisfaction of the other party(ies) with the implementation of the solution. If the unmet needs that originally caused the problem have not been satisfied, then start through the process again.

This chapter has described the importance of understanding ourselves and others in order to be more effective managers. People are the most important factors in determining the quality of our products, our organizations, and our lives. Increasing the quality in all these areas is a non-entropic growth process. It takes planning and work. Again, *people ultimately control all non-entropic processes.*

Matching the Skills of People and Positions

7

Earlier in the book I discussed, in a general manner, the model for skills assessment supported by Richard Bowles. This model divides skills into three general categories: people, data, and things. Again, I believe the word information better describes the targeted skill base than does the word data. Then in the chapter on models I expanded Hersey's model of management styles to include information as one of three basic behaviors. In this chapter I will build upon these models to define a system for evaluating both the behavior base levels of an individual and the skill base requirements of a position based on the required behaviors for the position. The overall objective of this system of skill evaluation is to achieve the best possible match between position and incumbent. The terms of the model are necessarily general and reflect basic skill categories. Although specific behaviors of an individual will fall into the general categories, I cannot give specific examples of the skill base terms that will apply to every position or person. That is part of the job of a leader of a specific organization.

The System

Again, the basic behavioral categories are People behavior, Information behavior, and Thing behavior. The responsibilities of each position will require an appropriate mix of these behaviors for the objectives of the position to be accomplished and for the individual to be motivated within the position.

Note that there is a definite difference between behavior and skill. The word behavior implies both ability and action. Because an individual possesses a skill for doing something does not mean that the individual wishes to or can effectively utilize the skill integrated into an environment and exhibit a behavior. Hersey uses the terms "willing" and "able" as quantifiers of a behavior. These two terms model the actions of the behavior.

For example, I very much like wood working. I build custom furniture. Our house is full of the products of my labors. I possess high-level skills for designing, engineering and setting-up to build furniture. But I do not choose to make my living building furniture for others. In fact I struggle when I have to make the same piece twice. I am *able* but not *willing*. Outside of home I have a skill. To my family and personal friends I exhibit a behavior.

Skills are talents or capabilities an individual possesses. Because an individual possesses a skill does not mean that the individual actualizes that skill into outwardly visible behavior. There is a dramatic difference. Skills do not necessarily impact on the environment of the individual unless the individual actualizes a skill in behavior. A person may be extremely skilled as a computer programmer but unless the person uses this skill either in actual programming or in mentoring and evaluating the work of others, the skill is not a behavior.

The model in Chapter 4 gave relationship and task behavior a ranking from one to nine. I agree with this model but I integrate it with the third parameter, information behavior.

My system utilizes a procedure for first ranking the requirements of a position. Each of the three behaviors is evaluated and given a required behavior quantification. The product of the quantification of the three behaviors gives an approximate maturity requirement for the position. Once the three behavior levels for a position are determined, then the task is to assess the three behavior levels of candidates in order to find the person whose behavior is the closest match to the required behavior.

Maturity level can be constituted by numerous mixes of the three behaviors. Maturity is an indicator of the relative worth to an organization. Different mixes of behaviors have the same relative value to the organization. The design engineer may be high in task and information behaviors but low in people behavior, say $5 \times 8 \times 8 = 320$. A manager of the planning department may be high in people and information behavior but low in task behavior. Again, $10 \times 8 \times 4 = 320$. According to the system, both behaviors are of equal value although quite different. A top-level manager would need to possess skills in all three areas with the dominant behaviors being information and people.

Again, the difference in skills and behavior is important. As an individual rises higher in an organization the more he/she is responsible for motivating and directing the activities of others. The dominant behavior necessary becomes people yet the position may require latent behaviors used for evaluating and directing the activities of others. The scale of the people behavior rating is expanded because as people rise in an organization the importance of people behavior increases. At the very top the need for people behavior may diminish and information behavior may become paramount. People and task or thing behaviors are, to an extent, delegated. In Hersey et al's model, top management exhibited little people or task behavior. What is not shown in that model is the high level of information behavior necessary.

Such a system is not exact. For example, we may state that the Thing behavior required for a position is six. Such a statement does not mean that a five or a seven rated person would not be successful, or would be bored in the position. Think of the actual number assigned to the behavior as being the mean of a distribution of behavior level that will meet the requirements of the position. For some positions the distribution of the quantified behavior may be wide, and in others the distribution may be fairly narrow. As we get into the system it will, ideally, become apparent to the reader how to assess the end points of the behavior distributions appropriate for a position. Such an assessment requires wisdom.

People Behavior

Returning to the assessment used by Richard Bowles, the general classification of people behaviors are helping, taking instructions, signaling, speaking, persuading, diverting, supervising, instructing, negotiating, and mentoring. These behaviors are applied to a scale shown in Figure 18.

Definition of each of these behaviors will be helpful. First be aware that higher level behaviors also incorporate the lower level behaviors. It is not possible to mentor effectively without the skills of negotiating, instructing, supervising, etc. The same is true in the other major behavior categories.

HELPING—Giving of aid; assisting. (Under the direction of another.) For example, my daughter helps me weed the flower bed, or a Boy Scout helps an

Figure 18

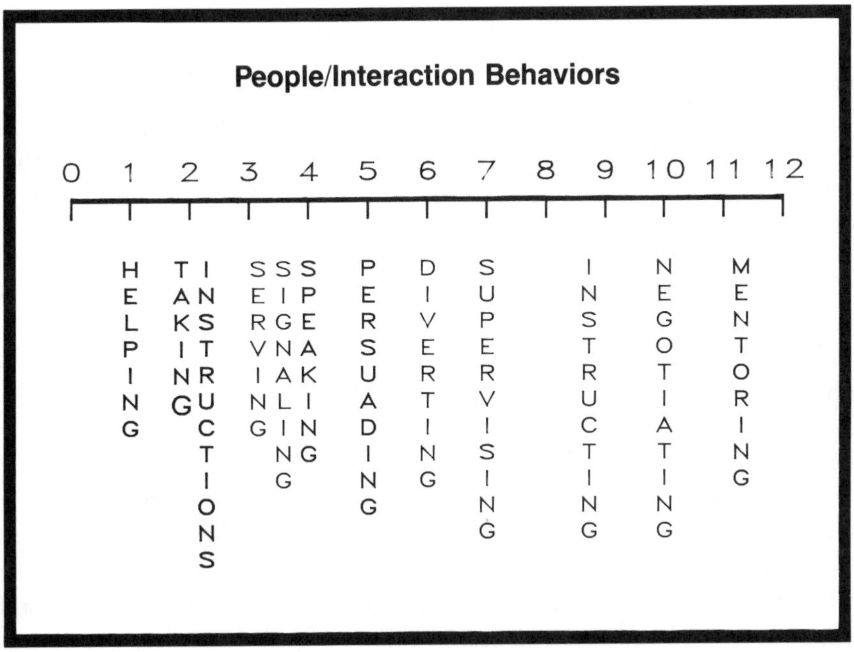

People/Interaction Behaviors

0 1 2 3 4 5 6 7 8 9 10 11 12

HELPING TAKING INSTRUCTIONS SIGNALING SERVING SPEAKING PERSUADING DIVERTING SUPERVISING INSTRUCTING NEGOTIATING MENTORING

elderly person across the street, or a person helps a mechanic by handing the mechanic the tools requested.

TAKING INSTRUCTIONS—Taking direction or orders effectively. Reacting in accordance with clear, concise, and detailed directions. The person is able to comprehend and execute the instructions given by another person.

SERVING—To do tasks for others. To provide for the needs of others. Serving is an integration of helping and taking instructions along with a degree of self-direction.

SIGNALING—To indicate or make known to another when certain previously established conditions exist. To communicate a certain condition through gesture or action.

SPEAKING—To express or communicate facts, ideas, opinions, feelings with the voice; to express the feelings, sentiments, ideas, etc., of a group. To effectively communicate by voice.

PERSUADING—To cause someone to do something, especially by reasoning, urging, or inducement; prevail upon. To induce someone to believe something; convince.

DIVERTING—To turn (a person) aside from a course of thought or action.

SUPERVISING—To oversee or direct work, workers, a project.

INSTRUCTING—To communicate knowledge to; teach; educate; to give the facts of the matter to; inform.

NEGOTIATING—To confer, bargain or discuss with a view to reaching agreement.

MENTORING—Being a wise and loyal advisor. Promoting growth for the welfare of the mentored. Possessing wisdom and acting with wisdom for the good of others.

Information (Data)

The information behaviors of comparing, copying, computing, compiling, analyzing, innovating, coordinating, and synthesizing are quantified using a similar scale.

The following are definitions for these terms.

COMPARING—The ability to examine and determine similarities or differences.

COPYING—To transcribe from an original data set to another set of data. The copy usually is an exact duplicate of the original according to the strict definition.

COMPILING/COMPUTING—To gather and put together in an orderly form. For example, an employee may be asked to put together a list of all customers who purchase product X. The same employee may be asked to COMPUTE the average order size, and the total dollar volume sold last month.

ANALYZING—(1) To separate or break up into parts so as to find out their nature, proportion, function, relationship, etc. (2) To examine the constituents

Figure 19

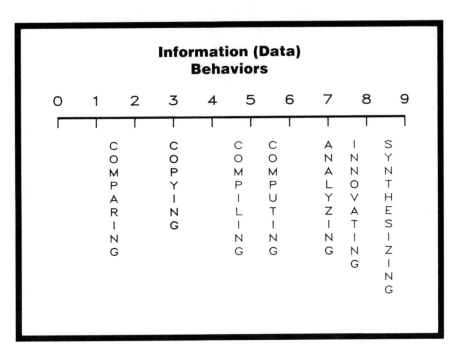

Information (Data) Behaviors

0	1	2	3	4	5	6	7	8	9
			COMPARING		COPYING		COMPILING	COMPUTING		ANALYZING	INNOVATING	SYNTHESIZING

or parts of; determine the nature or tendencies of. The employee mentioned above may be asked to analyze the sales trend for product X by looking at the average sales over the last 12 months and making a conclusion based on the data, such as "sales have gone up 12 percent in the last year."

INNOVATING/COORDINATING—To introduce new methods, devices, etc.; change in the way of doing things. To bring into proper order or relation; harmonize, adjust.

SYNTHESIZING—(1) To bring together into a whole by synthesis. (2) To form by bringing together separate parts. This book is a synthesis of psychology, statistics, philosophy and management, to produce the whole, a synthesized system for excellence.

Things (Tasks)

Finally, the Thing categories of skills and behavior are handling, off-bearing, feeding, tending, manipulating, driving-operating, operating-controlling, precision working, setting up, and designing-engineering.

The definitions of the terms used to describe the Thing behaviors follow.

HANDLING—To touch, lift, etc., with the hand or hands; to manage, operate, or use with the hand or hands; manipulate.

"Thing" or Task Behaviors

```
  0     1     2     3     4     5     6     7     8     9

        H     F  O  T  M     D O  O C  P W  S D  E
        A     E  F  E  A     R P  P O  R O  E E  N
        N     E  F  N  N     I E  E N  E R  T S  G
        D     D  B  D  I     V R  R T  C K  T I  I
        L     I  E  I  P     I A  A R  I I  I G  N
        I     N  A  N  U     N T  T O  S N  N N  E
        N     G  R  G  L     G I  I L  I G  G I  E
        G        I     A       N  N L  O      N  R
                 N     T          G G  N    U G  I
                 G     I            I       P    N
                       N            N            G
                       G
```

FEEDING/OFF-BEARING—To provide material to be used up; to provide with material in a prescribed manner. For example to feed coal to a boiler or to feed parts to a machine. Off-bearing: To remove material in a prescribed manner. For example, to off-bear cartons from a conveyor belt and place on a pallet.

TENDING—To be in charge of, as in tending a machine; to control within guidelines of action; to insure proper operation.

MANIPULATING—To work or operate with, or as with the hand or hands; handle or use, especially with a skill, like manipulating a milling machine or a computer program.

DRIVING/OPERATING—To control the movement or direct the course of a machine, usually mobile. For example, driving a bulldozer or tractor trailer truck. To bring about as an effect; to put or keep in action. Examples, operating a typewriter, computer, lathe, production machine, switchboard, etc., to produce the desired effect.

OPERATING/CONTROLLING—To exercise authority over; direct; guide; command; restrain to wanted or from unwanted variation from the desired mode.

PRECISION WORKING—Working to high accuracy and minimum variation; a very accurate level of controlling with minimum variation; working to very close tolerances; in extremely close compliance with procedure and specification.

SETTING UP—Physically working with equipment to adjust variable settings for precision working. Establishing the standard procedures for close tolerance work. For example, setting up a lathe so a precision worker can produce multiple shafts with minimum variation.

DESIGNING—To make original plans, sketches, patterns, etc.; to plan; make preliminary sketches of; sketch a pattern or outline for; to form plans, etc., in the mind.

ENGINEERING—To contrive; manage skillfully; the planning, designing, construction, or management of machinery, equipment, processes, buildings, etc.

I hope these standard definitions are definitive enough to give the reader an idea of the various levels of each behavior. They are necessarily general and for a given position must be made more specific. For example, an electrical engineer may not possess the skills and exhibit the behavior necessary for building a bridge. The mentor of excellence may not be a mentor of finance, and the synthesizer of computer programming may not be a synthesizer of financial statements. Each position requires specific skills and behaviors that fall into one of the general levels.

Management Maturity

Although the three behaviors are assessed separately, there certainly is interdependence between the three. It would be a mistake to take a non-

Figure 21

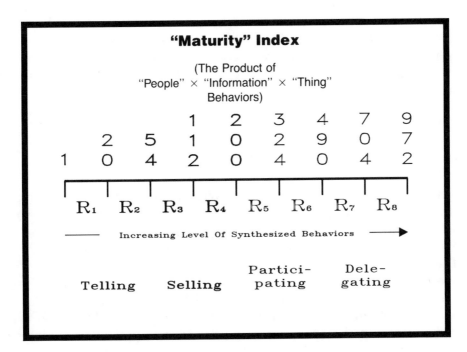

holistic approach in the skill and behavior assessment. As the three behaviors develop in an individual the overall effect becomes synergistic. Therefore, in my model I assess maturity as being the product of the quantifications of the three behaviors. A $6 \times 6 \times 6 = 216$ individual will have a higher impact on an organization, will more effectively analyze, communicate, and implement change, than will a $7 \times 3 \times 9 = 189$ individual. The latter individual may have high-task behavior but not be able to effectively communicate desired task behavior to others for implementation.

The term "management maturity" has become a cliché, indicating the level behavior exhibited by an individual. The term has not been well-defined. I have attempted to do so. The term does not necessarily imply psychological or physical maturity, although there may be some correlations.

Figure 21 shows how the product of the quantifications fits on a scale of management maturity, effective styles of leadership, and synthesized behavior. In a behavior-based organization, the R levels indicate the appropriate impact, authority, and responsibility capability of the individual.

Assessing Position Requirements

In assessing the value of a position, the input of those individuals most familiar with the behavior requirements of the position is utilized. The manager of the position, the incumbent(s) of the position, and person(s) reporting all rank their expectations of the three behaviors necessary to successfully accomplish the position responsibilities. They independently state the highest behavior level required within each major category and give a specific example of a situation requiring that behavior level. The ranking individuals then meet to reach a consensus on the proper value and an acceptable spread within the People, Information, Things categories. These behavior levels are given their respective numerical rankings, then multiplied to give the maturity level of the position. The form on the following page can be used for this purpose.

Assessing Behaviors of an Individual

Once the required behaviors and maturity level of a position have been established, a similar system is used for evaluating and/or interviewing candidates for the position. The quest is to determine the highest levels of the three behavior categories actually exhibited by the candidate.

The candidate is interviewed directly and/or people very familiar with the behavior of the candidate are interviewed to provide the necessary information.

I again return to a procedure used by Richard Bowles in *What Color Is Your Parachute?* The candidate or person being interviewed is asked to give a detailed account of the three or four activities or projects, not necessarily

Figure 22

Position Evaluation Form

Position _____ Evaluated by _____
Maturity index _____ Date _____

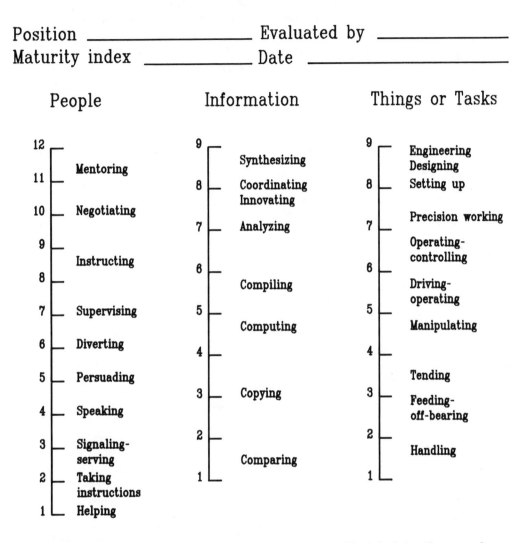

State in detail the specific required behaviors that led to the number assigned to each general category.

People _____

_____

Information _____

_____

Things or Tasks _____

_____

_____

work-related, that have been most fulfilling to the candidate. A two or three-page written description is best. A verbal account of the project can be given to a trained evaluator as an alternative.

Because the three or four accountings of activities are of activities where the individual felt the most fulfillment, and were chosen by the candidate, the skills and behaviors of the candidate will come close to reaching equality. The individual behaved using the highest level skills. This statement is not necessarily true for any one accounting or activity, but should be true when three or four different activities are analyzed.

The following open-ended questions may be helpful in stimulating conversation about the activity.

- What was your (the candidate's) role in the project?
- What was the goal of the project?
- Tell me about the other people involved in the project.
- How did you plan for the project?
- What did the project accomplish?
- How was the project implemented?
- What part of the project did you like best?
- What part of the project did you like least?
- Who was in charge of the project?
- Tell me about that person (the person in charge).
- What did other people think about the project?

It is not necessary to ask all the questions. Once the individual starts talking about the project he/she will probably volunteer enough information to make the behavior evaluations.

If input is obtained about the behavior of the candidate from more than one source, the evaluations must again be merged to find the highest competent behaviors of the candidate. Each person evaluating the candidate should record the specific behavior that led to the assessment of behavior level. The form on the following page can be used for both individual assessments and to consolidate the individual assessments into an overall assessment.

Most important in determining if there is a match between the position requirements and an individual is the pattern of the three major behavior categories: People, Information, and Things. The exact match will be rare, but it will not be hard to find a candidate with a behavior match that falls within the expected behavior requirement distribution necessary for both success and gratification in the position.

Figure 23

Candidate Evaluation Form

Candidate _____ Evaluator _____ Date _____
Maturity index _____ Written ☐ Verbal ☐

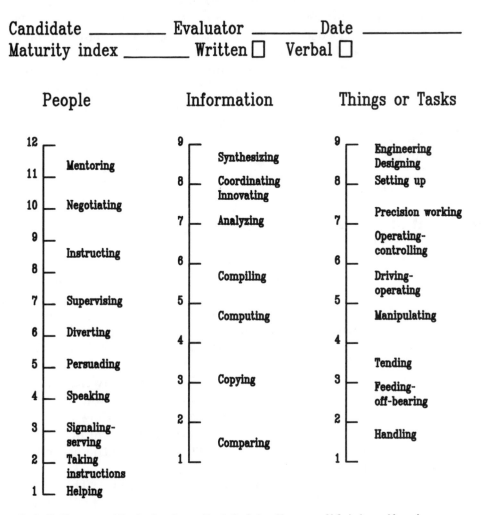

People	Information	Things or Tasks
12 —	9 —	9 — Engineering Designing
Mentoring	Synthesizing	
11 —	8 — Coordinating Innovating	8 — Setting up
10 — Negotiating		Precision working
	7 — Analyzing	7 —
9 —		Operating-controlling
Instructing	6 —	6 —
8 —	Compiling	Driving-operating
7 — Supervising	5 —	5 —
	Computing	Manipulating
6 — Diverting	4 —	4 —
5 — Persuading		Tending
	3 — Copying	3 — Feeding-off-bearing
4 — Speaking		
	2 —	2 — Handling
3 — Signaling-serving	Comparing	
2 — Taking instructions	1 —	1 —
1 — Helping		

Detail the specific behaviors that led to the candidate's rating in each category.

People _____

_____

Information _____

_____

Things or Tasks _____

_____

_____

Skills and Behavior and Growth

Another significant factor that must be evaluated is the difference between the exhibited behavior of an individual and the individual's desire and capability for growth. It is the nature of most people to want to continue growing in skills and behavior until either senility or death occurs. The growth is not always work-related. It may be focused in outside activities. When an individual stops seeking growth mental death has begun.

In an interview a review of the candidate's activities that exhibit both desire and activity for growth may shed light on growth patterns that would make the otherwise unqualified individual appropriate for a position. If the growth desire can be channelled into the work environment both the organization and the individual will benefit. Such a situation will make the position challenging to the individual.

Individual and Team Contributors

It has become common in industry to label people as either individual or team contributors. This system provides a quantification and definition of these labels.

The behaviors of the individual contributor are not evenly balanced and often are extremely slanted toward one category. The individual-contributor engineer would exhibit a behavior pattern similar to $3 \times 5 \times 9$. The pastor or counselor might exhibit an $11 \times 5 \times 2$ pattern. The individual-contributor statistician might have a pattern of $2 \times 9 \times 3$. Any strongly skewed pattern of behaviors is a strong indication of an individual contributor.

The generalist contributor's pattern of behaviors will show balance. The pattern on the behavior assessment will be relatively horizontal. This is true at all levels of maturity, whether R2 or R8. The CEO and the assembly line team player both require balance for effectiveness.

Some degree of slant may be appropriate in behavior. The CEO of a company would be expected to favor people and information behaviors yet have enough task-latent behavior to determine the validity of the information presented. The team player engineer will exhibit a maximum level of thing behavior, slope to information behavior and then possess enough people behavior to be successful in the interactions necessary to implement projects within a team.

Good and Bad Behavior Patterns

There are no good or bad mentally healthy behavior patterns. Good and bad are subjective evaluations and often belittle the talents of an individual. Such evaluations deflate the self-esteem of the individual. Almost all individuals have skills they are able and anxious to contribute. The purpose of this system of behavior and position requirement matching is to allow organizations to utilize the behaviors of an individual for the benefit of the organization, the individual, and society.

Neurotic, schizophrenic, and psychotic behaviors are behaviors that might be called bad because these behaviors are inconsistent, unpredictable, or dangerous. Such behaviors require professional attention and possibly eliminating the individual exhibiting such behaviors from the organization for the overall good of all the other individuals who constitute the organization, and for the good of society.

There are patterns that are appropriate and inappropriate for the requirements of a position. Such a differentiation is elementary to the concept of HQM. This system produces simultaneous maximization of benefit to employees, stockholders, and customers. That is *quality!*

Education and Training

8

Education in America has deteriorated to an embarrassingly low level. We no longer educate people. We train technicians—human machines. We teach people to very efficiently do repetitive tasks. Tasks that in the next two or three decades will be done more effectively with computers and automated machinery. Few courses in the mainstream of current education, especially at the secondary school level, teach people how to think for themselves, how to interact with other people, how to innovate and create. We are systematically suppressing these behaviors in our employees and in our education system.

We say we want employees to be inquisitive. But schools and industry often consider the overly inquisitive person disruptive.

We want team players. But we praise and reward the selfish individual achiever that plays win-lose games. We overlook the less flashy group contributor.

We seek original thinking, yet only support the research of a graduate student or the projects of an employee when there is reference and precedent.

We spend billions of dollars on capital improvements, yet most teachers are compensated far below the average income level. The true mentors have been driven from the profession.

As parents, we consider school to be a means of relieving the burdens and obligations of parenting. We send children off to school so that we can pursue our own desires. We take little interest in their education. Many parents are not even aware of what and how their children are being taught. We are quick to criticize a school board, principal, or teacher, yet extremely slow to offer praise for excellence or other support.

We build fantastic corporate centers, yet send children to learn in condemned buildings.

We support a welfare system that does not promote and reward achievement and learning because the system tranquilizes social distress. As long as those supported by the welfare system do not cause disruption to our lifestyle we consider the system adequate. Out of sight, out of mind!

Our education system is based on an antiquated society of the previous century. It values the convenience of the educational bureaucracy, society, and its administrators more than the true education of the students. The inquisitive and creative mind is constrained and molded toward mediocrity. The truly gifted are unchallenged and bored. The slow or underprivileged are left behind and socially promoted to get them out of the system, untrained for any reasonable means of contributing to society and providing self-support.

Few of our teachers are mentors. Many are glorified baby-sitters. In our public and many private education systems we are doing a grave injustice to the future generations that will be responsible for leading societies.

Education is one of the gravest long-term problems facing American society and business. It overshadows work ethic, capital systems, or equipment obsolescence. The inadequacy of education leads to the inability of the American employee, laborer and manager, to think inductively and deductively, divergently and convergently.

This lack of ability to think hinders fulfillment of societies' needs—the summation of the needs of constituting individuals—as well as self-leadership, self-responsibility, and self-determination. Managers are reluctant to delegate authority to individuals who have not demonstrated the ability to think and make sound decisions and are frustrated because they are not able to hire individuals able to do so at any price.

The American economic system and industry must bear much of the blame for this situation. The system has promoted the mass training of workers for the specialized industrial tasks of a low maturity system that met the current business needs. Education in the trades, engineering, accounting, and scientific specialization have received a mandate through the economic votes, dollars, of American society. Study of the humanities, courses where people learn to think, have been slighted. Such courses produce long-term benefit as opposed to the short term returns of the specializations.

We are committing slow societal suicide. Technology and society are changing much faster than the focus of our educational system. The narrowly trained engineer, scientific specialist, and business administrator, without a strong internal drive for continuing education, is obsolete and marginally productive five to 10 years after graduation. The task-oriented tradesman's skills are inappropriate for new technology in an even shorter time. The recent graduate with only a task-based education is not current with the new developments of technology being incorporated into the work place at the start of his/her first job.

The focus of education must shift from learning only specific technology to include teaching the skills of thinking and continuous learning.

No individual can totally assimilate information and technology at the rate it is being developed today. This phenomenon has driven us toward specialization. Yet the specifics learned in specialized formal education are outdated by the time the individual is ready to apply them. Only with a focus in education on training people to think, evaluate, investigate, question, and reason, to gain necessary information and reach sound conclusions, will the individual of the future be able to continuously adapt to the changes of the environment.

Workers want to do a good job. They want to receive strokes for doing a good job. Most do not know how. With the rapid changes in society and the work place it is not enough to be able to repeat the same task over and over. Such tasks can and are being automated. The new worker who is truly valuable is expected to analyze each problematic situation and arrive at a solution without extensive direction and as part of a group. The problems, when understood in detail, are seldom the same as previous problems. A previous solution may not be appropriate at the present. To make such a determination requires that the worker think—and we have stopped training people how to think.

Again, one of the trends detected by John Naisbett and Patricia Aburdene is the transfer of effective and relevant education from the public sector to the private sector. This is happening in the progressive and visionary organizations; it has been a defensive reaction. More and more corporations are either sponsoring education through compensation to the employee of expenses or actually establishing and staffing internal educational facilities. And much of the education is focused on skills other than tasks. Courses in leadership, motivation, interaction, listening, participative management, information skills—including SPC and computing, and problem-solving techniques (which are really organizing and thinking techniques) such as Kepner-Trego are growing rapidly as a percentage of total industrial training.

Yet it is hard to find universities that include courses in statistical and process analysis thinking in their technical curriculums. Few technical programs of higher education mandate courses in psychology or philosophy for their students. Few technically trained students graduate with any conscious conception of their own value system. Very few technical graduates have had training in the people skills necessary for successful contribution, even as individual contributors, in their respective technical fields.

Enough said about the situation. Anymore would be a game of "Ain't it awful!" There is action that can be taken to address these problems by both the individual and the organization. The common theme of all these actions is *support excellence through behavior.* Reward positive behavior. Confront and correct behavior counter to excellence.

Both individuals and organizations will need to take a longer term view toward the dividends of their actions. Behaviors do not change quickly. Rubrics and bureaucracies are tenacious.

As an individual one can support institutional excellence on a micro level. Support through your actions your own broad-based continuing education. Get involved with the programs of local schools. Interact with the teachers of your children. What you do to promote excellence of your children's education will also aid the education of the other children under those teachers. Let the teacher know when he/she is doing a good job. Support superior compensation for proven superior teachers, not for the total system. You are paying for the education of your children with your tax dollars. Be assertive when you do not get the services you are contracting for. Confront teaching practices that are not in line with excellence.

Promote excellence in your own family life and the home education of your children. And provide a home environment that is nurturing and reinforces positive behavior. Make the micro decisions that support a nurturing environment that promotes excellence.

Promote and support excellence in each environment—work, clubs, schools, etc.—where you are a member. Confront untruths and unhealthy motivation. Realize that the difference that you can make as an individual is not short-term. It may take years for the influence you can have to be manifested.

Realize that how you spend your dollars is voting for or against excellence. In our society the economic votes of the consumer direct the actions of business. Each time you support shoddy goods or services with your dollars you vote against excellence and for shoddiness. Be assertive when shoddiness is provided in goods and/or services.

The actions of individuals constitute the actions of organizations. Contrary to belief, no organization makes decisions. The individuals of the organizations make decisions, no matter how remote those individuals may seem to the person outside the organization. Organizations will not support training and education if the individual decision makers do not support education.

Organizations usually have greater resources and impact than individuals. The actions that can be taken as an organization parallel the actions of the individual. Again, the organization votes for the desired behavior with positive behavioral reinforcement and with dollars.

Selective hiring of graduates who are educated with both the technical skills and the people and information skills necessary for broad-based decision making supports the behavior of learning institutions of providing and including the necessary courses in technical programs.

Internal assignment and promotion based on behaviors in the three skill categories, as opposed to promotion by seniority or the "good-ole-boy" system makes a statement that skill development will be rewarded.

Providing time and mentors for continuing education and skill development supports growth of the individual. This may seem obvious, but in practice it is one of the most overlooked corporate behaviors, and one that severely blocks individual growth. In practice, organizations don't support this behavior by providing a buffer workforce or by approving overtime to fill-in during training or granting time off for education.

Organizations need to budget dollars for both internal and external education and training. The budget should be a percent of gross revenue, not just a percent of gross profits. The expenditure for education is a long-term expense of doing business. When it is neglected by a company it becomes a cost that is paid by society in general since the stockholders denied their responsibility in exchange for monetary gain. In the long term, such denial has been, and will continue to be, detrimental to the organization.

Internal training involves expenses for the training and continuing education of the individuals that are members of the organization. Later, in the cost of quality chapter, it will be listed under the major category of Prevention as an investment in the future quality improvement of the goods and services of the organization. Investment in general public education and training will promote the quality improvement of society in general.

The Specifics of Training: The Training of Management

It was stated earlier that 85 percent of the problems of American industry are problems of the system. W. Edwards Deming makes this point over and over again in his seminar, "Management Methods for Quality and Productivity." If training for quality and solving problems is to be effective the training must be addressed at the *root cause* of the problem. Training must begin with the training of management. Almost in conjunction but lagging slightly behind in timing is the training of the hourly worker.

There are two sides to any program of quality training. I term the two foci the "hard side" and the "soft side." The hard side encompasses rational data collection and analysis through statistical methods, technical problem solving, and technological improvement of "things" through research and engineering. The soft side includes the skills of the humanities, such as philosophy, psychology, and organizational sociology. These produce the behaviors of interaction, motivation, growth, and acceptance for change. Various organizations have advocated one or the other side of the quality thrust. I strongly believe the two are inseparable. In an effective quality program both sides are addressed in parallel. Programs begin to fall apart whenever the focus becomes disproportionate toward either side. Such interdependency is part of the holistic nature of excellence.

At the inception of a comprehensive quality program, the major problem and the first focus of training is usually management maturity and commitment to quality expressed through behavior. Management fails to fully realize that *we* make the decisions on the nature of the business. *We* decide what level of skills are necessary in employees. *We* determine the communications structure of the organization. *We* approve the capital expenditures for market research, innovative equipment and processes, and for training. *We* determine the quality of life in the work place. These are major responsibilities of management.

As society has changed, management has not met these responsibilities. The highly mature, highly intelligent, and highly motivated new breed of employees are sorely aware of the situation. Companies only offering lip service to quality will not be able to hire, or at least keep, the new high maturity employees. Training must begin with upper management.

Once management training has started and change in management style begun, training addressed downward will be reinforced through management behavior and can be effective. Until management supports the concepts and techniques addressed in training through behavior the training will be ineffective. This is the *root cause* of abandonment of the new skills learned by employees sent to seminars shortly after their return to the work environment.

The style and structure of this book is targeted as a training tool for training management. But it is also suitable for high maturity, highly motivated hourly employees, once management support is evident.

At the higher management levels the training is esoteric and philosophical. As the training is directed at lower levels of the organization it becomes more factual, procedural, and is addressed at specific skills and behaviors. The specific procedures of SPC need not be fully comprehended by upper management, although a thorough understanding certainly is beneficial. The concepts of changing for quality must be understood, endorsed, and utilized by upper management if middle management and operating level personnel are to endorse the policies with action. Only after upper and middle management have fully endorsed the atmosphere of change and the policies of comprehensive quality can the training of hourly workers be effective, lasting, and productive.

When a historically low maturity organization seeks to change, the most effective initial motivation is the directive and action of upper management. This change in action and endorsement by management is mandatory at the start of a comprehensive quality program. At this stage, benevolent autocratic, telling, behavior is the appropriate management behavior. The old way of doing business is not acceptable, "We will tell you in detail a better way."

The necessary changes and growth are not just in others; the required changes and growth are in each individual—including management. Each manager must be willing to change. When management guides and facilitates the change and growth, change and growth at lower levels will follow.

The second focus of training is on people skills. The topics are listening, understanding needs, rational Adult-Adult business behavior, mentoring change in others and win-win confrontation.

The third area of training is objective thinking and problem-solving skills. Although many managers do think objectively, many others do not. They allow past history, selective perception, fear, and unconsciously prejudiced thinking to interfere with their objectivity in problem solving.

Finally, variation theory, statistical techniques, and information assembly and analysis can be addressed. Managers now have the openness, objectivity, and skills for handling change. They now can handle the explosion of often painful but truthful information that statistics can and will provide. Management is now ready to use this information to solve tough problems and lead the worker in solving problems.

Moving people from the unconscious incompetent stage of learning into the conscious incompetent stage of learning can be done well in a group setting. This is the nature and focus of most seminars. But again, in reality, the discoveries of the seminar are seldom carried back and applied in the work place. Without coaching and behavior support, most people at the conscious incompetent stage of learning turn back and over time regress to the unconscious incompetent. Coaching and behavioral support must continue.

Continued training is most effective when it addresses a problem of the trainee. One-on-one or small group work utilizing the theoretical techniques to solve real problems brings reality to the new concepts and procedures. Coaching, again with real problems, guides the individual through the learning process until he/she is competent and confident to carry on alone.

I have found this to be especially true in teaching statistical quality control (SQC) and SPC. Theory has its place but theory is seldom made relevant and retained unless the theory is applied to a situation that is significant to the learner. Once such one-on-one or small group relevant application is made, the rationale of the theory becomes much clearer to the student. Then coaching must continue into another significant and different application; this time the student is coached to apply the theory previously learned in addressing the new problem. Eventually the student will reach the unconscious–competent stage of learning in applying the theory to practical problem solving. Thus the objective of the training is met.

In our eagerness to broadly train we tend to want to continue in a group setting in the later stages of learning. The net result of working with many is that none are truly trained. Although slower and requiring more time and resources, the individual training does produce the desired result. Unless our objective is to just put on a show for others it makes no sense to try to totally train in a group setting.

In Chapter 7 I developed a system for analyzing the competence level of an individual in the three major categories of skill and behavior. This quantification, in conjunction with similar position descriptions and the desire of the individual to move to a position requiring increased or different skill levels, highlights the target areas for training of an individual. The differences between the behavior requirements for a position and the evidenced behavior of the individual are the areas where growth must occur before the individual will be successful in the position.

For example, an effective trainer in a personnel department may desire to advance to a labor contract facilitator. The target area for people behavior development is negotiating behavior, and in information behavior perhaps growth to compiling, to analyzing.

Training and education are not complicated either in business or general society. The problem is that we do not support through facilitation, reward of desirable behavior or with monetary resources the process necessary to train. We don't support because the results seldom have a large impact on next quarter's or even next year's income statement, except perhaps as a negative result. *Education and training are responsibilities that we cannot afford to ignore.*

Communications, the Information Link

9

Effective communications links the behavior bases of people, information, and things. Without effective communications synthesis is blocked; there is no synergism of the group, nor is there mutual appreciation and utilization of the many individuals that constitute an organization. If one individual could be proficient in all three behavior bases then there would be little need or justification for the amalgamation of talents. We would all be totally self-sufficient "individual organizations."

No person possesses all the behaviors necessary to survive in today's complex society. We have become highly dependent on others for our own survival. Accepting this dependence we are, for the most part, sorely deficient of effective communication skills, yet our specialization emphasizes the need to be effective communicators. The business and technical communities have previously emphasized other areas of education. Such specialization, without growth in the ability to communicate concisely and effectively, will eventually result in loss of our ability to meet the needs of our customers. I classify communication skills as a synthesis of people and information skills.

The Information Explosion

Naisbitt and Aburdene point out that while communication has been de-emphasized in education we have plunged into an information-based society. So much information is available at any one time that any person attempting to incorporate all the information available in just one field becomes swamped and flounders in a sea of confusion and inactivity. This overabundance of information has led to further specialization and specialization within specializations. The impact of this specialization, again, has changed the way we interact with other individuals and the dynamics of organizations.

In the previous chapter on education I addressed the impact of specialized education. Here we are concerned with the impact of specialization on communications and the ability to achieve excellence in communications.

If we, as individuals in an organization cannot communicate effectively, our skills are of little benefit to the organization. The skills of the organization are the sum total of the skills of the individuals of the organization. If these skills are to be fully additive then communication provides the link between human data bases and results of activities. Even original thinkers and individual contributors must possess sufficient communication behaviors to translate the impact of their work into the efforts of the organization.

Sending and Receiving

Communication is a two-edged sword. There must be a transmitter and there must be a receiver for communication. The two must operate with a degree of commonality. Communication is analogous to the riddle "If a tree falls in the forest with no one around is there sound?" If someone speaks, writes, publishes a report, etc., and no one understands, there is no communication. I often see examples of "falling tree" communicators who, regardless of the quality of the communication, believe they have met their obligation to communicate. There is no transfer of observation, technology, concern, desire, or action in their communication. These communicators have not established nor confirmed a shared understanding between the sender and the receiver.

Many of our attempts at communication today are designed to meet the needs of the transmitter with little focus on the receiver and little consideration of the objectives and constraints of the receiver. Our communication is not user-friendly. These attempts are like a super-powered FM radio station operating when all the receivers are AM. No one hears or understands. The effort is wasted.

Quality and Quantity

Targeting the Receiver

Communication should be designed to meet the needs of a target customer. It should not tell all that one knows. It should transmit relevant information to the receiver. Prior to initiating communication, the transmitter should mentally reverse positions and determine what information is desired or needed by the receiver, what information is insignificant to the receiver, and what will be the benefit of communicating the information to the receiver.

The first step in the communications process is determining who is the customer. Too often we talk to hear ourselves talk, to boost our own ego. We try to transmit far more detail than is desired by the receiver. We often do not transmit the potential impact of analysis of the data.

Recently the concept of the one-page memo limit has been implemented in companies. Specialists shudder in horror. They ponder how they can tell all they know in one page. The point of the one-page memo is that mature customers do not want to know all that the specialist knows. The customer wants to know the impact of the analysis and wants a recommended action to be taken because of the analysis—not the details of the data collection or of the analysis. The specialist is part of the organization because he/she is competent. The role of the specialist in an organization is to thoroughly examine the details and arrive at conclusions based on the analysis. Just listing the details in a report drops the role of the specialist from analyst to data compiler. Compilation of data is a significantly lower informational behavior than are analysis and synthesis.

The modern information customer only expects the results of analysis and the recommendation of action. If the approval of that action by the customer is not necessary then, in the high maturity organization with sufficient trust, the communication is not warranted.

Active Receiving

The transmitter of information has an obligation to meet the needs of the receiving customer. The receiver also has an obligation to actively perceive and request clarification of the communications of the transmitter. Selective perception enhances the ability to comprehend. The receiver can block other stimuli and focus on the transmitter.

Continuing the analogy of the radio system, confusion would result if, given a program transmitted on a specific frequency, our radio receivers could not selectively tune to just one transmitter. Although transmission is technically correct, receiving results in mass confusion of sounds meaning nothing. All that is received results in only noise.

It would be just as confusing if a single transmitting station fed more than one program through a transmitter at one time. This analogy is parallel to subject jumping in communication or to shared attention listening. Changing topics before the development of a mutual understanding leads to confusion. These analogies apply all too often to actual communication.

Adult-Adult Transactions

Previously, we looked at Transactional Analysis' definition of the three states of each personality, Parent, Adult, and Child. Effective information transmittal for problem solving and establishing long-range direction is an Adult-Adult transaction. Parent directives block open response and expression of valid concerns by the receiver. Non-valuing pre-judgment blocks an interactive communication process that allows all concerns to be addressed. Parent-Parent and Child-Child transactions express dogma and emotion but do not facilitate problem solving. As mentioned, tone and body language communicate as much or more of the mental state of the communicator as do the actual words.

Effective communication is accomplished in two stages. First, information must be transmitted with control of the nature of the transaction. The second stage is verification of the effectiveness of the transaction. This second stage is often overlooked in current communication patterns. We think that because we said it or wrote it the receiver understood it. Such is often not the case. Listeners are not mind readers. The easiest way to confirm understanding is to ask the receiver to repeat his/her understanding of the communication. Usually some clarification will be necessary. Often several interactions will be necessary to verify that a shared understanding has been established. Such a process is an Adult-Adult transaction.

When an interactive communication process is desired but the initial speaker is Parent, the usual response of the listener will be that of a fearful Child acknowledging understanding when, in fact, no shared understanding exists. Thus is derived the necessity for control of both the information transmitted and the personality state of the transaction.

Two techniques of the professional salesperson are highly relevant to effective communication. They are emphasis of benefit and the trial close.

Emphasis of benefit is targeting the transaction to the needs of the customer—the listener or reader. Why communicate if the communication will not benefit one of the two parties of the communication? Of course, the transmitter is not always the initiator of the transaction. We initiate communication not only to tell information but also to seek information. Benefit is the purpose of communication. The communication should stress what the customer will gain, or what loss will be minimized, by the transaction. Such emphasis will increase the attention and comprehension of the customer of the communication.

The trial close is a sales technique where verification of mutual agreement is attempted on a minor point. Often when we attempt to communicate major benefits the decision process for the customer is complex and confusing. By breaking a decision or understanding down into a number of smaller attempts at agreement the seller is helping the customer work through the confusion one step at a time. In some communication the customer and vendor roles are not very clear but in any transaction there is a provider-customer relationship. Often one communication involves a number of transactions; the effective communicators sort out the transactions. The trial close provides a system of sorting and systematically establishing effective communications.

Abstract and Visual Perception

There exists a spectrum of individual ability to think and communicate. Two extremes of the spectrum are purely abstract and purely visual. A preponderance of either type of thinking and communicating has no correlation with wisdom. These two extremes are associated with left brain and right brain dominance. Some individuals understand abstract concepts and communications easier and some individuals comprehend quicker with visual and pragmatic examples in communication. Some people are theoretical and some are pragmatic. A continuum exists between the two extremes. To broadly communicate the transmitter must style communication to both types of perception. In individual communications an understanding of the dominant style of the receiver facilitates comprehension and effective communication.

For example, I struggled in calculus with the theorems and equations. Not until I saw a graph of a curve with the area under the curve broken into rectangles and understood that the sum of the areas of those rectangles approximated the total area under the curve, and that as the width of the rectangles was decreased, and the number of rectangles increased proportionately did the accuracy of the area under the curve estimation increase, did I grasp integration. After the visual comprehension the formulas made sense. Such is an example of visual perception. Other students in the class could look at the equation and read the theorem and fully grasp the power of the mathematical tool. They were more in tune with abstract thinking and communicating.

Similarly, I find graphically representing statistics far more effective in communicating the power of statistics to manufacturing people than citing abstract formulas and concepts.

Neither abstract nor visual communication is "right." Usually one or the other, or a combination of both, will be most effective in communicating. In this book I have attempted to use both methods of communicating. I have written about the concept, presented examples, and included graphic illustrations. A reader may have found one method of communicating most effective in establishing a shared understanding of a concept and wondered why others are included. Several methods of presentation are included so other readers may also easily reach a shared understanding. The reader who has noticed the variety of methods of presentation has a good start on understanding the nature of the communication style that is most effective for his/her understanding.

I am amazed at how often an individual with a different style of perception is labeled dumb or slow, when in fact the person is extremely smart. We often do not appreciate the abilities of individuals who are different. The problem of shared understanding is often one of communication, not of intelligence.

As a further example, consider the two methods of communication presented on the following page. Both communicate the same information. One presentation is graphic (Figure 24) and the other is tabular (see p. 101). Again, it is narrow-minded to think that only one method is the right way to communicate.

Another parallel example focuses on verbal and written communications. The intelligence levels of two individuals may be equal but the effective communication styles are different. Neither method of communicating should be associated with intelligence or creativity.

Figure 24

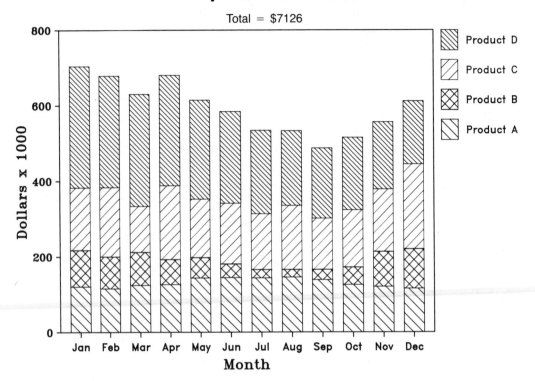

Concept versus Detail

Another parameter of communication style is a propensity for concept versus detail. Some communications balance both extremes but more often the emphasis is on one or the other. Again, understanding the customer's needs dictates the emphasis of the communication. The objective of the communication is development of shared understanding. Different "customers" develop that shared understanding through different processes. Some want the concept first and will ask for details to verify *their* conclusions of detail. Others want details, and mentally derive or ask for the concept. Generally, individual contributors, or specialists, will want the details first. Broad-based generalists want the concept first and then will ask for details as desired. Theoretically, the greater and higher the leadership of an individual the more the individual focuses initially on concept.

Targeting communication to meet the concept or detail needs of the customer increases the effectiveness of the communication. Rapid and effective communication improves response in a competitive environment.

XYZ Corporation Annual Sales
Dollars × 1000
Total = $7137

	Total	Jan	Feb	Mar	Apr	May	June	Jul	Aug	Sep	Oct	Nov	Dec
							Month						
Product A	1570	121	116	125	127	144	145	144	146	139	126	121	116
Product B	734	96	84	87	66	54	36	22	20	27	46	92	104
Product C	1981	166	184	122	196	155	161	148	170	136	152	166	225
Product D	2852	321	295	297	292	262	243	221	198	186	192	178	167
All Products	7137	704	679	631	681	615	585	535	534	488	516	557	612

Information Systems in Organizations

Seldom do the actual systems of information transmittal within an organization fit the structure of the organization. Networks of communications often develop to circumvent roadblocks to effective communication, whether the roadblocks be individuals or systems. Such networks are often systems of contacts or just the grapevine.

Previously, I discussed three organizational styles described by Chris Jensen: formal, informal, and achievement. Information systems develop differently in each type of organization. That development is highly correlated with individual access through normal channels to the information necessary for achievement of his/her organizational responsibilities. Low-maturity managers often underrate an individual's ingenuity for obtaining the information needed.

In the formal organization, only a small amount of task-specific information flows downward. Only requested information flows upward. The horizontal flow of information is formally blocked. Management behavior is extremely parent-like. Individuals are forced to use underground information sources. The inflexible and ineffective structure of the organization becomes a hindrance to accomplishment and innovation. Management does not understand why individuals are not conforming to policy and in response put in even more rigid policy to gain compliance. The result is the development of an elaborate "grapevine" system of communication and getting things done, shelves full of policy manuals, and eventually an organization of non-thinking, non-innovative, task-oriented "yes men." Only when the formal organizational structure meshes well with the shared vision, the mission, and the individual basic needs is such an organization effective. A problem exists because the visions, missions, and the tasks of society change faster than the adjustment of the bureaucratic formal organization.

One of the big problems of the formal organization underground information network is the accuracy of rumor and "the grapevine." Many tasks accomplished are not in line with corporate vision. The vision and the process for achieving that vision are not shared with the individuals charged with implementation. The net result is an organization struggling with purpose and full of "foxhole wars."

The formal organization has been the typical American business structure of the last 50 years. It has outlived its effectiveness. It marginally meets the needs of employees and customers. Now with increased global competition we see signs that the formal system will prove marginally effective at meeting long-term needs of the stockholder. It is losing in the new world economy to a higher maturity system.

The informal organization promotes effective "polite" communication. But the informal organization lacks a sense of shared purpose and an understanding of process for achieving that purpose. Polite communication flows because few members of the organization are willing to confront behavior that is not consistent with the shared purpose. Problems are seldom addressed or solved. Many individuals remain in the organization who either do not have the necessary behaviors and/or do not share the vision of the organization. They stay because it is a nice place to work. The employee's needs are being met at the expense of meeting the needs of the customers and stockholders. The informal organization first slights its responsibility to its stockholders, then to its customers. Finally the organization loses its ability to gratify the employee's needs with loss of profitability. The informal organization self-destructs!

The *root cause* problem of the informal organization is not systems of communications, although there may be little drive for improved communications. The problem lies in its balance and organizational neurotic behavior— fear of conflict and confrontation. The drive for a grapevine in such an organization is not the protectionist attitude toward information and "turf," but the complacency of the members toward communicating effectively.

In the Achievement organization the information system is dynamic. Change is endorsed because there exists a shared purpose and an understanding that the roles of the members of the organization are all directed toward achievement of the shared purpose. Taboos do not block horizontal or vertical communication between suppliers, customers, and a member with a different role. Contacts are promoted to gain information pertinent to a decision. Fear is seldom used as a motivator, and then only as a last resort for addressing behavior destructive to the ability to meet the needs of the stockholders, the employee group, and the customers. Because fear is seldom used and motivation is achieved through appropriate need gratification of positive behavior, communications flow openly. Direction may be necessary to continuously improve the quality of the communications. Individuals communicate in a personality style appropriate for the situation. The communication style for business, including most confrontation, is Adult-Adult.

In the achievement style organization, the grapevine is minimized. The needs that led to the development of the grapevine in other style organizations are addressed through the dynamic information system described. Systems of role definition, purpose, and communication are still necessary in the achievement organization. Such systems are discussed in a later chapter on the Achievement organization.

The contributions an individual can make toward achieving a shared vision and toward organizational development are highly dependent upon effective communication by both the originator and the receiver of the communication. For such effective communication to exist there must also exist an environment conducive to effective communications. The organization must strive for high maturity. Recognition of these facts is fundamental to growth in organizational culture and quality improvement.

Defining a Process, Any Process 10

Before we can address the quality problems that face us we must understand the processes that produce those problems. Such an understanding is mandated by the relationship of *effects, direct causes,* and *root causes.* The *effects* and the *root causes* frequently do not occur at the same stage of a process. The specialist of one step of a process scratches his or her head in disbelief as undesirable variation occurs. The *root cause* and even the *direct cause* often are in other areas of the process.

In the quest to define the process and the controlling factors of quality I found that processes are much larger than usually defined. The significance of what I call the macro process became more and more important. The macro process starts with procedures and basic raw materials and ends with the final customers' disposal or long-term satisfaction with the good or service. Finding and addressing *root causes* of variation often mandates that the investigator look outside the immediate organization. Partnering with customers and suppliers is necessary if the true *root causes* of variation are to be identified, addressed, and eliminated.

Within an organization there is often insufficient attention paid to the definition and understanding of the macro process. In manufacturing processes different departments often limit their concept of "the process" to the immediate departmental environment. Limited vision produces frustration with addressing *root causes* related to *effects* and often leads to "foxholes." A supplying department is not aware that variation in a property that does not directly affect the productivity of that department produces havoc in the customer department. Meanwhile, the customer department goes crazy trying to handle the variation introduced by the preceding department. As we will see, definition of the macro process addresses these frustrations.

Manufacturing departments do not have a monopoly on this type of frustration and limited vision. Planning, scheduling and shipping departments play havoc with sales departments. Purchasing departments frustrate maintenance, engineering, and production departments. Quality departments play havoc with meeting shipping, production, and invoicing schedules. The examples could go on for many pages. The significant point is that actions of any individual, department, or organization significantly affect the ability of others to manage their functions. By defining a macro process all these interactions are defined and *communicated*. Defining the macro process is a significant step in eliminating turfdom and filling foxholes.

The computer world has added much to the concept of process management. In the binary world of the computer, processes must be defined exactly. The larger processes of computers, programs, are broken down into manageable sub-processes, or sub-routines. Each sub-routine has a specific and limited function. Yet no sub-routine can accomplish the overall purpose of the program alone, and without the overall process the sub-routine is worth little. The total program must be considered holistically. The overall purpose of the program drives each sub-routine.

In computer programming, after defining the general purpose of the program, the flow diagram provides the overall vision of the process of producing the product and the interactions of the sub-routines. The skills, structure, and discipline of the systems analyst can be applied to any process.

The macro process of a business can be broken down into functional processes. Functional processes can be further broken down into functional sub-processes. The objective is to break down large processes into sub-processes where significant control parameters can be identified and managed. Definition of the function and control mechanisms of each sub-process, in light of the macro process, provides a system of meeting the overall objective of the macro process.

When significant control parameters for each functional sub-process are defined, process control plans for that sub-process can be formulated. A process control plan defines the standard operating expectations for each significant controllable parameter.

The macro process, sub-process, and process control plan may sound complex but, in practice and through the aid of SPC, they aren't. Through division into smallest common denominator functional sub-processes, development and definition become simple. The hardest task is usually convincing the organization of the benefit to be gained through the macro process concept.

The development of a macro process requires the definition of a common denominator that runs throughout the organization. The most typical common denominator is end-product; in most cases the macro process is best defined by end-product.

When an organization produces many end products, the sub-processes of the macro process for each product are often similar or identical. Some products may require extra unique sub-processes. Some may not require certain otherwise standard sub-processes.

Many control parameters for the required sub-processes of a product-defined process are often identical with the parameters of other products utilizing the same sub-process. Only the target values of the parameters change. A building block approach effectively defines each functional process and each functional sub-process in terms of the macro process. The product control plan for each individual process can be assembled to define the macro process for that product.

The basic tool for defining the macro process is the block diagram. Each block of a block diagram defines a sub-process. The sub-process blocks can be divided further into sub-process blocks as required to achieve a manageable and significant functional sub-process. The critical values and flows of material and information are shown on a block diagram.

Block diagrams have been used to describe process flows for a long time. The unique properties of these block diagrams are the inclusion of the *statistically significant* control parameters and, as the diagram resolution is increased for a specific product, the target value of each parameter for that process and product.

Block diagrams can be as simple as the basic problem-solving model shown in Chapter 1. Or they can be complex, with the block shapes relating to the function of the sub-process. Reflecting production lines, block diagrams can show a central single path of process flow. More often the highly defined macro-process diagram will incorporate many branches and loops.

The first step is the assembly of the block diagrams. At this time it is not necessary to be concerned with the significant parameters of each sub-process or with the parameter values for a specific product. The short-term objective is to define the process.

Once the initial macro process block diagrams are completed, the objective is to determine the significant few control parameters for each sub-process. Such a determination of significance involves considerable work. If the diagram is to be an effective operating tool, the parameters must be highly significant, not just someone's hunch of what is important. Incorrect past practice must be overcome with proper statistical analysis and determining the truth of the hypothesis.

Effective parameter definition is fundamental for effective macro process flow diagrams. The 80:20 rule almost always applies to control of any sub-process. Twenty percent of the controllable parameters control 80 percent of the variation of the sub-process. The insignificant many parameters are locked down and recorded elsewhere but are not initially part of the process control diagram or plan. The significant product properties controlled in a sub-process are the significant 20 percent. These few parameters are the high-impact independent parameters of the sub-process. Many of the remaining 80 percent will be brought into control either by being locked down or, as dependent variables, by the efforts to control the significant 20 percent.

Granted, other control parameter variations will cause property variation, but such variation is relatively minor when compared to the property variation caused by variation of the significant control parameters. Once a process control plan is successfully implemented, continuing process improvement will address the remaining control parameters in descending order of significance.

The gains to be made in product and process quality are large at the start of a process stabilization. Initial effort produces highly significant results. As more and more parameters are included in the control plan, returns diminish.

An initial common mental block to implementing process control plans is the belief that all parameters must be brought into statistical control in one giant step. Many process control plans have died due to over-engineering. The concept of the 80:20 rule was not understood nor utilized. Process control plans are a *process*, not a project. *The process control plan is dynamic. It is a process for establishing statistical control. It has no end-point.* It is continuously and systematically improved and updated.

Few of our American manufacturing processes are in statistical control. The first step in quality improvement is to bring the most significant of these processes into control. An out-of-control process cannot be fine-tuned. Much of the processing engineering effort I have seen attempts to fine-tune out-of-control processes. It can't be done! The major shifts in an uncontrolled process far outweigh the significance of fine-tuning. The first step in controlling a process is to define the process. Our bent for specialization, solution, and instant results drives us to overlook the basic first step.

Properties controlled through dynamic decisions may or may not be significant but often the insignificant many are relatively static. The significant few require the frequent decisions.

On the following page is a block diagram for the macro process of a system for producing a paperboard product. The process is not highly defined yet the diagram provides a tremendous amount of significant and actionable information. The flow diagram shows the significant sub-processes. Under each sub-process diagram is a line for listing the significant parameters of that sub-process. At this point the diagram is generic for all products produced on this system. For each product produced with the system a control value can be defined for each parameter. Now the process diagram is specific to that product. The diagram can be used for each product of the system simply by filling in the proper value of the parameter.

The concept of "customer" is extremely important in the design of this diagram. The intended customers are line operators. This is one of the simple tools those charged with control of a process need in order to fully understand what is required to "do a good job." The customer here is not the manager nor the engineer. This diagram does not provide all the information engineers need for design change and major shifts of process capability. The objective of the diagram is consistency of operation and resulting consistent product properties.

One of the main advantages of a macro process diagram is quick, effective, and broad communications of the significant control values and target settings for the process. The diagram does not attempt to include so much information that it becomes confusing, incomprehensible, non-communicative, and effectively unusable. It communicates the highly significant and highly dynamic control parameters. The many other control parameters are either relatively insignificant or their control is relatively static. These control settings are locked in place and do not require operator decision.

In application, the process flow diagram is the main tool of "running to target," or center lining. It provides a benchmark for the manufacturing process. Any operator change of settings should be traceable to an assignable

Figure   25

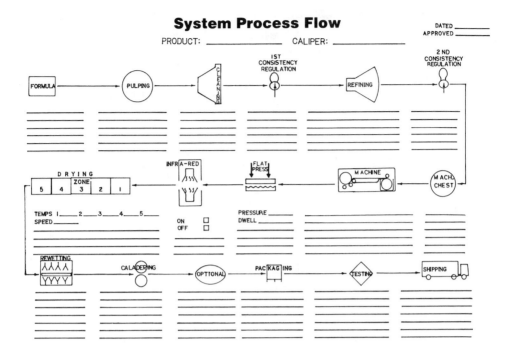

cause of variation in the production system. An assignable cause might be a shift in raw material property, a shift that the quality-conscious organization will be addressing with the supplier. There are other reasons for deviation from the benchmark. The decision to move away from center line must be rational and related to an assignable cause. Settings can be modified as the process is changed, or for a different reason, by rational consensus of the team. Such a decision should be made based on truthful information and actual need. Ideally, the process will be continually improved. Continuous improvement mandates frequent revision of the process control diagram and plan.

Process definition is not limited to the manufacturing plant. A similar diagram was made for the well-executed sales call. A process flow diagram of a sales call is shown on page 110. The same construction process was followed. In this situation the common denominator is the customer.

The macro process flow diagram is the end product of much work. It is the product of an interactive system of definition. It is a high maturity tool. No one individual will be able to produce a detailed and accurate macro process diagram. Accurate construction requires a team. Construction requires input and refinement by many people with expertise in numerous areas. For the team concept to be effective, the organizational maturity must be high.

In the next two chapters statistical concepts and tools of process control will be addressed. These tools and concepts are a new business language. They are essential prerequisites for a truthful and effective process control diagram and plan.

Figure 26

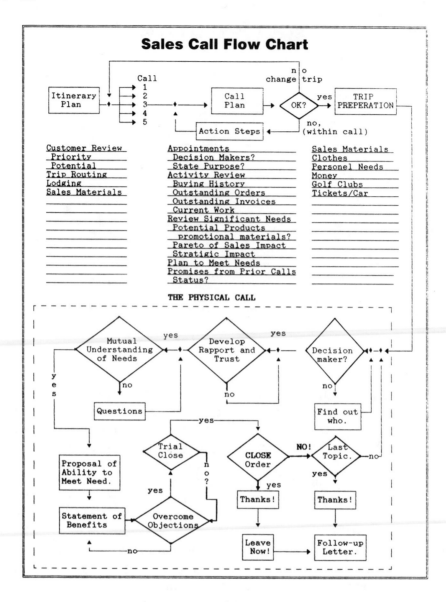

Sales Call Flow Chart

Call
1
2
3
4
5

Itinerary Plan → Call Plan → OK? → TRIP PREPERATION

no change trip

yes

no, (within call)

Action Steps

Customer Review
 Priority
 Potential
Trip Routing
Lodging
Sales Materials

Appointments
 Decision Makers?
 State Purpose?
Activity Review
 Buying History
 Outstanding Orders
 Outstanding Invoices
 Current Work
Review Significant Needs
 Potential Products
 promotional materials?
 Pareto of Sales Impact
 Stratigic Impact
Plan to Meet Needs
Promises from Prior Calls
 Status?

Sales Materials
Clothes
Personel Needs
Money
Golf Clubs
Tickets/Car

THE PHYSICAL CALL

Mutual Understanding of Needs → yes → Develop Rapport and Trust → yes → Decision maker?

no → Questions

no → (back to Develop Rapport and Trust)

no → Find out who.

yes → Proposal of Ability to Meet Need.

Trial Close — yes → CLOSE Order → NO! → Last Topic. → no

no?

yes → Statement of Benefits

Overcome Objections

yes

CLOSE Order → yes → Thanks! → Leave Now!

Last Topic. → yes → Thanks! → Follow-up Letter.

no → (Statement of Benefits)

Charts: Tools for Information, Knowledge, Communication, and Control

11

Charts are a visual presentation of data. And charted information is rapidly assimilated. Charts also expand perception. A picture of a situation is visible in one glance. Charts minimize selective perception, a situation common with data presented in tables. Charts communicate accurately and rapidly. A chart, therefore, is worth a thousand words.

This chapter focuses on several basic charts. These charts are both information and analytical tools. My intention is not to write a text on charting but to acquaint the unfamiliar reader with basic types of charts and the terms of the new business language. The charts are presented in ascending order of sophistication.

The Run Chart

The simplest of all graphic illustrations of process, the run chart, usually presents the value of one or more parameters over time. Sometimes batches, skids, or runs replace an actual time basis. These units are time-based or related.

The dependent variable is plotted on the Y axis and the time variable is plotted on the X scale. The power of the run chart is that it presents a large amount of information showing the variation in the dependent variable. The sophistication of the run chart can be increased, especially when sample size is one, by including $3\hat{\sigma}$ (sigma hat, meaning one estimated standard deviation, or variation, unit) action limits. This form of run chart is the simplest form of control chart. Many process control problems can be solved with the simple run chart.

Figure 27

The Run Chart

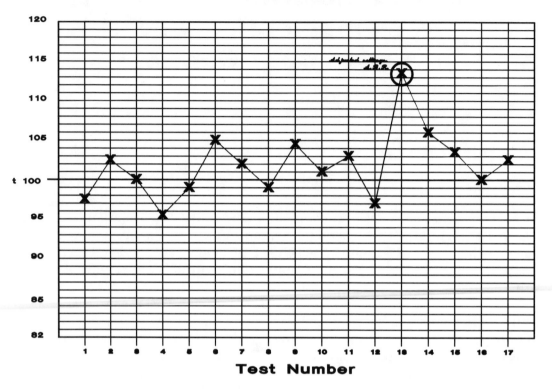

Test Number

The Ishikawa or Fishbone Diagram

Solving problems requires developing a cause-related solution. Action orientation drives us to jump to implementing a solution. Often we implement a solution not related to the direct cause. Then improvement doesn't result. The improper solution may even introduce more variation into the process.

After *effect* detection follows problem analysis not solution. The goal of problem analysis is to find a cause-effect relationship. The fishbone diagram helps identify and communicate potential *causes*. It is especially powerful when individuals have preconceived ideas about the significant *causes*. It forces open minds. The skeleton of a fishbone diagram is shown on the next page. This skeleton organizes *direct causes* into five categories, people, methods, materials, environment, and equipment. First, in a group, state an *effect,* then fill in the skeleton with possible *direct causes*. All suggested *direct causes* are entered under the proper category. Other categories, or other names for similar categories, are often used and are appropriate. Next, gather quantitative data to support or reject selection of probable *direct causes*. This activity

Figure 28

"Fishbone" Diagram

(A Brainstorming Tool)

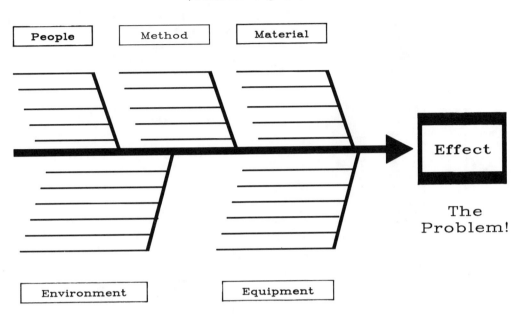

will lead the group toward a consensus focus on one or two *direct causes*. These *direct causes* become the focus of solution activities.

A fishbone diagram may also be used to select *root causes* related to *direct causes*. The *direct cause* replaces the *effect*. The procedure is the same.

The Pareto Chart

The significance of causal factors can be shown in a Pareto chart. As mentioned, 20 percent of the *direct causes* are usually responsible for 80 percent of an *effect*. The Pareto analysis quantitatively focuses on solutions that will produce maximum results. The Pareto chart summarizes an analysis and directs the group's focus toward solutions of the most significant problems.

The Histogram

The histogram is a simple method of showing the distribution of sample data. The range of sample data is divided into equal increments. The increments are spread across the X axis. The number of measurements in each increment are shown on the Y axis. The histogram often appears as stacks of boxes, or X's.

Figure 29

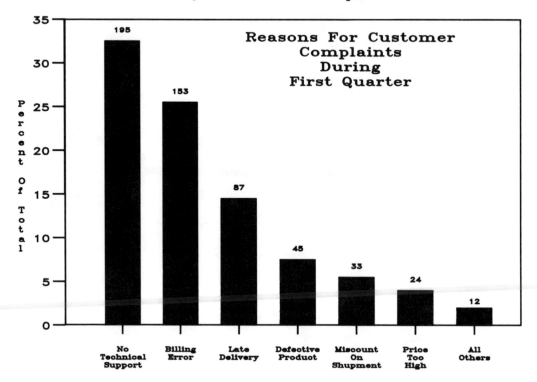

Example of a Pareto Analysis

The shape of the histogram indicates the range and pattern of sample variation. Multiple peaks indicate a *multi-modal* distribution. A multi-modal distribution occurs with a shift in process, or when data are collected from two systems of production.

The X-Y Chart or Scatter Diagram

The X-Y chart can be sophisticated or it can be simple. The X-Y chart is a graphic multiple regression analysis indicating relationship between two factors of a process. X-Y charts can be used to find correlations between measurements, instruments, or procedures. They can show a relationship between *direct cause* and *effect*.

An X-Y chart with high correlation between *cause* and *effect* can be used to determine the proper adjustment of a *cause* for a desired change in *effect*. Most X-Y charts will show a linear relationship, but curvilinear relationships also occur. Often X-Y chart analysis of a curvilinear relationship is simpler

Figure 30

Histogram

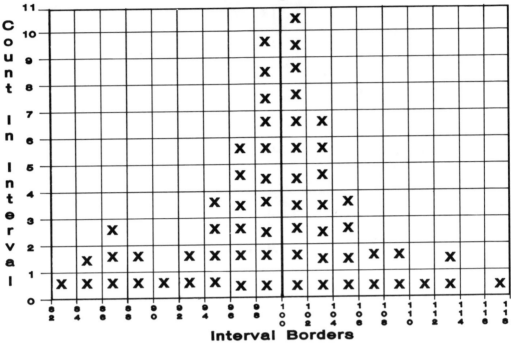

Of Testing Results

(Count In Interval vs. Interval Borders)

than curvilinear regression analysis. Several X-Y charts, varying in sophistication, are shown on the next page.

The X-Y chart is very useful in comparing the test results determined with two different instruments, two different operators, or two different procedures. A chart is prepared with equal scales on the X and Y axes. A line of equality passes through equal values of X and Y. One axis is labeled "instrument" or "procedure A." The other axis is labeled "instrument" or "procedure B." Test at least 30 duplicate samples, or samples as close to identical as possible. Span the range of expected test values: Test one paired sample on each instrument, or one by each procedure. With paired samples, results of one test procedure are the X coordinates and results of the other test procedure are the Y coordinates. Plot the X, Y values on the graph. If the test procedures yield near-equal results, the plotted points will fall close to the line of equality. Plotted points will not all fall on the line of equality because variation always exists in test data. The perpendicular distances of the points from the line of equality indicate amount of variation and degree of correlation. If a great majority of points fall on one side of equality a bias is indicated. If test values trend away from equality, estimate a line through the points.

Figure   31

X-Y or "Scatter" Diagrams

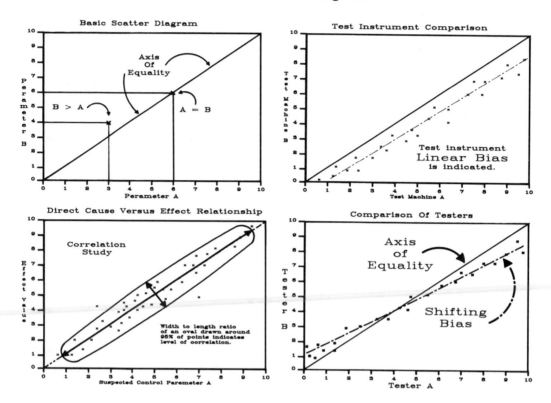

Half the points should be on each side of the estimated line; and the line will usually be straight, although occasionally it will be a curve. The drawn line can be either parallel, at an acute angle, or can cross the line of equality. A parallel line indicates a correlation with a constant bias. An acute angle line indicates a changing bias, such as a percent bias. A crossing line indicates a bias changing with test value. If the drawn line is a curve the bias relationship is exponential. In testing, two methods or procedures with a defined relationship can both be used. Determine which values will be used for control or certification, if applicable.

X-Y charts can show degree of correlation. The point pattern indicates the degree. Correlation connotes a mapping between the independent variable and the dependent variable. A perfect mapping exactly follows an equation or rule. Because of variation, a perfect mapping seldom exists. Testing and other variation not dependent on process can effect the value of the dependent variable. Figure 32 represents the two extremes of relationship. Random points indicate no relationship, while tight patterns indicate strong relationship. Statistically, the tightness of the pattern is analogous to the confidence level of the correlation. Strong *direct cause* to *effect* relation-

Figure 32

Actual Cause and Effect
Scatter Diagram Studies

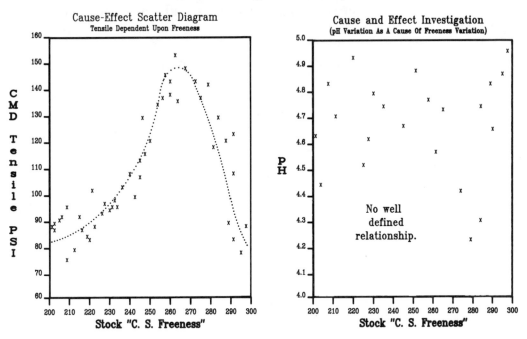

Cause-Effect Scatter Diagram
Tensile Dependent Upon Freeness

C M D Tensile PSI

Stock "C. S. Freeness"

Cause and Effect Investigation
(pH Variation As A Cause Of Freeness Variation)

P H

No well
defined
relationship.

Stock "C. S. Freeness"

ships can be used for predictions. High confidence predictions can be used for process control.

Control Charts

The control chart has become the backbone of modern dynamic process control and quality improvement. Control charts were first developed by Dr. Walter Shewhart of Western Electric after World War I. They were since used by AT&T, classified during World War II, by the Japanese in their post-war recovery, and during the early postwar period by some American companies. But they lost favor in the United States in the 1950s. The power gained from charting was then not handled properly. Charting was delegated and centralized by top management. Animosity developed toward individuals who exposed problems through charting. And the 1954 recession provided top management the opportunity to fire the proponents. When American industry began to feel the economic crunch of global competition, and after the NBC White Paper "If Japan Can Do It Why Can't We?" American industry revived the control chart.

Control charts represent variable and attribute data, constant or variable size samples. Numerous variations are based on these and other factors. The $\overline{X}$ & R chart (pronounced X bar and R chart), the $\overline{X}$ & σ chart, and the moving $\overline{X}$ and R chart represent variable data. NP, P, C, and U charts represent attribute data. For a full description, preparation, and application of each type of control chart refer to: Ford Motor Company's *Continuing Process Control and Process Capability Improvement;* Grant and Leavenworth's *Statistical Quality Control;* the AT&T *Statistical Quality Control Handbook;* or to Juran's *Quality Control Handbook.*

Control charts estimate the average value and distribution of a process parameter. Control or action limits mark a shift in distribution. Points outside the action limits, or certain data trends within action limits, indicate a shift in the true parameter distribution. Only when points fall outside the action limits or trends develop within the action limits is there high confidence the process has shifted. Points and trends indicating a process shift warrant action. Normal point distribution inside the action limits indicates normal process variation. Direct causes of variation stem from materials, methods, environment, process and testing. When points indicate no process shift (i.e., not outside action limits and without a statistically significant pattern), no process correction should be made. Action on controlled variation produces over-control.

Four common control charts are shown on the following page: the $\overline{X}$ & R chart (variable data, n>1), the moving $\overline{X}$ & R chart (variable data, n = 1), the P chart (percent non-conforming, attribute data, near-constant sample size), and the C chart (counts defects) (attribute data, constant sample size). The NP chart is similar to the P chart but measures the number non-conforming. The U chart is similar to the C chart but does not require constant sample size.

Attribute charts have applicability, but more information will be gained if attribute parameters can be quantified for variable control charting. Extra understanding and effort are required. Sometimes this is not possible.

Although useful to the manager and engineer, the operator realizes the greatest direct benefit from a control chart. The operator should do the control charting, since the operator is ultimately responsible for process control. Appropriate control parameters are dynamic. If direct causes are to be immediately identified, and if corrective action is to be taken quickly, the chart must be plotted and responded to by the operator. Charts plotted by an engineer or clerk just aren't as effective.

Initially, an operator should plot points on the chart and know how to respond to the chart; he/she does not have to know the statistics behind the chart, or even how to calculate action limits. Chart preparation and action limit calculations—less dynamic decisions—can be done by a supervisor, engineer, or manager until the operator is trained.

The moving$\overline{X}$ & R chart is special. Many continuous process parameters are homogeneous at one point in time. For example, multiple samples from a tank of well-agitated liquid usually show little variation. The liquid is essentially homogeneous. Testing variation is greater than true variation. It is

Control Charts

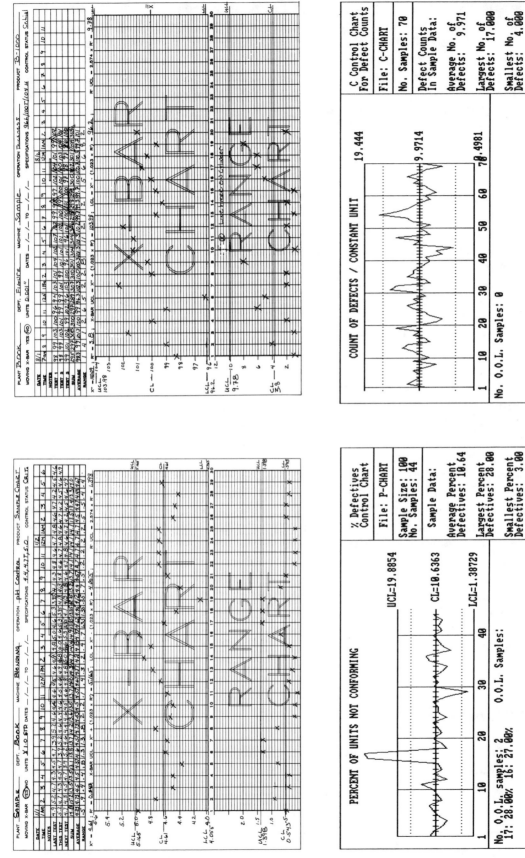

statistically and economically sound to use only one sample for testing. In a homogeneous continuous process, variation is time-dependent. One sample is an accurate snapshot, but the standard $\overline{X}$ & R chart requires more than one sample. There is no range in a sample size of one. The range and action limits of the moving $\overline{X}$ & R chart utilize time variation. Two or more test values, either current and prior, or prior, current, and following, define a range. Action limits of the moving $\overline{X}$ & R chart reflect normal variation of the process over time.

Whisker Chart

The whisker chart is another special chart. Its glory is in its people engineering. The whisker chart works best when normal variation, action limit range is tighter than specification limit range. The typical $\overline{X}$ & R chart system requires two scales, one for average and one for range. If a process requires charting several parameters the chart shuffle gets ridiculous. Charts are everywhere. Consolidated charts are huge and unmanageable, or worse, compact and unreadable. The whisker chart allows plotting both average and range on one scale. And more charts can fit on one large sheet. This simplicity facilitates operator acceptance.

Whisker charts can be either normal or moving. The normal chart uses a sample size, n>1. The moving whisker chart uses the moving $\overline{X}$ & R principles. The average is first plotted on the scale. Next the range is calculated, divided by 2, and the result added to and subtracted from the average. These two resulting points are plotted above and below the average. A line is drawn from the upper point to the lower point, which indicates the estimated process range, the center point being the average. Action limits control reaction to the average. Initially, specification limits control reaction to the range. Before the sophisticated statistical reader rises in fury, I must agree that theoretically the range response should be to the range control limits. This is a proper response of the advanced user. In the battle to get operators to use control charts I make this compromise. My conscience is calmed by the knowledge that the improper interpretation of the range increases conformance to specifications. Later, statistically sound interpretation will lead to continuous improvement. Excellence is thus not achieved in great leaps but with small steps.

CuSum Chart

The CuSum (cumulative summation of value deviation) defines, at selected confidence, shifts in process average of selected amount. The CuSum chart can

Figure 34

Whisker Chart

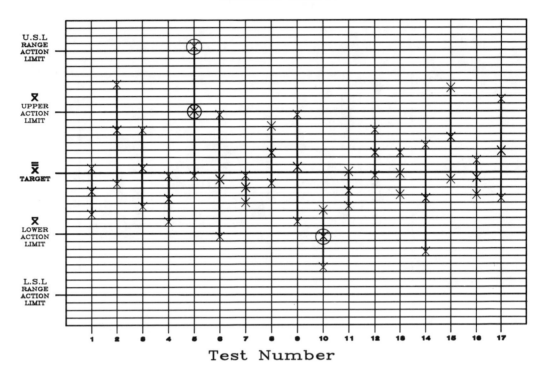

Test Number

verify effectiveness of designed process changes, detect a change in an untargeted parameter during adjustment of another parameter, and find unauthorized process changes. For a detailed discussion of the preparation and theory of the CuSum chart see Juran's handbook.

Cumulative deviation of sample value from target value or historic average is plotted against time. Samples should be consecutive. A triangular template is placed over the graph with the point at the last time and entry (X, Y). The triangle acuteness determines the amount of shift to be detected and at what confidence level. The line of cumulative deviation touching or crossing the triangle indicates a process shift. CuSum charts are not usually used by operators. They are complex, awkward and time-consuming except with computerization. They basically are an engineering and management tool.

These are the basic charts. With them most processes can be controlled. There are others, mostly hybrids, with special applications. The non-statistical reader familiar with these charts will seldom encounter process control illiteracy.

Figure 35

Example of a CuSum Chart

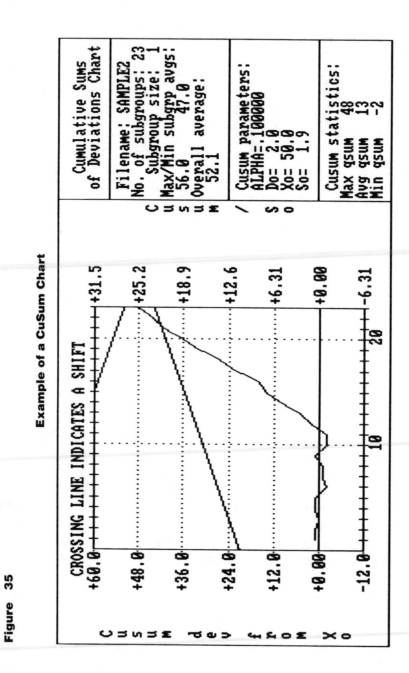

Managing for Excellence

Process Control Concepts 12

SQC Defined

The term "statistical quality control" is often used loosely without the speaker or listener understanding the term. The listener often must either clarify the communication or continue without really understanding.

SQC is statistical information assembly and analysis. It detects changes in systems.

Statistical process control (SPC) is the utilization of SQC to determine the direct cause and root cause of system changes and action to minimize future undesirable system changes. SQC does not stand alone as a philosophy of management. SQC quickly provides accurate information (knowledge) for defining appropriate action to solve problems. SQC and SPC are elements of larger categories: information tools and problem-solving behaviors.

Total Process Control for Quality

As previously mentioned, this book is not a text on SPC. For that, refer to *Continuing Process Control and Process Capability Improvement* published by Ford Motor Company. This chapter emphasizes concepts not adequately covered in many texts.

There are two foci of total process control. The first focus is information assembly, problem identification, designing and/or redesigning a process for control and implementation, and verifying control. The second focus is establishment of management systems that insure control is maintained. The majority of effort is usually directed at the first focus. The second focus is often neglected. Once a system of control is established and its effectiveness verified, the process manager must follow through with management and information systems. Once these system changes are implemented attention can again be directed to the first focus.

Sophistication in Problem Solving

Process control problems and techniques follow the 80:20 rule. A Pareto distribution applies. *Eighty percent of process control problems can be solved using 20 percent, the least complex 20 percent, of the techniques.*

Advanced techniques are sometimes applicable, but not knowing advanced techniques is no excuse for not acting on the simple 80 percent of the problems. Obsession with only the advanced techniques often results in few, if any, solutions. Using advanced techniques to solve most problems is like using cannons to kill flies! Many non-specialists *can* use the simple techniques; they simply must be empowered to do so. Highly skilled people should focus on really difficult problems. Correct allocation of behaviors benefits the individuals, the customers, and the stockholders.

> SQC IS A PROBLEM-SOLVING TOOL. IT IS
> AN INFORMATION ASSEMBLY BEHAVIOR.
>
> THE PURPOSE OF SQC IS TO QUICKLY OBTAIN THE BEST
> INFORMATION POSSIBLE FOR SOUND DECISION MAKING.

The All-Embracing Nature of Process

Process control has often been limited to the production environment, yet every aspect of organizational activity embraces process. All processes warrant control. Sales, purchasing, invoicing, research, product development, employee motivation, fiscal reporting, communications, advertising, training, and manufacturing all warrant control. All exhibit variation. All have *effects, direct causes,* and *root causes.* Control techniques and principles vary but the need for process control is widespread. I define process control broadly and advocate applying the principles wherever applicable.

Limited perception of the scope of process and process control can destroy an organization. Application limited to manufacturing misses many *direct causes* and *root causes* of poor quality.

Empirical Data

"Empirical data is never complete!" Deming declares this repeatedly in his seminar. And the concept warrants his repeated pronouncement. Conclusions reached through analysis of empirical data (data of observation and measurement) always have a degree of assumption. A degree of risk is inherent. Predictions and decisions based on empirical data cannot be absolute. The environment in which we gather data is dynamic. Who would pretend to have evaluated the significance of *every* possible cause of an *effect*? Only with limited perception would one believe *all* conditions of a previous situation were accurately measured and are now exactly the same. We are never 100 percent certain with empirical data. There are no absolutes with empirical data.

The assumed absoluteness of empirical data flares up at the worst times. This property is the foundation of Murphy's Law. An open mind acknowledges the basic nature of empirical data.

Let's look at some examples of conclusions incorporating assumptive thinking. $5 + 5 = 10$. True? In the octadecimal (base 8) number system $5 + 5 = 12$. You *assumed* I was talking about the decimal system. "Hydrogen reacted with oxygen yields water." Not true when the conditions exist to produce hydrogen peroxide. "Matter can neither be created nor destroyed" was blown apart by Einstein's discovery that matter could be converted to energy. A less assumptive statement prior to his work would have been "we have not been able to detect the creation nor destruction of matter."

"Everything is the same!" "Nothing has changed." "We've done it this way for the last 30 years." "Last month the regulator broke. That must be the problem now. Get maintenance to replace the regulator!" These statements disregard the nature of empirical data and assumption. How much of our knowledge is correct? Does it hold true with expanded perception? Does it hold true in a dynamic environment? When we correctly utilize empirical data we acknowledge that we take calculated risks.

The Nature of Variation

Variation is inherent in measured parameters. Our "A/not A" heritage wants to deny this. Usually there is a continuum between extremes. The world isn't black and white; the expected situation is for variation to occur. And it occurs in somewhat predictable patterns. Instrument capability and/or data validity both hide variation. Undetected variation is either due to lack of measurement sensitivity or perhaps wishful thinking by the measurer.

If variation always exists, then variation is inherent in any defined process. Variation usually has a definable pattern. Attempts to fine-tune a stable yet varying system that are not modifications to the system produce increased variation. "Over control" is very prevalent. When an operator or manager attempts to adjust closer to a target value and the measurements are within the expected or normal variation and show no pattern, variation will increase. Autocratic direction and/or internal desire to do one's best motivates people to take inappropriate action. The goal is less variation and tighter control. These actions are counterproductive and as much a source of poor quality as not taking action when a true system shift occurs.

The power of control charting is differentiation of normal variation and assignable cause variation. Assignable cause variation is caused by a shift in the process. *Only assignable cause variation warrants operator adjustment. If the amount of normal variation is not satisfactory it is management's responsibility to redesign the system to reduce inherent variation.* The values on control charts termed upper and lower control limits would be better termed, from a process control point of view, "action limits."

Control charts have a defined probability of error. The chart will indicate action when a system has not changed 0.3 percent of the time, or stated inversely, the chart will correctly indicate action 99.7 percent of the time. Remember, with empirical data there are no absolutes.

Defined sources of variation, problem-solving behaviors, time, and action maximize organizational effectiveness. Organizations waste time, ability, and effort chasing normal variation. Few, if any, organizations can afford this luxury. The probability of finding a *direct cause* of a single occurrence of normal variation with a control chart is less than 0.5 percent. Most of the time we don't know what type of variation we chase.

Sources of Variation

Knowing more about the sources of variation, normal and assignable cause, leads one to first track down sources of assignable cause variation and temporarily accept normal variation. The myopic alternative is to destructively assume that any measured variation indicates a process shift.

The possible sources of variation are overwhelming. Instrument precision and sampling methods can indicate or hide process variation. Tester ability to repeatedly duplicate the previous test method can introduce process variation. Inept mathematical ability in calculating test results can cause apparent variation. All of these variations are not true process variations: They are the result of variation of measurement.

Raw material variations may either cancel each other out or be additive. Multiple lines of process with output later merged introduce additive variation. All these sources of variation are in addition to the normal variation of the actual production system. Ambient temperature and humidity may even introduce variation. These sources are external process variations.

All these variations are part of the overall system. The job of process management is to understand and, when possible, minimize all sources of variation. Remember that to reduce the amount of normal variation requires a modification of the system.

Finally, test values are dependent on the testing procedure. This seems like an obvious statement, but it is amazing how often two facilities testing for a property get two different results. The true value, if there is such a value, has not changed but because the testing is being done using different procedures testing indicates different values.

For example, I became involved in a disagreement over the tensile strength of a paperboard product. I found two testing laboratories were using for one thing, two different tensile strength machines, and second, were pulling the samples at different speeds. We were able to standardize on one speed but we still saw differences. Neither lab could fund another tensile machine to match the other lab's machine. We were able to develop a correlation between the two machines and define a bias. We had to resort to the ASTM Standard Method Committee to determine what type of machine was used to set the standard. And so we made significant progress at filling a supplier-customer foxhole.

In another dispute, I found that two laboratories were both "conditioning samples." One lab conditioned samples in low humidity to low moisture content and the other conditioned to high humidity. If results are to be compared, it is imperative that testing facilities use the same test procedure or develop significant correlations between results. Test values cannot be compared without stating procedures.

An Immoral Love Affair

Statistics provide information and establish criteria for problem-solving action. Nothing more, nothing less. Information provides insight and power. Statistics reveal truth. Some individuals, for psychological reasons, recognize the power but are either unable or unwilling to take action. They don't effectively communicate the results to others with power to take action. They develop a "love affair" with the charts and numbers. Sometimes they will present information critically at the wrong time and the wrong place. The knowledge thus becomes an inappropriate power base to support a hollow sense of self-worth. They alienate others who could effectively utilize the information. They dig big foxholes. Statistics and charting are a means *to* action, not an end.

These types of individuals are only detrimental to a quality program, and the long-term success of the organization. Confront the immoral data lovers quickly. Fill those foxholes.

The Power of Statistics

Statistical power is the ability to gain information of definable certainty about a total population with reduced testing and analysis. The total population of results is all results obtainable with 100 percent testing. For example, it would be impractical to test the life of every similar light bulb made during a month.

Suppose the production line makes 10 million bulbs per month. Quality control could not test the burn life of every bulb produced. There wouldn't be any bulbs left to sell! These tests would be destructive. Instead, test the burn life of 35 representative bulbs. Use accelerated and correlated conditions. The average and distribution of bulb life of these 35 bulbs can be used to predict, with definable confidence, the average and distribution of the life of the 10 million bulbs. The predictions might be: "The average life of bulbs produced in January is 1,000 hours. 99.7 percent of the bulbs will have a life between 1,000 -3 estimated standard deviation (notated by $\hat{\sigma}$) hours and 1000 hrs. $+3\hat{\sigma}$ hours."

These statements are *estimates*. Their certainty never equals 100 percent. A 100 percent statement can only be made by testing all the bulbs. Increasing sample size increases certainty.

Classical quality control—testing quality after the fact—considered the previous analysis sufficient. The quality department reported the quality level to management. If bulb life was low and didn't meet specifications, then management, production, sales, and accounting had a problem. The quality department acted as a policeman. The estimate was generated after a month's production and perhaps even after shipment.

Classical quality control defines a static state of nature, yet production processes are dynamic. The *direct causes* and *root causes* of variation may have come and gone. Information about *direct causes* and *root causes* usually is gone. The only action remaining for management is to criticize and demand that the production be scrapped, retested and sorted, or shipped anyway. All we can say from this classical statistical analysis is that a percentage of the production did or did not meet specifications.

Classical statistical quality control adds cost to each unit of product produced. Extra manpower is required. The product is scrapped, reworked, or shipped anyway. Either the customers or the stockholders lose.

Novice interpreters of test data often believe that the extreme test values, without statistical interpretation, are the extremes of the population. Only as the sample size approaches the size of the population does this approach truth. A small sample does not definitely define the range of the population. Also, non-representative sampling and resampling for results only changes the estimation, but the population does not change. Reality cannot be modified through data manipulation. Yet all too often these events happen. It certainly reflects questionable ethics. It's a lose-lose game.

The Nature of Distributions

The most common distribution of data is the "normal" or Gaussian distribution illustrated on the next page. A truly normal sample data distribution isn't seen very often. Most data distributions show some abnormality. Two common abnormalities are skewness and kurtosis. Respectively, think of them as

Figure   36

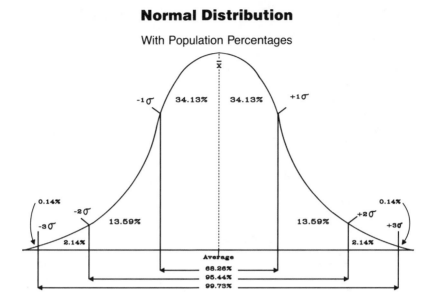

Normal Distribution

With Population Percentages

lopsidedness and flatness of the actual curve when compared to the normal curve.

There are other distributions. Many are variations of the normal distribution with a flatter curve, a sharper curve, or varying upper or lower tails.

The Poisson distribution is also significant. This distribution describes rare occurrences of very high significance. Examples are the defective O-rings produced for the space shuttle booster rockets, or high-speed failures of automotive steering mechanisms. Poisson (you might remember the name by association with "poison") events don't happen often. When they do, the results are disastrous.

The Pareto distribution, shown in Figure 37, is the basis of the 80:20 rule: the silent majority, the troublesome few, and setting priorities. A small number have high impact.

Processes Over Time

Processes are dynamic. They are subject to change over time. We view a process from the present. We look back at the past. We try to predict the future. Can we make a specification or establish a production rate? We look at the past and present and make a prediction. We empirically assess the relative stability of a process. We assess these factors over time, past to present. If we are smart, we look at a number of measurements. Often these assessments are intuitive, sometimes quantitative. We estimate a process "capability." Our estimate has

Figure 37

Cost of Rejected Product per Standard Unit

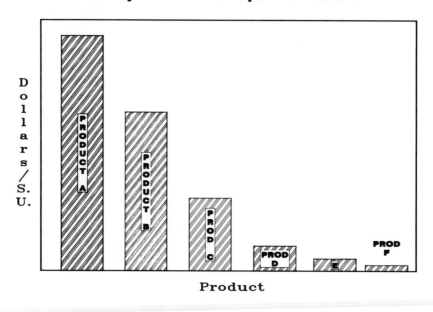

a confidence level. If we have no confidence we cannot make a prediction. *No prediction of future process performance can be made without past and present process stability.* This concept is graphically represented on the next two pages.

Control charting periodically assesses the stability of a dynamic process. Control charts quantitatively evaluate stability and instability, determine predictability, and indicate action. They detect process instability when it occurs. *Direct causes* can be found, and corrective action can be taken. Abnormal production will then be defined, and variability minimized.

In-Control and Out-of-Control Processes

When a process is "in control," the *true* process distribution is equal at every test. *Test* value variation is normal parameter variation and error inherent in testing. Test samples are a small part of the total population. Samples can come from any part of the distribution. One-hundred percent sampling would result in equal sample statistics, and these statistics would equal the population distribution.

Processes out of control are indicated by a change in process distribution or range. A shift in the process average, higher or lower, is a shift in $\bar{X}$. Both can happen at the same time. The action limits allow for the sample variation. Points outside the action limits, or certain patterns of points, indicate a probable process shift.

Figure 38

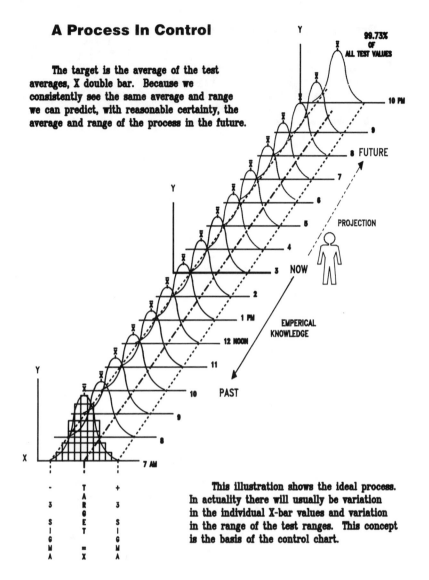

A Process In Control

The target is the average of the test averages, X double bar. Because we consistently see the same average and range we can predict, with reasonable certainty, the average and range of the process in the future.

This illustration shows the ideal process. In actuality there will usually be variation in the individual X-bar values and variation in the range of the test ranges. This concept is the basis of the control chart.

The Nature of Charts

Charts incorporate complex statistical concepts, yet they are relatively easy to use. They are visual. They communicate rapidly and accurately. Charts move statistical information power to the operator. Charts delegate authority and responsibility.

Figure 39

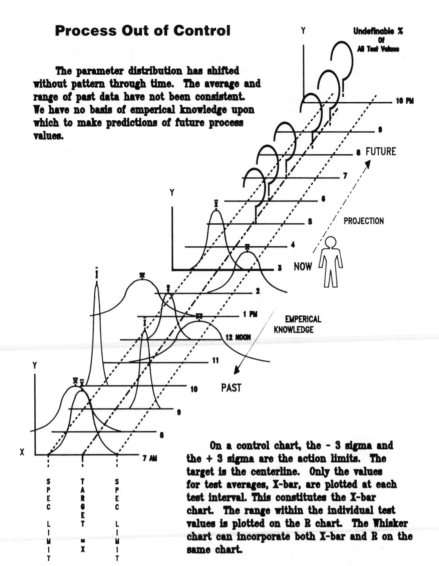

Process Out of Control

The parameter distribution has shifted
without pattern through time. The average and
range of past data have not been consistent.
We have no basis of emperical knowledge upon
which to make predictions of future process
values.

On a control chart, the - 3 sigma and
the + 3 sigma are the action limits. The
target is the centerline. Only the values
for test averages, X-bar, are plotted at each
test interval. This constitutes the X-bar
chart. The range within the individual test
values is plotted on the R chart. The Whisker
chart can incorporate both X-bar and R on the
same chart.

Time, Cycle, Position

Dorian Shainin endorses time, cycle, and position as factors of process. Most
abnormal variations correlate with these factors. They form a framework for
direct cause identification. Non-conformances may correlate with the natural
cycles of shift changes, lots, operators, seasons, batches, hopper loading, roll
diameter, billing, etc. Defects often occur in a pattern. When charts indicate a
problem, time, cycle, or position, macro and micro process knowledge, along
with the nature of the defect, help identify the *direct cause*.

Binomial Problem Solving

One way to find a *direct cause* is to examine every possible cause in the process. Who can be sure they have thought of every possible cause? We may or may not get lucky. Hunches sometimes are correct. A correct hunch may identify the *direct cause* quickly. Those are the easy problems. Finding the *direct cause* of a tough problem demands a systematic and effective approach.

Along with time, cycle, and position, binomial problem solving works. It is an appropriate application of "A/not A." It is no more than dividing the process in half. Then determine in which half of the process the problem exists: yes or no. If the problem is only in the latter part of the process then divide the latter part of the process into two parts. The analysis is repeated. If in the first division the problem is in both halves, then divide the first part *again*. The analysis is repeated until the *direct cause* is found. Exponential reduction of the examination area rapidly converges on the direct cause. The technique is extremely powerful.

"Would you rather work for a month for $1,000 a day or for a penny the first day and have your wage doubled each day?" This kids' game exhibits the power of exponential progression. We resist using binomial problem solving because we initially assume we know the *direct cause* of the problem. A good investigator first evaluates hunches, but when the first and second hunches prove wrong, he/she shifts to a binomial approach.

Capability Determination

The conditions for labeling a process "in control" or "out of control" have been discussed. Actually, we evaluate each significant process parameter for control. Before capability can be determined, a process parameter must be "in control."

Let's go over some terminology. Standard deviation units are indicated by the Greek letter σ, sigma. A letter with a line over the top indicates the "parameter" average. For example $\overline{X}$ means the average X. Now, process capability (PC) is the "in control" process spread. The spread is specified as $\overline{X} + 3\hat{\sigma}$ minus $\overline{X} - 3\hat{\sigma}$. The process spread is $6\hat{\sigma}$ wide. Most statisticians and organizations use $\overline{X} +$ and $- 3\hat{\sigma}$ for defining capability. The $6\hat{\sigma}$ process capability includes 99.73 percent of all normal variation. An $8\hat{\sigma}$ process spread includes 99.9 percent of the normal variation.

When all significant parameters are "in control" the product of the process is properly called "in control." *No highly confident statement about process capability can be made with out of control parameters.* We just cannot know! We can't predict. If identified *direct causes* led to the process being out of control, eliminate the respective data in a capability analysis, and determine an estimate of capability. The confidence of the estimate is significantly reduced. Still, the estimate may be useful.

In a process capability study, the process capability of a parameter and the specification spread, high-limit minus low-limit, are compared. This compari-

Figure 40

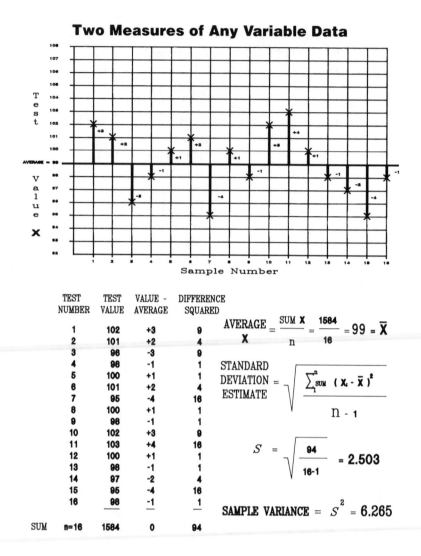

Two Measures of Any Variable Data

TEST NUMBER	TEST VALUE	VALUE - AVERAGE	DIFFERENCE SQUARED
1	102	+3	9
2	101	+2	4
3	96	-3	9
4	98	-1	1
5	100	+1	1
6	101	+2	4
7	95	-4	16
8	100	+1	1
9	98	-1	1
10	102	+3	9
11	103	+4	16
12	100	+1	1
13	98	-1	1
14	97	-2	4
15	95	-4	16
16	98	-1	1
SUM n=16	1584	0	94

$$\text{AVERAGE } \overline{X} = \frac{\text{SUM } X}{n} = \frac{1584}{16} = 99 = \overline{X}$$

$$\text{STANDARD DEVIATION ESTIMATE} = \sqrt{\frac{\sum_{1}^{n}\text{sum } (X_i - \overline{X})^2}{n-1}}$$

$$S = \sqrt{\frac{94}{16-1}} = 2.503$$

$$\text{SAMPLE VARIANCE} = S^2 = 6.265$$

son is expressed as a ratio called the process capability index. The most common method of expressing the ratio, specification spread divided by 6σ process capability, yields a *process capability index* of 1.0 and indicates the two spreads are of equal width. A 1.33 value indicates the 6σ capability spread is two thirds the width of the tolerance spread.

Because upsets to a normal "in control" process do occur many purchasers require a minimum 1.33 process capability index. What's good for the goose is good for the gander. Manufacturers also benefit from attaining a 1.33 process capability index. Even with upsets, the probability of producing unacceptable product is reduced. Producing unacceptable product costs more any way in which it's handled. Requiring a process capability index greater than 1.0 may in some minds define a tighter de facto specification.

Figure 41

Process Capability, "PC" Index

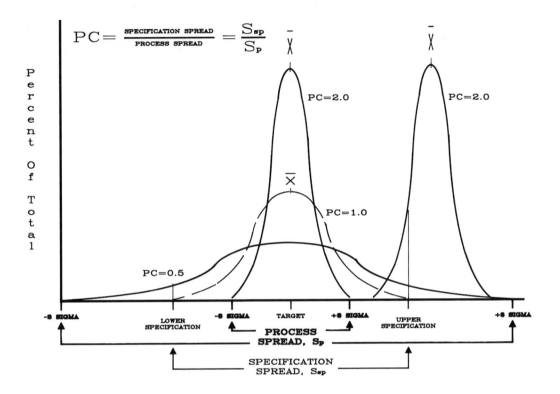

$$PC = \frac{\text{SPECIFICATION SPREAD}}{\text{PROCESS SPREAD}} = \frac{S_{sp}}{S_p}$$

Figure 42A

The C_{pk} Index of Performance

The C_{PK} index is a ratio of 1/2 the specification spread divided by the spread from target to the farthest 3 sigma. Technically two indices exist for any curve. By convention the smallest index is always quoted.

For the right curve, with PC=1.50, the C_{pk} is 0.60. Since the center curve is perfectly centered the C_{pk} = the PC = 1.50.

$$C_{pk} = \frac{.5\ S_{sp}}{\underset{\text{The larger value,}}{} |D_L| \text{ or } |D_U|}$$

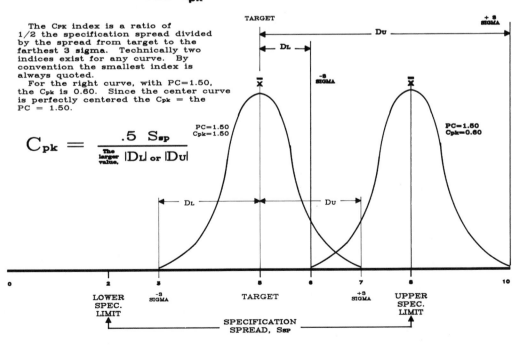

Figure 42B

Process Capability Studies

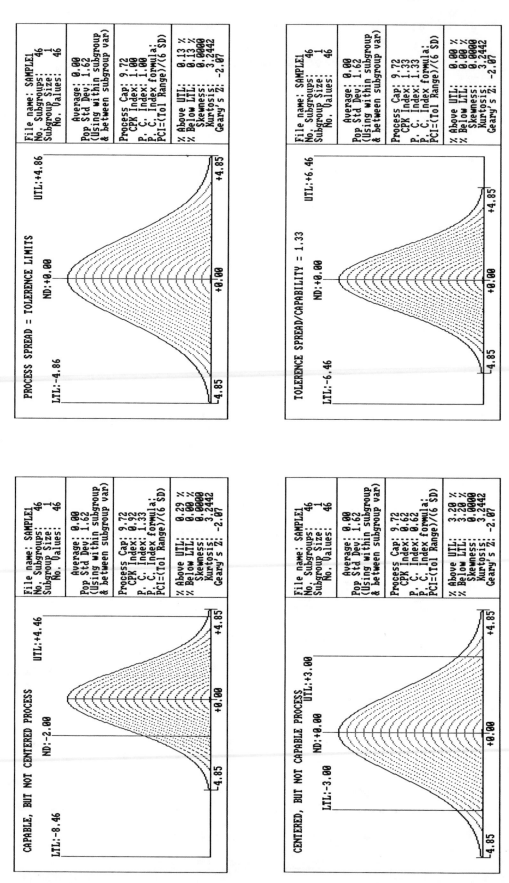

A process can be capable but not meet specifications if the process average is not centered in the specification range. A process could have a process capability index of 2.0 yet no test value would meet specifications. The index is merely a ratio of one spread to the other. The process capability does not have to overlap specification range. The two ranges would have no common values.

To address this situation, another test called the C_{pk} (pronounced "C sub P K") index was developed. The C_{pk} index takes into account both the spread ratio and the alignment of $\overline{X}$ with the center of the specification. C_{pk} compares the spread between the process average and specification limit with one-half the specification spread. Actually there are two C_{pk} indices for each distribution. One range is between the average and the upper specification limit and another range is between the average and the lower specification limit. The quoted C_{pk} index is the smaller of the two. Only when a process average is perfectly centered will the C_{pk} index equal the process capability index. The process capability index measures *ability* to operate within the specifications, while C_{pk} measures how effectively the capable process is operating within the specifications. At least one U.S. automobile manufacturer will require a 2.0 C_{pk}.

Z tests (calculation of percentage beyond upper and lower tolerance limits) provide information for economic decisions. With Z tests waste can be predicted. A capability study may indicate degree of process modification necessary to qualify a process or product. Knowing how much improvement is needed will improve cost projections. The capability study, with other analyses, can help predict product profitability before introduction.

Designed Experiments

Designed experiments can be simple or complex. Designed experiments are used to establish relationships between *direct causes* and *effects*. Examining the relationship between one *direct cause* and one *effect* is technically a designed experiment, but the term usually refers to investigating several *direct causes* and several *effects* and inter-relatedness. These complex relationships require the mathematics of the designed experiment to determine optimum settings for optimum properties.

Complex and powerful, designed experiments require expertise for design and implementation. Juran's handbook describes theory of designed experiments. Many texts are focused solely on designed experiments.

Establishment of Specifications

I believe specifications, as known today, are dying. Specifications are the product of compromise. Many were established with even less rationale.

I became involved in the quality process during the early 1980s when the automotive quality emphasis filtered down to suppliers and the suppliers' suppliers. We manufactured base material for gaskets. One early emphasis was manufacture to specifications. In accordance with the request, we did. We struggled to bring our processes and products in line with specification. Some properties had to be adjusted significantly. Customer complaints rose instead of fell. The complaints weren't from incoming quality inspectors; they came from operators and from our customers' customers. Product made "to specifications" did not work. It couldn't be converted efficiently. Our new material was a shift in their raw material. Nor did the material perform well in use testing.

Many of the specifications were over 20 years old. Many were established with the attitude that a specification was required "so just pick numbers that sound good." Other specifications were lifted from other products only vaguely similar to the current product. Over the years, unofficial, unsanctioned agreements between manufacturer and customer adjusted properties without changes to specifications. Red tape over-complicated such adjustments. There was little emphasis on incoming quality inspection prior to the quality emphasis. Unwritten specifications reflecting customer need evolved. "Manufacture to specifications" was a minor disaster. The customer received a different product not designed for their processes.

Specifications have traditionally been stated as either one-sided or two-sided. The one-sided specification defines either no more or less than a certain amount of property value or non-conformance. A two-sided specification specifies a maximum and a minimum value of a property. Sometimes, after production has started, the specification is found unacceptable.

Specifications reflect the limits of acceptability of the purchaser and the maximum allowable variation by the supplier. The specification system is an Aristotelian "A/not A system." It reflects little understanding of variation. For a customer *specifications state the thresholds of crises*. For a manufacturer they can be the freedom to ship less than optimum material. Production management often believes just meeting specifications is providing maximum quality. Given the definition of quality this "A/not A" situation just isn't true.

In our dynamic economy, rigid and static specifications soon become hindrances to quality improvement and value-adding innovation. When a sound understanding of variation is incorporated into the establishment of specifications, the specifications take another form. The specification involves two parameters. First is a statement of a parameter value at which quality is maximized. This target has no width. It is an optimum. At the optimum the holistic benefit is maximized. The maximization is a balance of long-term functionality and cost. Costs are not the manufacturing costs, but the costs to the ultimate consumer over the useful life of the product or service.

As the value of the property moves in either direction from the target the costs rise. On the negative side, lower engineered quality cost of manufacturing is lower, but customer satisfaction is less. If the product doesn't meet consumer needs value is lost. If the product is useless total value is lost. The consumer doesn't buy and the manufacturer loses the total value of the product.

With increased parameter value the cost of supplying the product rises. It gradually rises to the point where its value totally exceeds consumer need. The consumer chooses not to buy.

Figure 43

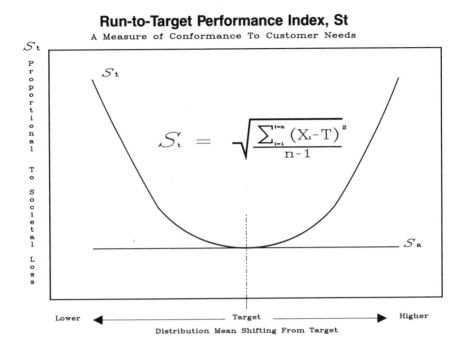

Run-to-Target Performance Index, St
A Measure of Conformance To Customer Needs

$$\mathcal{S}_t \;=\; \sqrt{\dfrac{\sum_{i=1}^{i=n} (X_i - T)^2}{n-1}}$$

Lower ◄─────────── Target ───────────► Higher

Distribution Mean Shifting From Target

A carpenter buying a hammer would not purchase poor workmanship, a hammer that bends nails and marks finish woodwork. On the other hand, the carpenter also would not buy a stainless steel, precision-machined, and gold-plated hammer. He/she would select optimum value for the intended use.

This example sounds reasonable. It deals with extremes. But how wide is the range of acceptability? There is no definite range of acceptability; just a relationship between loss as quality varies from optimum, and the cost of producing optimum. If the carpenter "dings" a piece of finish molding once a year a small cost is associated with the variation. If the hammer is priced slightly higher than the optimum product then there is only a small cost associated with high engineered quality. There is a small cost associated with a small movement in either direction.

Even with a properly targeted product any variation from target creates loss of value. The slightly imperfect hammer will probably sit on the shelf longer than the optimum hammer. Even if it sells quickly the buyer will probably experience some dissatisfaction during its life.

Of course, as a businessman, if the carpenter repeatedly experiences higher costs they will be passed on to the customer. These costs are costs to the manufacturer, to the home buyer, and to society.

Societal costs and the costs of reducing variation reach a break-even equilibrium. Only with innovation can total costs be lowered.

New specifications will state a target, but the supplier will also state the capability of the process in statistical terms, $\overline{X}$ plus and minus 3σ. Purchasers will compare capabilities with other suppliers to find the lowest cost manufac-

Figure 44

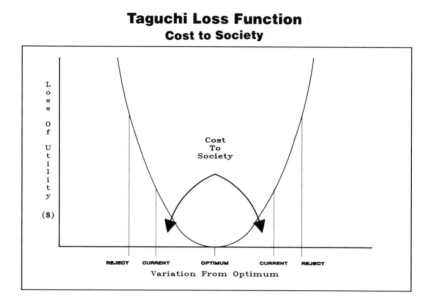

Taguchi Loss Function
Cost to Society

turer. Process capability will determine the highest existing level of innovation, resulting in the minimum societal cost. Competition will be to produce the optimum product at the lowest cost to society.

An index that can be used is a modification to the concept of estimated standard deviation from average s_a, standard deviation from target, s_t. When a process is perfectly centered with average equal to target, s_a equals s_t, but as the process average diverges from the target the s_t index increases in a parabolic manner. This parabolic curve is related to the Taguchi loss function curve.

One advantage of s_t is that no lower or upper tolerance limit is needed, only a target. The concept of s_t promotes the concepts of continuous improvement, not the "A/not A" attribute view of conformance.

The cost to society will be determined using the Taguchi loss function. The Taguchi loss function is a parabolic mapping of variation to cost, as shown in Figure 44. Thus any variation from optimum has a quantifiable cost.

Customer and competitive pressure will force minimum costs through reduction of variation countered again by the cost of process improvement. Short-term, break-even analyses will be slow to move but long-term, competitive pressure will drive innovation and process improvements, resulting in lower societal costs.

This whole concept isn't radical. It isn't even new. It's being used now against the American economy and we're losing. We'll look at the Taguchi cost function again in the chapter on cost of quality.

There are other, more complex, concepts in SPC. Again, 80 percent or more of the process control problems can be solved using the concepts discussed in this chapter. I purposely did not discuss more advanced techniques here. Walking comes before running. Advanced techniques might draw focus away from the first tasks, defining the processes, improving basic behaviors, and bringing processes into statistical control.

The Computer as a Tool for Process Control 13

No development of the twentieth century has had more impact on the nature of world-wide society than the digital computer. It is the means of the information explosion. It has accelerated the development of society at an astounding rate, a rate to which many people cannot adjust. It has modified how we think and how we solve problems. The computer has bestowed knowledge power on those technically competent to manipulate it and interpret its output.

At first, the power and knowledge of the computer rested in the hands of a few. The experts of the mammoth machines of the 1950s, 1960s, and early 1970s provided a function previously either not filled or filled only with masses of people. The computer experts provided high-impact information to the decision maker. This ability to provide information gave these people power.

In the late 1970s, two teenagers started a second phase of the revolution. Steven Jobs and Steve Wosniak developed the Apple personal computer. This was the first mass-produced small digital computer available to the general public. The concept has now exploded, hindered only by the rubrics of the ignorant and the defensive behavior of the power brokering experts of the mainframe computer.

As the personal computer, or microcomputer, developed, a battle began between the controllers of the mainframe computers and the advocates of the personal computer. The battle continues in many organizations. It is largely a battle over power and control of information.

The two machines are two different tools playing different roles in our information society. There is some overlap but the prime applications of each system are different. The mainframe is a tool for crunching huge masses of data and network distribution of that information. The personal computer, PC for short, is a personal productivity tool. It aids the individual in solving localized and specialized problems, whether fiscal or engineering analysis or effective customer-oriented communications.

In undergraduate school forestry courses I spent many evening hours in the laboratory computing standard deviations on an adding machine. In graduate school I spent much less time at a mainframe terminal doing similar calculations. Now I can make the same calculations in a matter of minutes at my personal computer. I estimate that the time ratio is greater than 1000:1 and the accuracy ratio is greater than 100:1. Now I can present the results of analysis quickly and can present the results in highly communicative customer-oriented graphics.

Today many schools require freshmen to show up with a personal computer. Some institutions include a computer in initial tuition. The computer is a required tool of the students' courses just as a slide rule was a required tool for the courses I took 20 years ago. Students are taught to use the personal computer as a basic problem-solving tool. If we expect this new breed of problem solvers to function at full potential then they need the tools of their trade. The argument that personal computers are an excessive cost holds little water when subjected to objective analysis. The $2,000 to $3,000 price of a system is quickly recovered. The initial cost is more than offset through rapidly solving one small problem that would otherwise go unsolved.

The battle between the two groups advocating digital computing analysis must be addressed. It is a destructive foxhole war that benefits no one.

Automated Process Control

Automated process control instruments alone will not solve process problems. Automation is certainly an effective method of reducing costs and providing continuous control. Before automation can be effective, the process to be controlled must be thoroughly understood. The process must be brought under control manually. The *direct causes* and *effects* must be correlated, and the critical *direct causes* of variation must be identified. Instrumentation offers the advantages of 100 percent inspection and one-time capital expenditure. Instrument control is subject to the same problems of over-control, under-control, and control of the wrong *direct cause* to produce the desired *effect*. When the normal parameter variation is known, the sensitivity of the control instrument can be set to react only to assignable cause variation.

Even the best instruments cannot reduce the amount of normal variation. A reduction in the normal variation requires redesign of the system. Over-control with instruments will have the same effect as manual over-control: the amount of variation will increase.

Instrumented control leads to a reduction of semi-skilled labor. The requirement for highly skilled management, engineers, and maintenance increases. Unknowledgeable management seems to believe instrumentation will reduce total labor costs and solve all problems. Actually, when low-skilled people are charged with using and maintaining the systems of automated control the problems and costs increase. Highly skilled, qualified people are scarce and expensive. And the costs get higher as more processes are automated.

When an instrument *does* falter, the instrument is often faulted, when the true *root cause* problem is the skill levels of management, engineering, and maintenance. When instruments are properly installed, regulated, and maintained, skills must increase. Instrumentation increases conformance quality and productivity. It does not increase engineered quality. It does not decrease the demand for skills.

The current move in computer control of processes is called distributed control. Many small computers interact to control the macro process. No one computer controls the overall process, and failure of one system does not disable other parts of the system. This is the second generation of computerized control. The concept is sound if the macro process and micro process *direct causes* and *effect* relationships are understood. Again, the knowledge to control manually is necessary before distributed control can be effective. Distributed control is not a valid solution for local computer control that is problem-riddled.

Computers and Charting

There are tasks of process control where good computer software is beneficial, and there are procedures for which computers should not be used. Computers quickly produce control charts, but cannot easily replace the operator-plotted charts used to control a process. Control response time is critical. Only when computer terminals with graphic feedback can be placed at each work station are computers suitable for on-line control charting. In an effective distributed control system, effective control charting and problem area identification can be done by computer. Again, the effective potential problem analysis behind a distributed control system is massive.

The speed and ease of computerized control charting coupled with inadequate operator training has led to the desire for computerized charting. Data are often collected manually and taken to a personal computer. This procedure converts a dynamic process control tool into a static tool that only defines what happened in the past. Computers can be used for X-Y charts, histograms, capability studies, CuSum charts, Pareto analysis, and presentation quality chart preparation. They even have applicability, as mentioned, for on the floor charting and control, provided they are programmed properly, the control plan is relevant, and the feedback to the operator is rapid. The computer also allows rapid deletion of aged data, the addition of new data, and rapid recalculation of control limits. It can save time in doing repetitive quality graphics and calculations. Computerized automation and robotics are effective and real. Again, with such computerization great increases in skills are required.

Computers are one of the prime instruments driving change in our society. They have advanced to the level where they are tools of many trades. Computers have their applications in communications, general problem solving, statistical information analysis, and process control management. Only in certain specific situations are computer control charts and control schemes preferable to manual charting. Computer-controlled processes require an extensive base of manually controllable systems. Computers are *not* a substitute for training operators in the proper procedures of charting and reacting immediately to the charts.

The Process Engineer 14

The role of the process engineer is to design and control processes. The skilled process engineer requires more than the specific skills of engineering to fully understand the technology of the total production system. He/she also must utilize additional skills in information systems, information analysis, in mentoring, and controlling the actions of people. As stated in previous chapters, people are an integral part of a non-entropic process. The management of processes is not just the task behavior of addressing problems with things. Task management has previously been the role of the process engineer in most organizations. The true process engineer cannot be an individual contributor. To manage process requires the ability to design, maintain, and modify systems that effectively meet the objectives of the process.

Based on my experience I find few process engineers possess behaviors necessary for process management. They are limited in their breadth and vision. The majority tend to focus narrowly and be overly concerned with things and tasks.

Emerging are a few truly outstanding process engineers. Where are these people coming from? Certainly not from our engineering institutions of higher learning. They continue to produce the task-oriented specialist who has a hard time producing broad-based original thought. These engineers are specialists without wisdom. They do not generally come from our formally organized multinational corporations. These organizations continue to pocket individuals into specialized task behavior and maintain systems of centralized control and policy that denies "intrepreneurship."

The common themes I see in outstanding process engineers are a broad experience and education base along with some classical engineering skills. Almost all are in tune with themselves. They are self-confident in their abilities. They are aware of an overall purpose and a process for improving the quality of life for the organization and mankind. Some decided to be engineers after a period of education in another curriculum that emphasized the ability to think and understand people behavior. Many have experience in positions that involved heavy people behavior such as sales or teaching. Some are on second careers. These second careers were chosen through a conscious Adult decision, not through peer pressure, an inappropriate desire for money, or by choice of parent. These people know who they are and what they are about. They understand their role. They work not for the approval of others but for the fulfillment of a greater vision. The minor setbacks are seen as part of the process of quality-of-life improvement, not just for themselves but for all people touched by their actions. The new breed of process engineer is technically skilled and knows how to think broadly. He/she has some knowledge about many subjects instead of lots of knowledge about one or two subjects.

In hunting for these people I look for sound basic technical training, training not in specifics but in principles. I hunt for evidence that they understand the behaviors and motivations of people, including themselves, and have a drive to influence the actions of others for overall benefit. I hunt for exhibited leadership behavior. The leadership behavior does not have to be in previous process engineering positions. There are far too few organizations that offer the opportunity for such leadership. The leadership can be in clubs, community, church, or any other outside organization. I hunt for evidence of a desire to continuously learn and a disdain for rubric behavior. A humble disdain of ineffective systems and procedures aids in the ability to promote change. I hunt for evidence of the ability to communicate in a manner that recognizes that the other party is the customer of the information the individual is offering.

Finally, I hunt for the ability to handle information in a systematic and simple manner. The exceptional process engineer has the ability to condense analysis to a simple, effective, and communicative procedure. The individual is not in love with the procedure in itself but with the ability of the procedure to benefit.

In Chapter 7 I detailed a procedure for determining the behavior requirements of a position and the highest behavior levels of an individual. Using this procedure, I submit that the qualifications of an outstanding process engineer are as laid out in Figure 45.

This person possesses considerable balance. After all, the true process engineer is not an individual contributor but a broad-based contributor. Processes involve people, information, and things, and a strong understanding of the interrelatedness of all three is mandatory for control of a process. Expertise in only one area is not sufficient.

In relating this concept of the process engineer to other people I have observed reactions ranging from strong approval to extreme defensiveness. Almost always the strong defensive reactions come from people who feel threatened by the excellence of such an individual and fear the change such an individual will demand. The person who reacts defensively does not usually understand the concept of excellence and change for the overall good. They view the individual as a person with whom they will have to compete in a win-lose game. The game the critic knows is achievement of glory for self. The

Figure 45

Position Evaluation Form

Position _Process Engineer_   Evaluated by _The Author_

Maturity index _640_   Date _____

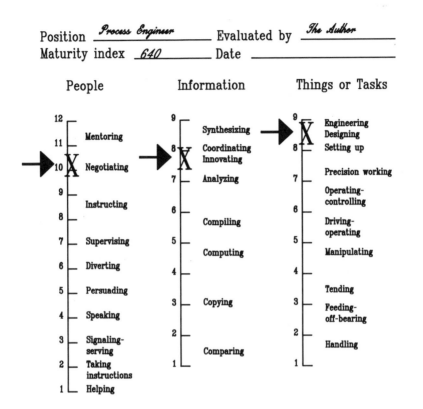

People	Information	Things or Tasks

concept that fulfillment of self is achieved through benefiting the overall organization is foreign.

Soon perhaps our institutions will recognize the benefits of sound broad-based thinking abilities and a balance in the skills and behaviors of the individual. The institutions will incorporate mandatory humanities courses into technical curriculums. There is some indication this is starting to happen at a few institutions. Perhaps our elementary schools and secondary schools will incorporate courses and exercises that teach children how to think for themselves instead of mandating that students follow "cookbook" rules. Ideally institutions will stop trying to program human robots.

Quality in Things 15

Quality in things is not fully in line with the premise of this book. My emphasis in this book is on the areas of the quality process that have not received the necessary attention for the process to progress properly. For the most part, I think, those who excel in the "quality of things" behavior in our society do an excellent job. My premise in this book is that for excellence there must be balanced growth in people, information, and things behavior. As part of this process, excellence in thing behavior is demanded. I cannot attempt to go into the same detail about the skills and behaviors of things that I devoted to people and information. Technology is just too broad and multi-faceted. There are, however, basic categories of behaviors and principles, trends, and observations I want to discuss.

For clarification, I define "thing" behavior as dealing with inanimate and theoretical entities. Addressing these entities involves task behavior. Accomplishment of "task" is the primary objective. People and information behaviors are not significant factors in the utilization of purely thing skills. Things include physical sciences and technology, equipment design and control, and independent task accomplishment. Pure thing behavior encompasses almost all activities where people and information behavior is not relevant.

For the most part, our "thing" oriented manufacturers are outpacing the ability of society to keep up in the other two categories. Our technology rules and drives our society. Much confusion results because people cannot assimilate, accept and communicate as fast as technology is growing. Often this phenomenon leads to threat and conflict.

I do not advocate a slow-down in the pace of technological and thing development. Throughout history there have been periods where such a position was taken. The Church tried to suppress the findings of Galileo because the Church felt the people were not ready for such change and revelation. But such positions did not slow the development of technology. Suppressed revelation forced technology to be exported to other societies. I advocate increased focus on the other two behavior categories, people and information. Broader focus will allow and facilitate forward progress of our society. If any one category outpaces the other two, turmoil will result.

An example I have heard used compares the progress in the process of excellence to a team of horses pulling a wagon. If one horse slacks forward progress is erratic and uncontrolled. If one horse outpaces the other horses the effect is the same. *All units must pull together in balance.*

The Theoretical and Specific Nature of "Thing" Behavior

Progress in technology is closely coupled with our specialized society. The forward progress of technology now occurs incrementally. Individuals or small organizations develop new technology with broad impact. A multitude of small contributions add up to an overall effect of rapid forward progress of the category.

Every few years, a new breakthrough in theoretical technology stimulates a burst of forward progress by the specialists. These breakthroughs are happening at an accelerating rate. The theoretical is being converted to the applied by the specialists as fast as possible.

One of the interesting contradictions is that the original thinkers of new theoretical "thing" technology are often not limited by specialization. A review of their lives and works reveals that they are much broader thinkers. Their ability to think effectively and not be limited by rubrics opens them to the innovations in thinking patterns necessary for the breakthrough. This same openness and innovation carries over into other parts of their lives. They are motivated not by financial reward but by a search for truth in nature. Their motivation is a self-actualization that is not limited by the constraints of man and the pettiness of society. Although gifted with genius in certain disciplines they also were or are gifted with the ability to think and excel across a broad variety of disciplines. Aristotle, Galileo, Newton, Descartes, Pasteur, Einstein, Currie, and Deming have contributed or excelled in areas other than the special technologies for which they are most known. Most saw both good and bad for mankind in the application of their discoveries, and proceeded in their search because of their philosophical desire to know the truth of the universe. They were above the specifics of application. Whenever possible they removed themselves from the specific applications of their discovered theories that we term good and bad.

The specialists of limited thinking ability produce the applications of basic truths that are constructive and destructive for mankind. A limited vision of the impact of the applications has produced effective artillery, germ warfare, ICBMs, the atomic bomb, as well as vaccines, weather satellites, nuclear medicine, and atomic power.

One of the great struggles for the twentieth and twenty-first centuries will be to keep the development of technology directed for the benefit of society and to prevent the destruction of society. Such destruction could come rapidly, as through our increased capability for totally destructive war, or, I believe more probable, through the dehumanization of the individual so that mankind is controlled by technology and a few myopic specialists instead of the consensus of society controlling the application of technology.

Mankind will not stop, and should not want to stop, technological progress. We can only hope to increase our abilities to constructively utilize technology through increased effectiveness and growth of our people and information behaviors.

Technological Specialization and Pocketing

The specific nature of things and technology breeds the specialist. The sub-categories listed as the skills of thing behavior in Chapter 7 are general levels of ability. The concepts and basic principles are similar across technologies. The technology of each industry and organization is specific. Each has its specific technology where the skills of design and engineering are unique. The more an individual specializes in the specific technologies of an application, the less transferable that technology is to other organizations. Competence at one level in one technological application does not necessarily indicate competence at the same level in another technological application.

This phenomenon is not as prevalent in the other two categories, people and information. Generalities are more applicable there. In thing behavior the principles are applicable but cannot be implemented without specifics.

Task Increases Through the Quality Process

At the beginning of the quality process there appears to be a balance between the tasks accomplished and the need for accomplishing tasks. This is deceptive. The balance is often achieved not through accomplishment of all that could be done but through limitations on what is believed to be necessary. In the stage 1 organization, maintenance is shoddy, equipment is obsolete, and projects are put aside because of short vision cost concerns or lack of response from the engineering/maintenance group. Such occurrences are not obvious on first examination. Demoralized people just stopped asking. Experience has taught them that the answer to requests will either be "no" or the requests will be ignored. When they *do* get action from the maintenance/engineering function, the quality of work done is shoddy. The requester wishes the request had never been made.

During stage 2, people start to realize the nature of their "thing" problem. Maintenance and capital improvement projects are assigned faster than even the top-notch department can accomplish. Years of backlogged work needs to be done. Much "bailing wired" equipment must be overhauled or replaced. At the same time the push for quality, productivity, and profitability demands maximum production time and reliability on machines. Accomplishing these tasks requires human and monetary resources. This phenomenon is one of the two major reasons for an initial increase in the cost of quality, but short-sighted management wants to see a *reduction* in the cost of quality.

There are two prongs to the drive to improve the quality level of tasks and things. The major emphases, assuming the physical assets of the organization have not been heavily "cash cowed," must be to establish reliability and availability. Equipment reliability and availability will establish noticeable quality and profitability improvement. Statistical control cannot be established on equipment always in either start-up or emergency shutdown mode. Once basic statistical control can be shown for a major percentage of the operating time, present equipment deficiencies can be rationally determined. Action plans for upgrade can be made and implemented. The alternative method is a shotgun approach—repair without proper problem analysis. Both approaches increase the cost of quality.

Establishing reliability of existing equipment is often blocked by quality and quantity of personnel. Upgrade requires extensive training or replacement of existing crews. Enlarging the work force will probably be required.

Outside contracting, wherever possible, offers a short-term alternative. The quantity and quality of people necessary can be acquired from outside—for a price. In the long run, unless outside maintenance is seen as a long-term alternative, the skill levels of maintenance and engineering must be upgraded. Once equipment is brought up to tip-top shape it must be kept that way.

Effective preventative maintenance programs and equipment redesign must become a way of life in the quality-driven organization. As the process progresses focus moves from reliability to streamlining procedures and increased maintenance accessibility. Availability of mechanical equipment will probably never be 100 percent. The goal is continuous improvement in availability.

As a company anticipates entering the quality process the decision makers of the company will want to take a long hard look at the tasks to be accomplished and the human resources available to accomplish these tasks. And these tasks must be accomplished to move into stage 3. Plan and establish a shared vision before confusion and demoralization set in. The road is not easy to traverse. There must exist a drive for excellence meshed with a realistic appraisal of the capacities of the organization.

Figure 46

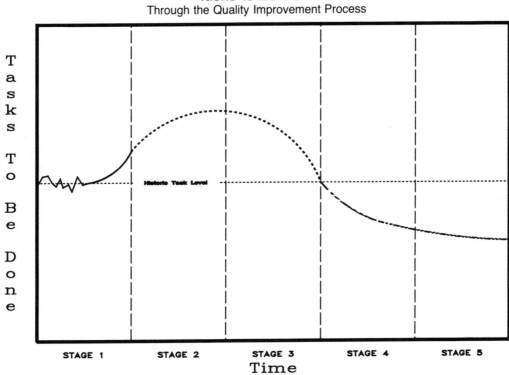

Tasks to Be Done
Through the Quality Improvement Process

Tasks To Be Done

Historic Task Level

STAGE 1   STAGE 2   STAGE 3   STAGE 4   STAGE 5

Time

Assessing the Cost of Quality 16

The fiscal value we call the cost of quality is a result, or *effect*. It is a report card on how well we manage the process of comprehensive quality improvement and control our systems of doing business. Cost of quality can be adversely affected by inappropriate action toward meeting responsibilities to customers, stockholders, and/or employees. Effective action cannot be taken on an *effect*. Action can only be taken on *direct causes* and, preferably, on *root causes*.

Cost of quality figures give insight toward sources of problems and toward needed action. *Appropriate action to solve problems is the only effective procedure for reduction of the cost of quality*. The objective is to minimize the unnecessary costs that limit the ability to provide for the needs of customers, employees, and stockholders.

Low cost of quality does not always mean lowest cost. Pragmatically, the sting of the "low bidder" has been felt all too often. There always seems to be someone with short-term vision who is willing to provide a shoddy good or service for less money. In quality terms, engineered quality is sacrificed for cost. Usually in such a situation where price alone is paramount the purchaser sacrifices both engineered and perceived quality. The provider of low-price/poor-quality is different from the provider of low-price/exceptional-quality. The supplier who can provide low-price and exceptional quality has traversed through the quality process and has realized the cost and quality benefits achievable from quality improvement. The low-cost/high-quality company has reduced cost of quality and realized increased productivity.

Of course every wise buyer wants to find the supplier who has traversed the process. The role of the buyer is to find maximum value for the lowest price per unit of real value. Almost without exception companies that can provide low price and high value are proud of their quality and will provide evidence readily of statistically determined product design and statistically in-control processes. This is their competitive edge. And they have worked hard to achieve it. It is a strong selling point for them. They will be willing and able to talk true quality with the buyer.

The low-price/low-quality company will not be able to provide statistical backup for its claims. It will talk of its "high quality" in vague generalities. The queried salesperson will skirt the issue of quantified quality with the "old school" sales methods. The fact is these companies cannot provide the value to go with their price.

The Western hemisphere quality community has developed a system for quantifying and tracking total cost of quality, defining the individual sources of cost of quality, and differentiating the major sources from the minor sources. Once sources are defined, the course of action is to allocate problem-solving efforts and fiscal resources toward making reductions in the major sources of cost of quality. This process is dynamic and continuing. It takes internal cooperation and the cooperation of suppliers and purchasers.

A company must realize that it cannot do everything to reduce the cost of quality that could be done at one time. Yet it must do something and what is done must be significant. The following procedure quantifies the priority of the necessary actions.

The cost of quality evaluation is divided into three categories: cost of appraisal, costs of failures, and costs of prevention. Within each of these categories are numerous sub-categories. A listing of possible categories and sub-categories follows. Each company will have to develop sub-categories that are specific to the activities of that organization.

Cost of Quality Determination

I. **Appraisal**

1. Quality department salaries + burden.
2. Quality department wages + burden.
3. Depreciation, quality department related.
4. Percentage of other salaries indirectly involved in quality appraisal.
5. Operating supplies of quality department.
6. Expenses of setting and adjusting specifications.
7. Training of audit mode quality personnel.

II. **Failure**

1. Internal Failures
   A. In-process waste.
   B. Rework costs.
   C. Down-graded material differential.
   D. Scrapped work in process.
   E. Scrapped finished product.
   F. Capacity utilization cost.
      1. Unscheduled down time.

2. Preventative maintenance differential, (actual minus ideal).
3. Rate deficiency (state-of-the-art capability mean rate minus actual).
G. Chronic steps not required with state-of-the-art equipment, process, and materials.
H. Administrative costs associated with resolution of failures. (Raw materials, work in process, and finished goods.)

2. External Failures
   A. Returns net of inventory recovery.
   B. Sales and administrative credits.
   C. Price reductions.
   D. Customer contact to resolve complaints.
   E. Business lost because of quality and price.

III. Prevention

1. Training
   A. Internal (formal and percent of salaries and wages of those involved in on-the-job training).
   B. External.
   C. Meeting expenses.
      1. Internal—coordination, communication, establishing vision, and problem resolution.
      2. Partnering with suppliers and customers.
2. Process engineering.
   A. Salaries + burden.
   B. Operating expenses.
   C. Productivity reduction while trying out new processes, equipment, and materials.
   D. Learning curve productivity reduction due to new process modifications.
   E. Research devoted to process and product improvement.
   F. Charges for outside help (consultants, etc.) for process improvement.
3. Preventative maintenance (ideal time).
   A. Salaries.
   B. Wages.
   C. Materials.
   D. Percent of maintenance operating expenses.
   E. Percent of maintenance depreciation.

Attention to the significant few root causes of internal failure will be more significant in reducing the cost of quality-failure than will be working on any other combination of the *root causes* of failure. Information from a reporting system is used by cost of quality teams to select projects for targeted project task forces. At this point, the financial cost associated with a problem has already been determined. With a target ROI, a pay-back period, and probability analysis of the potential savings achievable, a probable annual savings can be determined. A total expenditure budget figure can be set for the project. Potential solutions must meet the financial criteria just established. A project is not complete until both the cost of the project and the actual realized savings are determined. A project may be continued if the savings potential of further work meets the same criteria as a new project.

The achievable savings through Paretoized task force projects is initially great. As more and more projects are successfully completed, the cost of quality as a percent of standard production cost becomes smaller. The potential return on investment of future projects becomes less. More sophisticated analytical techniques are now needed to identify root causes of the cost of quality. The projects become increasingly more complex. The impact of each project in terms of the percent reduction possible diminishes. Market demand, societal changes, and financial criteria determine when projects are no longer viable.

Not all projects directed at cost of quality involve manufacturing process and capability. If projects are to be successful they must address *root causes*. Basic education, training, employee health, information systems, equipment, and motivation are the *root causes* in the decline of American quality and competitiveness. These *root causes* must be addressed. Our accounting systems are not designed to evaluate these costs. What is the cost of inadequate training? What is the cost of not being able to hire the best and most talented people? What is the cost of not having the right information to make a sound decision? What are the costs of poor employee mental health? What are the costs of lack of innovation? These costs are *real!* They are just hard to quantify. To address the *root causes* requires investment.

Competitors in the United States and throughout the world are addressing these *root causes* with investment. But current accounting procedures do not adequately account for these costs. With current accounting procedures we cannot adequately calculate the ROI of these investments. Therefore we have assumed there is none. This is certainly a false assumption. These costs reduce the long-term profitability of the corporation. These costs are borne by society in general through higher prices, lower wages, and lower dividends.

We hunt for *root causes* of long-term decline in profitability. The *root causes* are staring us in the face. But we are so caught in our rubrics that we refuse to see them. In our new society there is no long-term viability for an organization that refuses to address these *root causes*.

Taguchi Loss Function

The Japanese have developed a system for quantifying the costs of both inappropriate conformance and engineered quality to an organization and to all of society. Dr. Taguchi's loss function equation for a normal distribution is:

$$L_s = K(T-D)^2$$

Where:

L_s is the loss to an organization and society. K is a constant specific to the product and organization. How K is calculated for a product is shown below. T is the target value of the property. This value provides maximum utility to the customer. D is the variation in property value from the target. Then let S = a specification limit.

The dollar cost of quality of a unit with maximum $3\hat{\sigma}$ variation is the mapping through the function of $T \pm 3\hat{\sigma}$ on the X axis to the dollar value on the Y axis. The total cost of quality associated with variation of the property is the area under the curve from $T-3$ to $T+3\hat{\sigma}$, or $T-D$ to $T+D$.

The specific equation can be determined if any point on the curve is known. This point often is one of the specification limits. The assumption is made that specification limits are also the limits of usability, i.e., the specifications reflect customer utility. As I have stated, specifications must be verified. They often are set arbitrarily and do not reflect customer utility. At the specification limit the total cost of production of the unit, including overhead, etc., minus any scrap value (or the cost of rework, whichever is less), is the cost associated with a property value of $T-S$ or $T+S$. With one of these two points and a normal distribution a value of K can be determined.

Figure 47

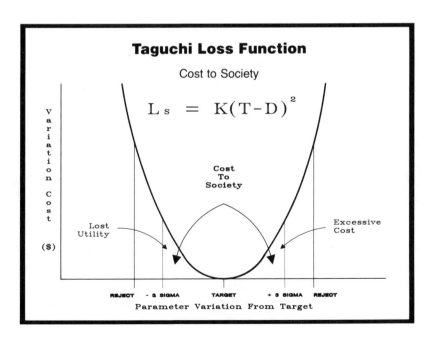

Now that we know the cost of variation from target (C) at S, K can be determined by:

$$K = C/D^2$$

The Loss Function equation can be solved for any value of D. For more information on the Taguchi Loss Function, I refer the reader to *Introduction to Quality Engineering, Designing Quality into Products and Processes* by Genichi Taguchi.

There is a loss function for each property of the product or service provided. Using a Pareto diagram of the perceived lack of quality according to customer response the significant cost of quality properties can be determined. The significant properties are listed with the dollar value of that property as calculated through the Taguchi Loss Function. The sum of the property loss function dollar values gives the total cost of quality.

Taguchi Loss Function Cost of Quality
(Based on Six Sigma Capability Spread)

Pareto Property *Product A*	TLF Property COQ
Density variation	$ 1234
Color variation	2243
Delivery date variation	956
Quantity variation from order	487
Invoicing errors	225
. . .	. . .
Total Cost of Quality, Product A	$ 5145 +
Gross Sales, Product A	$28487
COQ as Percent of Gross Sales	**18.18%**

The improved control of some properties is proportionally related to improved control of other properties. When it can be shown that addressing the *root causes* and *direct causes* of one property will equally improve the control of two or more properties, only the cost of the most significant property should be included in the cost of quality calculations. When the control mechanism of two or more properties is totally independent then both costs should be included. Although a unit of product can only be rejected once—even though it exhibits two or more defects—effective action on the most significant variant will not produce an acceptable unit. In the case of rework the product or service would need to be reworked twice, once for each property not in compliance. The same is true for acceptable properties with variation around target. The independent problems have independent costs and require independent action plans. Only when the property is exactly at target is the full utility of the product realized throughout the expected life of the product by society.

One of the problems of acceptance by American upper management of the Taguchi cost function cost of quality system is that the Taguchi loss function system is not a precise cost accounting of the cost of quality. It is a statistical estimation. It is not the step-by-step accounting procedure that satisfies a desire for detail and accuracy. Nor is the Western system an accurate system of assessing the cost of quality.

There seems to be fear of the Taguchi loss function because it is a statistical *estimation* and therefore "is not a proper accounting figure." True, the loss function is an estimation but it is a sound method. The cost of quality determination is several large estimations. It indicates relative improvement over time. The classical Western method of calculating cost of quality involves many small estimations and/or expensive systems of accounting for time and materials allocation. Every classical accounting system for the cost of quality I have worked with involved a tremendous amount of ball park figuring. The categories where quantification becomes too difficult, such as loss of gross margin from sales lost due to less than optimum quality, are generally eliminated. If a cost accounting number cannot be determined, the category is considered not valid. Because they are eliminated from the system does *not* mean that these costs don't exist and that they aren't real.

Arbitrary elimination is a problem because the numbers cannot be used in justification of process and technology improvement. With the Western system, investment for quality improvement is often hard to justify.

Yet the Taguchi method is much more inclusive of the total long-term costs to society and requires far fewer resources for calculation. It provides a system that quantifies that which exists but cannot be easily quantified with our current accounting systems.

There is another aspect of the Taguchi school of quality management which I will only mention. In the later stages of the quality process, quality and the minimization of variation is a significant design criteria. Through designed experiments products and processes with lower variation and less possibility of varying outside the limits of acceptance can be selected during design. In the earlier stages the effort is to control variation in products that already are out of the design stage. Initial design of the product and process with variation minimization as a significant criteria is the starting point of consistently producing a product with maximum value and minimum cost.

Budgeting for Quality Improvement

As an organization traverses through the quality process, the cost of quality follows a pattern. This pattern is shown in Figure 48. One of the most striking

Figure 48

Cost of Quality
Through the Quality Improvement Process

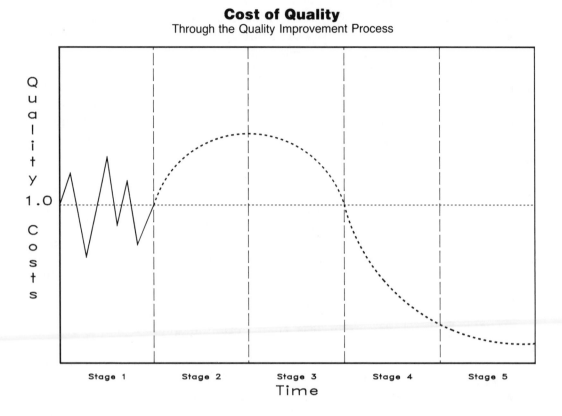

properties of this graph is that as an organization leaves the unconscious incompetence of the first stage the cost of quality starts to rise. It rises for several reasons. First, the organization is going through dramatic change. Truth about the real costs of doing business as it has always been practiced is being exposed. The drive for improved processes and resources far exceeds the ability of the organization to provide. If the drive for quality is external, the external failures, claims and returns, rise rapidly. The company becomes more conscientious about selling material that does not meet specifications. Slowly, as the truth of the ability to produce to specification is learned, the cost of quality shifts to internal failures. Pareto graphs of the sources of the costs are assembled. Action plans are formulated to address the *root* and *direct causes* of the cost of quality. Repair and equipment upgrading escalates. Slowly but surely the cost of quality levels off then starts to drop. The rate of drop accelerates through stage three and then starts to slow as the easy problems and the highly significant problems are solved. The tougher and less significant sources require more intense work with less reward. Toward the end of stage 4 the focus is not as much on bringing processes into control as it is on research and technical innovation for improved quality and lower cost. Quality becomes a significant factor in the design of product and process.

One of the big problems of the quality process is the initial upward trend in the cost of quality. Often management enters into the process without knowledge of the process and expecting instant reward. After a few months to a year, management panics because the quality costs have actually risen. The resources of the organization are strained. Organizations often turn back at this point saying quality engineering, statistical analysis, and team organization do not work. The organization reverts into the old rubrics. Meanwhile competitors struggle through the process and encroach on the markets of the company. Competitive position and profits erode.

The quality process can be tracked using the Western cost categories of appraisal, failures, and prevention. In stage 1 all three categories are at modestly low but uncompetitive levels. When the company enters stage 2 the cost of external failures and the cost of appraisal rise rapidly. Next, external failures are traded for internal failures. Not until mid-stage 2 does the cost of prevention take a sharp jump upward. As the organization enters stage 3 the rewards of the investment in prevention start, while internal failures start to decrease. At about the same time, the dependability of equipment increases and the demand for initial upgrade diminishes. Further upgrade and reliability continues to reduce internal failures, and the other costs of prevention continue. This trend continues through stage 4 until in stage 5 there is little cost associated with failure, and the cost of appraisal is minimal. The majority of the cost of quality in stage 5 is prevention. Much of this cost is continued training, education, and research targeted at improved process and product. Further growth is dependent on producing a better product with inherently lower cost while the competition struggles further back in the process.

The cost of quality figures provide a means of budgeting and control of the progress of the process. In most organizations dedicated to the process it will take four to seven years to start to realize increased profitability. Much planning and effort should be devoted to getting through stage 2 and stage 3 as quickly as possible. The timing depends on growth in the people, information, and things as discussed previously in this book.

Policy for Quality and Achievement 17

In the new organization, the nature of policy shifts to match the maturity and structure of the organization. Policy becomes a means of expressing vision, values, roles, and general guidelines. Policy moves away from the Parent role of "Thou shalt not and Thou must." High maturity individuals and task forces establish methodology for accomplishing the necessary activities that drive the organization forward. Trust based on organizational values continually directs each individual toward a shared vision.

Such a system works when the actions of the individuals of the organization are consistently highly mature. In the next chapter I discuss a high maturity organizational structure. This chapter is directed at policy that directs the new organization.

Establish a Vision

First, establish the vision of why the organization exists. In the vision state the purpose of the organization, the direction the organization wants to move, and the benefits to all members of the organization and to society that will be gained because of movement toward the vision.

A vision is properly established with input from all levels of the organization. Senior management listens, suggests, coaches, condenses, negotiates, analyzes, and finally composes the vision. Mutual development and "buy-in" make the vision truly a shared vision for the organization.

After establishment, communication and reinforcement of the shared vision becomes a continuous objective. The vision must be kept in the forefront of consciousness. When new employees seek to join the organization, the vision and values should be expressed clearly to the candidate. Differences should be brought out and discussed candidly and thoroughly. Major conflicting differences in values are grounds for not asking the employee to join the organization.

The vision states a process, not a project. An over-defined and limited vision leads to a burst of effort and then, once accomplished, possible dissolution of the organization. When the vision is accomplished the organization is left with no vision. A properly defined vision will be viable for the life of the current form of the organization. Only major reorganization and refocus will necessitate change of the properly developed vision.

Develop and Define a Value System

The value system is the basis for mutual trust within the organization. The actions of all levels of the organization should be in accordance with the values of the organization. Well-developed trust allows the organization to be governed by the vision and the values. Continuous effort is needed to communicate and reinforce the values. Only rarely, if the organization communicates effectively, will punitive measures be necessary for violation of trust and the value system.

There will be actions that do not conform to the value system. Such actions should be confronted constructively. Often they are due to either inappropriate skills or lack of understanding of the values. Actions reflecting a continuing difference in fundamental values are grounds for separation of an individual from the organization. But be sure there is fundamental disagreement and not just misunderstanding.

Earn and Demand Trust

Trust is the thread that allows the high maturity organization to utilize a multitude of behaviors for consistent movement toward the shared vision. Trust is based on a mutual appreciation of values and self-accountability. Without a high level of trust the holistic system of organization will not work. Trust, shared vision, and mutual appreciation of values are the critical policies of the new organization. Breaches of trust that are not confronted and resolved will lead to foxholes and degeneration of the organization back to an autocratic system.

Seek Truth (The Highest Confidence Information Possible)

In all quests for information seek the best information possible and drive for the highest confidence level possible, given time constraints. Make truth an obsession. Use every tool possible to gain increased understanding. Use such tools as statistics, psychology, listening, questioning, and history.

Finally, realize that almost all of our information is empirical. As people mature and their universe of perception increases they realize that there are few, if any, universal truths. All information becomes an estimation.

Synthesize Short-Term and Long-Term Objectives

Most conflicts over long-term and short-term objectives and actions arise from underdeveloped communication skills, lack of shared vision, low-esteem defensive behavior, underdeveloped and wavering values, narrow thinking, inadequate planning, archaic short-sighted accounting procedures, and short-term fiscal policy. The healthy organization will seek to resolve short-term and long-term conflict.

The long-term viability of the organization is dependent upon appropriate action to meet both objectives. When the short-term action is detrimental to long-term viability, the ability to meet the needs of customers, employees, and stockholders is compromised. The same is true when long-term action does not synchronize with the realities of the short-term.

The concepts of thought synthesis and win/win third way conflict resolution are key to solving long-term versus short-term conflicts, as mentioned in earlier chapters.

The optimum situation is the third way that meets long-term and short-term objectives. The minimum acceptable solution will not be detrimental to either set of objectives. Most conflicts occur when both sides of an issue are not understood by the parties in conflict. The first step in resolution is a non-judgmental presentation of all the facts. Each side must understand the values and rationale of the other side, even if they do not agree with the conclusions of the other side. Both sides need to be working with the same data base. Differences in values are almost never open for negotiation. Tangibles are easily negotiated. Mutual understanding is easily established with position reversal. Each side states the position of the other side to the satisfaction of the side supporting the original position. After understanding of position is established, discuss openly and honestly the alternatives. The ability to enter into such a discussion is a property of high maturity. Most issues will be resolved easily if the problem solving process can reach this level.

Reality is the other key factor of long-term and short-term, or any other, conflict resolution. Narrow focus often makes us blind to the effects short-term action will have on the long-term objectives. Over-idealistic expectations reflect a lack of understanding of the facts of the situation. A focus on the reality of a situation often leads to reevaluation of expectations, without a compromise of values.

Promote and Reinforce Positive Behavior

Promote, reinforce, coach, and reward the behavior in line with the shared vision and values of the organization. As described in *The One Minute Manager*, work to find and reward the correct behavior. The behavior of the manager described by Kenneth Blanchard is high maturity management.

Quickly, consistently, and constructively confront negative behavior. The key word in the last sentence is *constructively*. In a high maturity organization almost no negative behavior is due to insubordination. Negative behavior is due to lack of skill, lack of knowledge, lack of proper resources, or lack of communication. Expect that constructive growth, not punitive fear, will be the result of confronting negative behavior. If, after thorough discussion and investigation there is strong evidence that the negative behavior is the result of unwillingness to accept the organizational values, then separate the individual from the organization.

Demand and Reward Excellence

Don't settle for second best in people, information, or things. Demand and reward excellence. Many of the problems we face today in American business are because we have accepted and rewarded the mediocre. We drive the excellent to an average state and we deceive ourselves that the marginally acceptable is average. We have been afraid to correctly measure the quality of people, information, and things. Excellence will only be sought when it is rewarded with actions that satisfy the dominant basic need.

Facilitate Growth of the Organization and the Individual

If we are to demand excellence then reality also demands that we provide a means for excellence. In most cases we are no longer excellent. Our manufacturing facilities are obsolete. Our schools are archaic. Our people are under-skilled. Behavior does not reflect highest skill level. People who think creatively are shunned or chastised. If excellence and continuous growth are to happen consistently then these problems must be addressed with action plans and plan implementation. The role of management in this process is to demand, coach, and facilitate. As the individuals of the organization grow so will the organization.

Execute a corporate conscience. If the corporation believes in better education, demand and facilitate it internally and externally. We don't hire children yet we *do* hire the product of our archaic educational system and are amazed at the deficiencies in their education. We complain about the burden of welfare yet, with a few exceptions, we will not live up to a corporate conscience to provide an alternate system of developing the under-skilled, under-educated and underprivileged.

Provide continuous internal training not just in the tasks of a specific role but in the ability to think. Training in the ability to think is a leadership role that should be part of every action of the leader.

Make Positive Change the Norm

People shudder at change because the vision of the change, the benefit of the change, and the individual's role in the change are not well communicated. The rate of change now cycles faster than the life span of the average individual. Change is part of a new reality. I have empathy for those in crisis because of change, yet have little tolerance for their lack of willingness to be flexible. Flexibility is a property of maturity and, more than anyone else, the individual is responsible for his/her own maturity. No one else can make the decision for an individual to strive for increased maturity. Only the individual can make that decision.

Demand Effective Problem Analysis

Few situations lead to more confusion in an organization than ineffective and inappropriate problem analysis. Much effort is devoted to executing the wrong solution to a problem because either little or incorrect information was used in formulating the solution. Leaders must continually encourage growth in the information skills necessary for effective problem analysis.

Root Cause Analysis

The *root cause, direct cause,* and *effect* model of Chapter 1 applies to most problems. Long-term solutions demand addressing the *root causes* of problems. Don't be satisfied with the short-term fix based on addressing only the *direct cause.* As policy, drive the information search to the *root cause* and demand action plans that address those *root causes.*

Statistical and Probability Thinking

Make statistical and probability thinking the norm of problem identification and thinking. This Adult mentality must become a common language and a way of life at and away from work. It is a sign of maturity.

Discipline Toward the Vision, Values, and Growth

Discipline is one of the most misunderstood concepts in the structure of our organizations today. Discipline is directing and demanding focus of self and others toward the principal vision, values, goals, and objectives of the organization. It is not a blind demand for conformance to dogma. The autocratic organization often sees such blind obedience as a sign of loyalty.

But loyalty to what? Loyalty to a vision? Loyalty to values? Loyalty to the customers' needs? Loyalty to an autocratic individual, right-or-wrong? The only true loyalty is toward a vision and toward values or principles. This is the discipline to be demanded in the new organization. The conflict between individuals that may result from personality and personal objective differences is petty and is not a basis for loyalty. As individuals mature they become more tolerant of the differences in individuals. They learn to appreciate the positive in each individual. At the same time they become very intolerant of efforts to undermine or not contribute to a shared vision. The mature organization demands Kantian *categorical imperative* loyalty to the universal organizational values and the shared vision.

Promote Calculated Risk Taking

Mature organizations promote calculated risk taking. Without a reasonable level of risk, advances and positive changes are never reality. Support risk taking. Make failures a positive growth experience through immediate analysis of the errors of the risk calculation and the actions. Do not belittle an individual or group for taking a well-thought-out calculated risk. While risk implies the possibility of failure, it also has the possibility of increased benefit.

Delegate to the Lowest Possible Level

Our current concept of delegation completely changes in the new organization with high maturity leadership. Decisions can be made at the lowest possible level. And leadership is affirmed from those being led. Promote the concept of distributed control. Decisions are best made by those closest to the facts of the situation. The primary roadblocks to effective delegation are attempts to delegate responsibility without authority. Delegation without authority lacks a basis of trust between the delegator and the delegatee.

Continuously Plan for Excellence

Planning for excellence, as is planning for any objective, is essential. Effective planning utilizes the best information obtainable. Planning is at least half the work of reaching an objective. Quality, in the holistic sense, does not just happen.

From the discussions of *root causes* it should be apparent that the quality function cannot be effectively delegated to a single department. It must be a multiple focus process. It is a way of doing business. Quality is achieved by finding the *root causes* of any type of variation and taking action to change the system. The system must be changed to prevent recurrence of the variation. These changes are not the function of a single department or of the hourly worker. They are initiated by management.

Planning for excellence consists of mapping the current levels and defining needed growth in people, information and thing skills. Planning for excellence includes an emphasis on organizational change and management growth. Planning for excellence includes specific action plans based on factual information addressing significant and specific problems. For these actions to be effective they must be based on the best and most truthful information possible. Long-term success depends on increasing the behavioral levels of the individuals that constitute the organization.

A detailed plan for excellence is an integral part of a plan to achieve a long-term viability. Also inherent in planning for excellence in our dynamic environment is the acknowledgment that any approach to excellence must also be dynamic. W. Edwards Deming's principal contribution to Japan's rapid quality and productivity improvement was the introduction of the Shewhart control cycle of Plan-Do-Check-Action shown in Figure 49. As much as anything, the control cycle is a reflection of belief in the dynamic and never-ending nature of quality improvement. Quality and excellence thus never reach a satisfactory level.

Inherent in progression through the Shewhart cycle is the quality of information obtained in each step. Much of the non-statistical portions of this book address obtaining the best information possible upon which to make decisions.

Planning for excellence is highly dependent on ascertaining the current position in the process of achieving excellence, communicating the current position, and outlining the short-term and long-term action plans.

Several systems useful in planning for quality are the Action Plan, the PERT or GANTT project management plan, and the Control Plan. Customer contact reports, customer complaint reports, and telephone conversation reports provide understanding of the customer's concept of quality. The written nature of these documents allows widespread communications throughout the organization.

An Action Plan for a project details the objective of the project, what is to be done, who is responsible for doing it, the timing of what is to be done, the significance of the action, the anticipated result of the action, the proposed procedure to follow, and finally the required follow-up action.

The PERT chart is used in project design from market research through commercialization and full-scale production with statistically controlled processes to define the various steps of a project, the interactive timing of the steps, the manpower requirements, and the project costs.

Figure 49

Control Cycle

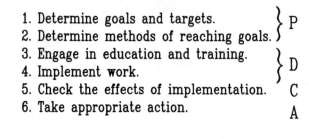

1. Determine goals and targets.   } P
2. Determine methods of reaching goals.)
3. Engage in education and training. } D
4. Implement work.   )
5. Check the effects of implementation. C
6. Take appropriate action.   A

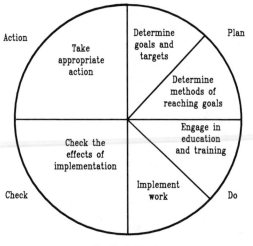

Control Circle

From *What Is Total Quality Control? The Japanese Way,* © 1985 by Dr. Kaoru Ishikawa. Published by Prentice Hall, Englewood Cliffs, NJ.

A control plan can be developed once the desired results of the action plan have been obtained. The finalized control plan specifies the raw material requirements, the process of production, the control parameters, the control procedures, and the finished product properties for a product. The control plan is the standard operating procedure for the production of a product.

When it is determined, either through marketing communications, direct contact, or complaints, that a currently commercialized product is not adequately meeting the purchaser's needs, minor changes in a control plan can be made through an action plan initiated and evaluated by process control management. Some major changes in properties may require a complete project to redesign the product. In such cases, the redesign of the product and processes should be managed in the same manner as a new product.

The Taguchi approach to product and process design should be used in such a redesign. For either product redevelopment or product modification it is essential in planning modifications that both the objections to the current product and the desired property modification be specifically and quantitatively defined.

To continually achieve greater levels of excellence an organization must continually determine objectives, plan for achieving objectives, do what has been planned, check the effectiveness of what was done, and act to fine-tune the benefits. To effectively carry out the last step, an organization must again plan what to do. The control cycle thus comes full circle and starts again.

Promote Partnering

Partnering with suppliers, customers, and purchasers is a high management maturity concept essential for quality. Partnering is developing a close, open, honest, and candid working relationship with another organization utilizing the products, talents, and capabilities of both organizations for greater benefit to both organizations than would be possible individually. Partnering is the ultimate in the supplier-customer relationship.

The partnering concept applies both externally between the suppliers and purchasers of an organization and internally between departments or teams within an organization. Within organizations it often appears that various departments do not realize that they are working together toward a shared vision and toward the more tangible objectives of a profitable and competitive position. Partnering requires filling both internal and external foxholes.

Partnering may initially appear naive. The foundations of partnering are trust, honesty, action, and a win-win philosophy of competition. Foxholes and the breakdown of trust are almost instantly destructive to partnering relationships. Yet the benefits to both parties are real.

There must exist a relationship where both organizations gain. Partnering is not an attempt by either organization to run the business of the other organization. Each organization is always responsible for its own actions. Each organization incurs an obligation to communicate, in a timely and honest manner, internal decisions that will affect the relationship and the operations of the other organization.

Partnering has tremendous potential but will not work for long in organizations without high maturity. The potential of partnering equals an influx of new capital without the equity dilution and without time constraints.

Demand Quality in Product Development and Design

When the production processes and the product design do not include quality maximization as design criteria, only a mediocre level of consistency and engineered quality can be expected. Currently, many products and processes are being extensively reexamined after reaching production. The reexaminations result in total product and process redesign, not just fine tuning. Resources are utilized that could have been directed elsewhere. Quality can and must be designed into the product and process before production ever starts. Make quality a major design criteria in the research and development process.

Emphasize People-Oriented Engineering

Because people ultimately control all non-entropic process, whether manual or highly computerized, a significant design parameter of process is facilitation and integration of the people into the process. Make the operator's ability to excel a design criterion.

Demand Maximum Value in Physical Assets and Purchases

Value is not reflected in the lowest nor the highest cost for an asset. Value is determined by maximum benefit for the price paid. The benefit received is far more than the actual asset purchased. The price paid may be far more than the dollars transferred. Both properties, benefit and price, can be either positive or negative from the obvious. Almost every purchase has hidden costs and benefits, pluses and minuses. They are often hard to quantify and justify, but they are real. The benefits of consistency of product and service from one supplier may far outweigh the price disadvantage of the supplier. Product life affects the overall benefit received.

All this sounds logical and obvious. Yet it is amazing how often our organizational actions are not consistent with this logic. The *root cause* of this inconsistency is our system of individual accountability.

For example, a purchasing agent may be rewarded for always obtaining the lowest price. The purchasing agent's responsibility ends there. Production is rewarded for maximum productivity but is forced to use the low-value product the purchasing agent was rewarded for buying.

Where is the shared vision and the organizational maximization of benefit? Conflicting individual accountabilities develop internal foxholes. Management can limit the foxholes by enforcing shared vision, group account-ability, and maximization of value in the assets and materials purchased.

Promote Employee Health

Companies have a responsibility to employees. How well this responsibility is met is a major part of the employee's and the community's perception of the excellence of the company. Companies that do not accept this responsibility no longer have access to the "best" employees. Investment in employee health is an investment in total quality.

This responsibility for employee health can be divided into two categories: a responsibility for physical health and welfare and a responsibility for psychological health. As our society and the work force have matured, the high maturity employees consider physical health and welfare prerequisite to employment. Employees expect a safe and healthy work environment. They do not expect to be subjected to undue hazards such as carcinogenic materials, toxic fumes, high-risk tasks, or any other unreasonable long or short-term threat to physical health. They expect some form of comprehensive health insurance. They expect a reasonable sick-leave policy. They expect group life insurance. Some employees in sedentary information-oriented jobs even expect access to physical exercise facilities. These are low-level needs that are met by the best, and even many of the not-so-good companies.

The new challenge and emphasis within the American society and American businesses is the *psychological* health of the individuals of the organization. This new emphasis is a response to growth and changing basic needs of individuals as our population psychologically matures. As was discussed earlier, much of the population is now seeking to fulfill higher level basic needs. The dominant basic need of today's most productive individuals is higher than ever before. The capabilities of the workforce are greater than ever before. Individuals want more from their vocation than a safe place to work, a steady income, and even a friendly environment. They now want recognition, valuing of their full talents and creativity, physical and psychological ownership, and the opportunity to live out their deepest ideas and beliefs. In terms of basic needs they are motivated by esteem and self-actualization. The new generation seeks to be respected and be all they can be. The term that has been used recently to simply state this shift in needs is "intrapreneurship." Today the best, the creative, the highly productive employee is highly driven for "intrapreneurship." The best companies harness this almost fanatical drive for the benefit of both the employee and the company.

As a policy, take advantage of this movement. Focus the drive for mutual benefit. Provide the employee with challenges and rewards that lead to mental as well as physical health.

Clearly Set Priorities

One of the functions of high maturity management in a team environment is to lead the teams to establish priorities that are in line with the shared vision. Resources are almost always limited. Team activities need to be directed toward obtaining maximum and balanced benefit for customers, stockholders, and employees using the available resources.

When teams stray away from proper priorities the interaction skills of leaders are utilized fully to reinforce the proper prioritization without usurping the authority delegated to the team. This involves restatement of the vision, expansion of team perception, coaching, and mentoring to bring the team to reset their own priorities in line with the vision and the available resources.

Promote Growth as a Process, Not a Project

The concept of process versus project is alien to much of Western culture. Our Greek heritage and patterns of learning naturally divide continuous activities into projects. Projects have end points and "A/not A" expectations. Management by objectives attempts to break processes into projects. Goals are almost always set aggressively at benchmark levels. When progress toward the vision is significant but misses the benchmark the emphasis historically has been on the fact that the benchmark was not achieved, not on the contributions made. In similar manner there is little reward for exceeding the benchmark. Contributions are a continuous variable, not an attribute. Excellence is a process, not a project.

In practice, projects do have end points. Installation of new equipment, or reaching the retail level with a new product can be visualized as projects, but these are significant steps in a much larger process. The concept of process emphasizes a broad understanding of the shared vision. The concept of project shields the shared vision from the broad membership of the organization. Leadership must continually keep emphasizing the process of striving for the shared vision and emphasize the *process* more than the *projects*.

Strive for Excellence in Communications

As policy, facilitate informative, accurate, and actionable "customer-oriented" oral and written communications. Value timeliness and effectiveness over formality.

Train in the skills and behaviors of informal communications. My experience leads me to believe that the most neglected behavior is the ability to actively listen.

Drive for conciseness. The 80:20 rule applies to most communications. Most mature managers are familiar with the mounds of insignificant and inflated reports and memos in their mail each day. I often see 10 to 20-page reports that can be effectively summarized in one paragraph. Tell people what they need to know. Don't hide the impact in the detail. The "One Page Memo" has great justification. It forces conciseness and emphasis on impact.

Verbally communicate what can be said and does not have a valid reason for being informally written. Informally write all that does not require typing. Copy machines and NCR forms allow us to broadly disseminate informal communications. Do not tolerate over-formality of communications when the root purpose of the formality is for personal image building at the cost of conciseness, actionability, and communication of significance and impact.

Formal communications are justified at times. Again, such communications are most effective when it is directed and oriented to the customer. Minimize the use of specialist jargon. Communicate what needs to be said and then *stop*.

The New Organization 18

The new economy and new roles for higher maturity individuals warrant new organizational structure. The old structures were designed for autocratic, militaristic organizations with a few top-level decision makers and many low maturity low-level task doers. Power flowed from the top. The formal autocratic organization does not promote growth of the individual in the higher basic need categories. Thinking and positive reinforcement of creativity and innovation are not part of an autocratic system. Change in a bureaucratic system is slow and often ineffective.

A new system of structure is needed. The structure must be based on the talents, values, and dynamics that actually exist at present or that are to be developed. First, let's look at the dynamics that are significant to the new organizational structure.

Transactional Analysis and Organizations

The principles of transactional analysis, discussed in Chapter 6, can be extended to organizations. Groups of people, whether informal groups, departments, plants, or corporations, develop personalities over time. These organizational personalities have the same three elements: Parent, Child, and Adult. As in individuals, one element of organizational personality often contaminates the Adult element. There are Parent organizations, Adult organizations, and Child organizations. These personalities correlate with the management styles prevalent within the organization and relate to the controlling personality element of other parties, i.e., customers, stockholders, other departments, higher management, and/or employees.

Parent-dominant top management desires Child-dominated lower levels of the organization. Parent organizations don't expect or want thinking. They want conformance to rules. The lower levels of the organization may in kind act from the Parent in transactions with even lower levels of the organization.

Parent-dominated first line supervision, if the transactions are not to be crossed, expects hourly employees to operate in the Child. In historic management there appears to be an expectation of this set up to continue down the line. As long as this system works, the transactions are not crossed. This is the classic system of American management.

In this classic system, top management is fully responsible for the organization. If top management has the skills and they can hire enough people to fill the positions the autocratic system works. It has in the past. Our American success story was built on this system. And it will probably continue to work relatively well in the near future.

But there is a growing problem with the classic management and current organizational transactions. As individuals and our society grow through Maslow's basic needs, the Adult in personalities becomes more and more dominant. The healthy gratification of the higher needs requires Adult-Adult transactions. Individuals seek ownership. They want to be significant contributors in solving the problems of the organization. They want responsibility and authority. They seek Adult-Adult transactions. They find gratification in Likert's level 4 organizational system of management. The Parent-Child transactions of "Do it because I said so!" are no longer acceptable. Individuals lose interest in the tasks of their work. The motivation for achievement and excellence diminishes, and they seek gratification of dominant basic needs elsewhere.

This is the *effect* the struggle to become the Eupsychic person is having on our organizations. This is an *effect* of the growth and maturation of humanity. We cannot overlook this change for long. Individuals with high self-esteem and self-confidence realize when actions are not producing sought gratifiers. They seek the gratifiers in other organizations. The bravest create their own organizations.

The threat of separation from the current organization and base gratifiers provided by the old style organization is becoming overridden by a drive for fulfillment of dominant higher level basic needs. Returning to the relative salience graph in Chapter 2, the reader will recall that when a person is seeking to gratify higher level needs the importance of lower level need gratification diminishes. A mentally healthy employee will take a cut in pay to be part of an organization with opportunity for gratification of esteem and self-actualization. Another individual will second mortgage his/her assets to create an organization that will allow gratification of dominant higher level needs. The new organization will have to accommodate the individual seeking gratification of high-level needs.

Not all individuals of the organization are as healthy as the individuals described. Some cannot overcome the threat to their lower level needs. These are the mentally unhealthy people who show no enthusiasm for their work. They work just for a paycheck. They do just enough to insure they will continue to do so.

There are a few individuals who just have not developed enough to seek gratification of higher level needs. They are mentally healthy and yet they seek gratification of lower level basic needs. We have eliminated many of them through our welfare programs. These individuals have had their basic needs met without gaining the basic skills usually associated with healthy fulfillment of the lower level basic needs. Are we doing a service to these people and to society or are our welfare programs just creating a monster? We have developed a system for avoiding the *root cause* of an *effect*. This short-term solution has the potential of destroying our society.

In our society there are these individuals seeking gratification of lower level needs, but not many. Ask yourself *why* these individuals are still seeking gratification of the lower level needs. It may be that they have not had the opportunity for fulfillment of lower level needs. This often may be the case with migrant workers. More often healthy low-level need gratification is strongly associated with low-level behavior and skills. Ability has not warranted rewards for gratification of lower level needs. Are these the people we want controlling the activities of our changing organizations in our dynamic society? These are not the creative and innovative people that will allow companies to gain and maintain a competitive edge. Low-level tasks can be done by these people, but again, fewer tasks remain, and not many people are willing.

The Alternatives

One possible solution to this dilemma is to export our organizational structure to Third World countries where the populous is still struggling to gratify lower level basic needs. There the worker will gladly follow the Parent directives in order to gain safety and physical security. We started doing this after World War II.

There are two problems with this alternative. First, as the lower level needs of the Third World populace are met, these people also grow and seek gratification of belonging/love needs and even the esteem needs. Again the management system becomes inappropriate. And this is happening in several developing countries.

Second, exporting jobs to Third World countries is suicide for our society. Exporting our management structures to other countries is not an acceptable long-term solution. This pattern, through conscious or unconscious intent, has been the historic method of growth of societies: the demise of one society and the rise of another higher level society incorporating the unimplemented innovations of the previously dominant society. Ideally we have risen to a level where we can learn from history and address the *root cause* of the cycle.

Another alternative is to allow the forces of nature to take their course. This is the truly competitive market system for change. The highly motivated individuals can start new organizations, incorporating the new methods of product development, production, and quality. From a strictly economic standpoint this is probably acceptable. This default method of change is happening. Big bureaucratic organizations are becoming a smaller part of the economy. New business starts are at an all-time high. Again an old society is being replaced by a new society, internally. This alternative is a revolution. The problem is, larger organizations employ many people, influence the nature of our economy, and carry much political clout. As they die a slow death they carry the quality of life of members and society with them. Tolerance of the slow death allows inroads by competitive societies and organizations into our society. We become dependent and at the mercy of other societies. We lose part of our self-determination. The flow is counter to the growth of the individual within the structure of the old organization. Individuals of old organizations face recessive gratification of needs. Managers lose the opportunity for self-actualization. The organization eventually loses the ability to fairly compensate employees. The death of the organization accelerates. As the old organization dies, the ability to gratify the needs of customer, stockholder, and employee diminishes. Of such situations are wars made.

We can change our organizational structures and gratify needs of customers, employees, and stockholders. If we don't, the cycle will continue. Our old-style organizations will die. We will become a has-been society.

A New Organizational Structure

There is a viable alternative: redesign our organizational structures. Incorporate a system that meets the current needs of society. Make the new system flexible to the changing needs of a changing society. The remainder of this chapter is devoted to describing a vision of a new method of organization. The vision involves the synthesis of the sociological, psychological, behavioral, informational, and technical concepts discussed previously in this book. It acknowledges and incorporates the dynamic growth of the individual and of society. It seeks continuous growth and improvement. It promotes Adult-Adult individual and organizational transactions. It simultaneously maximizes the dominant need gratification of customers, stockholders, and members of the organization. The new system emphasizes longer term planning and thinking. It requires favoring maximization of long-term balanced benefit, over the short-term individual gain, for customer, stockholder, or member.

The culture of an organization and the structure of the organization go hand-in-hand. By structure I am not necessarily thinking of the formal structure published for an organization. These published structures often do not reflect functional reality. Instead such diagrams reflect the mental ideal of old school upper management of how they *wish* the organization would function. It usually does not.

The true organizational structure is strongly impacted by the degree to which the behavior levels of the various people match the behavioral requirements of the respective positions. Mismatched behaviors force those charged with goal achievement to circumvent mismatched positions. Circumventing drives individuals being circumvented to defensive blocking. A vicious cycle develops. Rules, bureaucratic policy, and formal management become the predominant style. More energy is spent in trying to maintain the system than is devoted to solving problems and meeting needs.

The net effect is that many organizations have a hidden organizational structure. This hidden organizational structure often varies greatly from the formal structure. This hidden structure reflects how the responsibilities and authorities for carrying out business are actually delegated. Two indicators of inconsistencies and ineffectiveness in structure are predominance of a communications grapevine and "bootleg" methods of task accomplishment.

The high maturity organization continuously attempts to merge the actual organizational structure and the ideal by matching behaviors and roles. As was discussed earlier, structure should reflect the behaviors of the people assets of the corporation. Integrated into the structure is division of focus of the various areas and individuals. Individual contributors and low maturity individuals fill roles effectively that require those behaviors. Proper behavioral and role assignment is part of the culture of the prevention mode in quality driven organization.

Why do the structures of organizations have to remain rigid? The classic organization tries to lock in structure. Is this just another business rubric we are unable or not willing to break? Perhaps, like the analogy of the person driving to work who does not know of the new highway just a few blocks away that will save time, many organizations cling to their outmoded structures not cognizant of alternative structures.

Structure *can* be dynamic. Roles offer a "home base" of stability. Since tasks constantly change, structure must constantly change to effectively address tasks. Individual talents and behaviors are more consistent than tasks. An organizer of people can function in different organizations with different tasks. The top-notch mechanical engineer can be an engineer for a variety of tasks.

The need for effective interaction is growing in the organization. The need within the individual for effective interaction, the soft side of business, is also growing. The need for esteem and self-actualization is growing. The new organization must incorporate gratification of these needs. This aspect of psychology points to Likert's system 4 of interaction.

I have pointed out that societies are dynamic. The needs of people and their skills and behavior are dynamic. I hope you, the reader, will agree that change is reality. Change is accelerating. Yet we continue to lock people into fixed positions and organizational roles. Somehow we rationalize that the fixed roles for people fit the long-term needs of the organization. We do not facilitate their growth. We do not provide opportunity for the change in behavior that is part of growth. We do not effectively promote growth to benefit both the individual and the organization.

The concept of the team allows broad-based exposure for members of the organization. The team continually brings new ideas and thought processes together to strive for a mutual objective. Teams benefit the individual and the organization.

Synthesis of these factors leads to a new organizational unit, a unit that is a basic unit of organization. It parallels the old department but is not limited in function as has been the traditional department. The unit is focused but not limited by fixed and specific long-term accountabilities.

The team is a high maturity organization. The team consists of both individual contributors and broad-based generalists. The team, as a unit, is balanced in all behavioral categories. Specialized behaviors, in line with team focus and necessary for objective accomplishment, are purposely sought for team participation. The roles of the individuals are well understood, but not fixed long term. People are used in their most motivated and productive functions. Individual talents are recognized and utilized, yet individuals step out of role for the overall benefit of the team. Interaction and stepping out of role result in synergistic cross-training.

Team communications flow freely in all directions. Fear, as in an autocratic organization, is eliminated. Team membership is based on value to the team and the organization. Use of skills is valuable to the individual.

Within the team exists mutual recognition of the talents and shortcomings of each individual. There is a shared vision, in line with the vision of the greater organization, that drives the team to accomplishment.

Think of a holiday fruit basket. If the basket contains all apples it is monotonous. All are similar. The apples can be nothing more than apples. Now think of a basket with apples, oranges, peaches, plums, bananas, mangos, and nuts. There is an excitement to this basket. The variety offers diversity. It offers the opportunity to effectively meet the needs of a variety of customers. It offers multiple benefits that can be met by no homogeneous basket. The analogy is like the team. The team offers both the customer and the members variety, excitement, and expanded effectiveness.

The team also offers individual members the opportunity to learn and grow. The team is a forum for social, esteem, and self-actualization need fulfillment that benefits the individual and the organization.

What does the basic unit look like graphically? It looks like a three-dimensional solar system. It consists of individuals with varied talents and maturities orbiting around a high maturity leader. The leader is not an autocrat but a facilitator and driver toward growth and achievement by the individuals and team. The leader breaks down barriers to effectiveness and guides interaction for maximum utilization of talents. The leader reinforces positive behavior and coaches for change in negative behavior. The process of achievement warrants as much attention as the achievement, yet neither is degraded through unbalanced focus on the other. The achievements of the team are *shared* achievements. The team recognizes that no individual can achieve to the level of excellence achievable through the whole team.

Team leaders, and perhaps some other team members, are also members of a higher level team led by an even higher maturity leader. Again, diversity for achievement is the focus of the team.

Figure 50

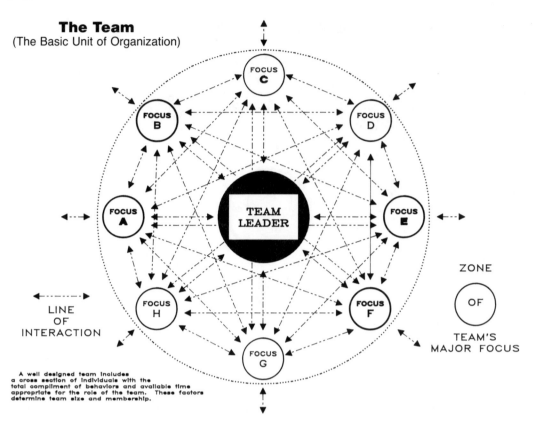

The Team
(The Basic Unit of Organization)

FOCUS C

FOCUS B

FOCUS D

FOCUS A

TEAM LEADER

FOCUS E

ZONE

OF

LINE
OF
INTERACTION

FOCUS H

FOCUS F

TEAM'S
MAJOR FOCUS

FOCUS G

A well designed team includes
a cross section of individuals with the
total compliment of behaviors and available time
appropriate for the role of the team. These factors
determine team size and membership.

The pattern continues through all levels of the organization. What emerges is an organization with only the drawback of its impossibility to draw on paper. It resembles many atoms melded into a large complex molecule with carbon atoms as leaders. Perhaps another visualization is a solar system with each planet having many moons and with satellites around each moon. I have attempted to visually represent part of such a structure in Figure 51.

The common bonds holding the organization together and driving movement are a shared vision, mutual appreciation of appropriate values, clear definition and appreciation of roles, and an openness to change in roles as individuals and tasks change.

Paramount in importance in this structure is the shared vision. Throughout history, mankind has been able to accomplish the unachievable when all team members were dedicated to a vision. When working toward a vision most differences would seem petty. Sometimes members were forced to participate in an autocratic system. Other times the members participated because the shared vision became a route to self-actualization.

The defense effort of World War II was a shared vision. The shared vision of a man on the moon overcame tremendous obstacles to achieve the goal. In sporting events the shared vision of victory is often the deciding factor in

Figure 51

The Mature Organization

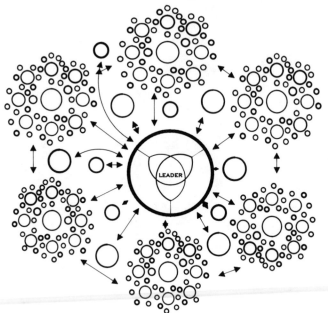

overcoming unfavorable odds. Within almost every organization exist numerous smaller examples of achievement overcoming great odds for accomplishment of a shared vision. For any structure of organization to be truly effective and achieve excellence there must be a shared vision.

What happens to an organization once the goal is accomplished? Often after a limited vision is achieved the organization loses focus. Petty infighting and bickering develop. The effectiveness of the organization diminishes.

I believe that in a business organization the shared vision is excellence. The vision is a process not a project. It is a never-ending process to achieve an ideal objective that can never be totally achieved. The vision of the excellence-driven organization must be focused on the process of continuous improvement in the ability to meet the needs of customer, stockholder, and employee, not on the achievement of arbitrarily set targets.

The People of the Organization

In this new organizational structure, one of the criteria of success is matching the people of the organization to the roles. In Chapter 7 I described a system for matching the individual behaviors with the position requirements. On the following page is a model summarizing this system.

At the outer bounds of the circle are the individual contributors. Each has value and the ability to contribute. At the intersections of the categories are

Figure 52

Quality Culture Behaviors

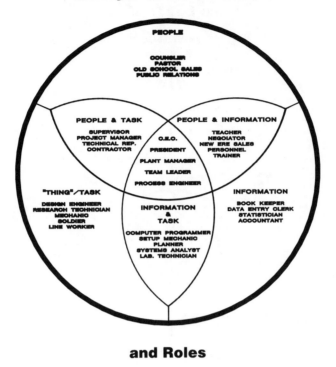

and Roles

areas indicating the synthesis of two behavioral categories. Individuals who have synthesized behaviors show initial signs of leadership. Their growth is toward greater breadth, not toward specialization. Movement toward the center of the circle indicates greater synthesis of behaviors.

Finally, at the center of the figure is the true leader of the high maturity organization. This individual exhibits fully synthesized behavior. The individual is both balanced and driven toward self-actualization. The individual has both the skill and behavior to function in all three arenas and the wisdom to know which behaviors are appropriate for a given situation. In the team concept the difference between leadership of lower level teams and the higher level teams is the depth and breadth of wisdom and experience of the leader. The leader of a lower team grows to become the leader of a higher level team. Figure 53 shows the full model I have developed to illustrate behaviors and roles in the mature organization.

Functional Reality

This quality philosophy and this book detail a quest for an ideal. We live and operate in an imperfect world. Not all people are honest. Not all suppliers are

Figure 53

Cone of Behavioral Maturity
and Leadership

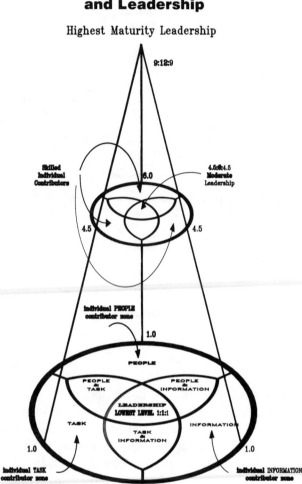

Highest Maturity Leadership

concerned with long-term viability. Not all employees can or will be motivated. Mutually beneficial needs between employee and organization sometimes don't exist. Not all stockholders are concerned with the long-term growth of their investment. They want quick gain and then will sell. Speculators let others bear losses from inconsistent short-term actions. Not all individuals have the mental capability to effectively analyze and solve problems. Many more such statements could be made. These statements reflect differences between what is reality and the ideal.

These statements are also made lest the reader think this organizational philosophy is a sophomoric synthesis of quality and reality. The stated philosophy is ideal. It is a vision of what can be. Our quest is to bring reality as close to the ideal as possible. It requires continuous never-ending effort. A societal shift will not be a quantum leap, but will be small movements, one project at a time.

I often think of the analogy used by my friend and sponsor, Jerry West. "How does one eat an elephant? One bite at a time." The quest is not for full accomplishment of the vision but for continuous progress toward the vision.

There exist conditions we just cannot change but cannot ignore. There will continue to be conflict. Perhaps we will handle it better. For some problems synthesized solutions will not be found. Perhaps someday economics, knowledge, education, and technology will produce synthesized solutions but perhaps not within the time frame we define as long-term. Decisions must be made in these situations; decisions that will not please everyone. Product lines may have to be dropped. A champion's project may not be viable. Employees may have to be terminated. Finances just may not be available for the long-term solutions that are sorely needed. Statements such as these are reality. Life is not totally rational nor is it always fair. We have to do the best we can in addressing these situations and recognize the accomplishment in the progress we make.

We operate our organizations in an imperfect world, yet if progress is to be made we must strive with each step to move a little closer to perfection. Each organization dedicated to excellence must always seek to move toward perfection. The wise person does all that can be done to move closer to perfection, yet knows when efforts would be in vain and tactfully refocuses efforts elsewhere.

Following is a list of points that I believe are fundamental to the new organization. They are a value system for development of this new organization.

Concepts for Developing and Maintaining Effective Quality-Driven Organizations

1. Develop an organizational philosophy that man (mankind) is basically good. Each individual initially wants to do the best he/she can. There are individuals who, because of their history, cannot endorse this basic philosophy. If, after counseling, individuals cannot endorse this philosophy, those individuals should be separated from the organization.

2. Accept that the long-term ultimate goal of any worthy individual and organization is to profitably nurture each individual touched by the organization, including self, to be everything the individual is capable of being. *Organizations ultimately exist for the benefit of people.*

3. Define the specific purpose of the organization and be sure every member of the organization knows that purpose. Be broad enough in such a statement to allow for the constant change of society. Don't define the organization out of existence.

4. Develop a value system for the organization in writing and communicate it across the entire organization. Most individuals and organizations have not clearly defined their values and thus have little on which to refer when confronted with tough decisions.

5. An organization, and each individual member of the organization, is answerable equally to the customer, the stockholders, and the employees. Imbalance toward, and/or neglect of any of the three, in the long run will lead to deterioration of the organization.

6. Seek truth. Truth is knowledge. Make seeking the truth an obsession. Knowledge leads to wisdom, and wisdom is the highest and least erodible base of power. Statistics uncover the truth of the variability of nature. The humanities seek to uncover the truth of human nature.

7. There are few if any absolutes. Discipline each person to learn to think in terms of probabilities instead of absolutes.

8. Change is inevitable. It cannot be avoided. It must be addressed. As technology increases the rate of change will accelerate exponentially. To stand still with the familiar is to fall backward relative to the progress of society. We are either the victim of change or we take the initiative and control and direct the changes.

9. Assume almost nothing. Most of the information upon which we make assumptions is empirical. Change is constant and there is no such thing as a duplicate of a previous situation. Conclusions based on outdated, not applicable empirical data are not valid. Data and information must be validated before reaching new conclusions. Small changes may produce large effects.

10. Understand the interrelatedness of our world. In the long run there is no such thing as an independent event. Every event contains both good and bad. The events of the world are holistic. History is filled with connections as are our everyday lives.

11. *All non-entropic processes are ultimately controlled by people.* The forces of nature seek constantly to move toward randomness. Mankind has continually grown in knowledge and wisdom and organization. This is counter to the entropy of nature. This organization of society and environment is solely due to the actions of people.

12. Accept and learn to appreciate the differences, varying talents, and fallibility, of people, including yourself. We humans are not perfect. Learn to like yourself. Appreciate the positive in each person. Utilize the assets of each person and steer clear of their liabilities. Utilize people in terms of their positive talents.

13. Learn to listen! Most great ideas are lost because we do not know how to listen. Listening is *active,* not passive. It requires training, effort, and energy.

14. Play win-win games. When we compromise each side gives up some of what they think is important. If you win and someone else loses the loser will target you to be the loser next time. There are more than two sides to each situation. Find the "Third Way" that best satisfies

the criteria of both parties. We become defensive about "our way" because of our own insecurities, not because we are working for our own good, the good of the organization, and/or the good of the other individuals of the organization.

15. Each person's personality can be visualized as having three parts: Parent, Adult, and Child. The Parent is judgmental, dogmatic, and blocks communications. The Child is playful, passive, and emotional. The Adult is rational, problem solving, probability estimating. Usually one state is dominant in each personality under given circumstances.

   Not only do individuals have these three aspects of their personality but organizations, corporations and departments also have these three aspects of group personality. The most effective way of doing business is Adult to Adult. Strive for Adult behavior.

16. Learn to understand the needs and motivations of people in general and specifically what the needs and motivational forces governing the activity of each individual are.

17. Operate with a synthesized understanding of both idealism and reality. Change what can be changed for the better and accept that effort to change some real situations may be a waste of time and effort. Use the talents and resources available for maximum effectiveness.

Constancy of Purpose 19

Deming's first point of his 14 points for management is "Create constancy of purpose toward improvement of product and service; with a plan to become competitive and to stay in business." Organizations without constancy of purpose often act in opposition to each other, dig foxholes, and lack forward progress. Each organization, especially larger organizations, will struggle to effectively establish and communicate the organizational vision, the values, and the mission. Start-up organizations and organizations in crisis usually know their vision and mission well—survival! As stated previously, many organizations cannot state succinctly their vision nor their mission nor have they defined their values. In practice their organizational values are a hodgepodge of situational ethics that support personal position or expediency.

Most production workers just respond with a blank stare when asked the vision and mission of the organization. The blank stares continue when they are asked about the organizational values. When asked about their role they may respond that they operate such-and-such a machine or that they supervise such-and-such a group. The connection between vision, values, mission, roles, goals, and objectives is unclear. People just react situationally instead of taking positive action toward the vision. There is no apparent constancy of purpose.

Most of us use the words values, vision, mission, role, goals, and objectives loosely, and sometimes interchangeably. These words have lost their true meaning.

In this chapter I want to briefly discuss the concept related to each word, the interrelationship of each concept, and a system for communicating them throughout the organization and to each individual of the organization.

Organizational Values

The organizational values are a foundation upon which all other statements, behaviors, and actions will be built. They are the ground rules of behavior and a framework of acceptable action and interaction. They state the moral principals we use with people, information, and things.

The Vision

The vision of a continuing organization states a usually never achievable but continuously sought ultimate purpose. It states an ideal. Vision statements are often short, sweet, and esoteric.

Subgroups of the organization may also have a vision statement, but if a subgroup vision is defined separately it *must* support both the vision and the mission of the overall organization. A subgroup's vision is closely tied to the subgroup's role in achieving the mission of the organization.

The Mission

The mission is a general statement of action and process. It states how the organization will continuously move toward the vision. As is true with the vision, the mission is impacted by the organizational values.

Within a complex organization there may be more than one mission. First, the organization in total must have a mission. Each functional group should also define its mission. The group is a subgroup because it focuses on a specific role. Its role—and its mission—is not precisely the same as the role and mission of another subgroup. Still all subgroup roles and missions must support the organizational vision and mission.

The Role

The role is a statement of behaviors within the mission. It is more a statement of activity and behavior than of purpose. The role can be described from two different perspectives: the organizational view of the role and the individual's view of her/his role. Hopefully, if the organization utilizes good staffing and assignment techniques based on exhibited or desired individual behaviors and behavioral requirements for the position, the two perspectives will be nearly the same. The intent of Chapter 7 was to provide the reader with a system of assessing both the individuals' asset behaviors and the behavioral requirements of a position.

When describing roles attempt to summarize the behaviors expected of a person in the position. Is the main responsibility leading people, counselling people, analyzing information, synthesizing informational systems, operating equipment, setting up equipment, engineering new systems of equipment? Does the role require a synthesis of behaviors? If so, a mix at what level of the three main categories of behaviors? By clearly defining roles the expectations, and the requirements for success in a position are clearly defined.

Teams also have roles. Again the roles reflect the expected main activities of the team in total. Establishing systems of in-process control, consistently running machinery to produce high quality product at a profitable level, and providing financial information to decision makers are all examples of team roles.

Goals

Goals are relatively short-term changes an individual or group wants to implement. Goals can also include maintenance of a status quo. The goal states the desired end result and the benefits of the result. For example, reduce production rejects by 10 percent to reduce the cost of quality; develop an in-process control and acceptance system to replace the current lot acceptance system so shipping can be done directly from the line and reduce inventory costs; reduce the month end closing period from eight days to four days so operations can better plan its activities.

In the team environment a team may have a number of goals for a future period. Not all individuals have the "lead" on all goals, but the roles of many team members may be utilized in accomplishing the goal. One person should have the lead on a goal. Others work in a mature team environment in support of achieving the goal.

Again, the goal does not state the implementation plan. It only states the desired result and the benefit. All too often goals and objectives are confused. By jumping to implementation when stating the goal we limit the creativity of the individual(s) charged with the goal.

Sometimes an objective becomes a goal. The person charged with the objective loses sight of the intended result and benefit of the activity, and believes that because the objective was completed the "goal" was realized. Completion of the objective is not the goal!

Objectives

Objectives support goals. A goal may be supported by a number of objectives. Objectives are statements of desired action, the timing of the action, the quality level desired for the action, and the lead person for the action. Actions that support a goal, when completed, result in realization of the benefit of the goal.

An example may help clarify the relationship. Given the goal "Implement an in-process system for production control and product acceptance on line A" the necessary supporting objectives might be:

1. Team member A determine the parameters of customer perceived quality for product X produced on line A by March 1. Prioritize them in descending order of significance and assign a relative weight to each.

2. Team member B develop a process flow diagram of line A by March 1, showing all operator controlled equipment and all engineering/ maintenance controlled equipment.

3. Team member A classify all operator controls as either "critical," "standard," or "audit" based on the control impact on the top three, middle 4, and remaining factors of perceived quality by June 30. Be able to support the conclusions with quantified data.

4. Team member C develop and teach in October an operator training program to teach operators how to fill out, interpret, and react to control charts. At the conclusion of the training the operators should be able to fill out, interpret, and properly react to actual control chart information in accordance with the control plan.

. . .

8. Team member B verify the effectiveness of the in-process system using before and after implementation lot acceptance data with a comparison of the pre and post program C_{pk}. At this point our program will be successful if we maintain at least equal C_{pk} and 90 percent of shipments can be made immediately.

9. Team member D reduce lot acceptance testing to a twice per month audit upon successful completion of objective 8.

As you can see all these objectives support the goal. They state desired action, measures of timing, quality level, and the ownership. In practice each objective may contain several more significant steps in the form of an action plan. Each step should include who, what, when, and to what quality level.

In a team environment a higher team, including the leader of the responsible team, will establish the goals for the team—with input from the responsible team to the leading team. The responsible team, as a unit, then develops the objectives supporting the goals.

Looking at the hierarchy in reverse order, the goals of the lower level team will usually be tied to an objective of the higher level team. The goal will be one of the action steps of the even higher level team assigned to the lower level team leader.

None of the objectives alone will insure realization of the goal. Only when all the objectives are completed on time and to a satisfactory quality level will the full benefit of the goal be realized.

Once more, objectives, goals, and missions are appropriate when they support a well-defined vision and higher level missions. If they do not further the missions and move the organization toward the vision then the goals and the objectives are not appropriate. Such activities waste the time, talent, and financial resources of the organization. Inappropriate goals and objectives prevent advancement of the customers' perception of the quality of the organization. The figure on page 195 graphically illustrates the interrelationship of all the previously discussed elements necessary to create constancy of purpose.

Creating Constancy of Purpose

It is important to organizational and individual success that the values, vision, missions, and the specific role be communicated to each individual in the organization and that others understand the missions and roles of other teams and individuals. The solution to this communication problem comes from a modification of the job description, the role description.

The organization has done the preliminary work of developing simple unencumbered vision, mission, and value statements. These statements should be included in every role description. Along with these statements should be statements of the role of the position, the behavioral requirements of the position, and criteria of role fulfillment, and what is expected of the person in the role to be deemed successful.

I intentionally did not include specific goals and objectives in the role description. Goals and objectives will change from period to period. They are an important aspect of communicating expectations but they do not belong in the role description. Also the role of a position is prescribed by higher teams while goals and objectives should be developed by the team of membership and the individual.

On page 196 is an outline of the significant elements of the role description.

Figure 54

The Elements of Establishing Constancy of Purpose

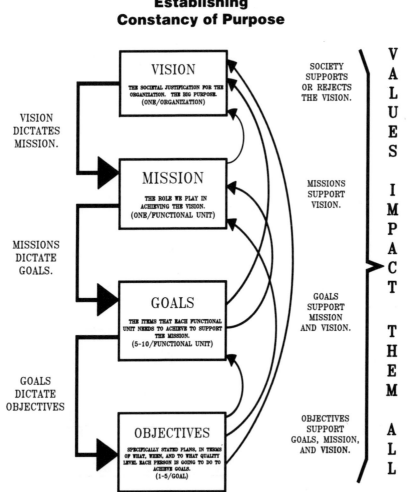

Role Description

Position _____   Team _____

Candidate _____   Team Leader _____

Organizational Vision Statement

Organizational Mission Statement

Organizational Statement of Values

Team Mission Statement

Role of Position

Expected Impact of Role

Behavioral Requirements

Criteria of Role Fulfillment

Signed:

_____   _____

          (Candidate)   (Team Leader)

Date_____

Fellow Team Members:

_____   _____

_____   _____

_____   _____

_____   _____

_____   _____

_____   _____

The Quality Process, a Final Look 20

Throughout this book I have presented models, as well as the basic concepts and the vision of a process for moving an organization from adequacy to excellence. If the reader considers these concepts applicable the next step is analysis of the current organizational position. The next step is development of a detailed action plan for moving from adequacy to excellence. Excellence is not achieved immediately. The movement involves many small steps.

This chapter is structured in line with Glenn Hayes' five stages of the quality improvement process. This review progresses through the stages detailing points significant in defining the current position and in developing a quality improvement plan.

First, realize that upon initially looking at an organization without a well-defined shared purpose and without a shared culture, the observer will find departments and individuals exhibiting different levels of maturity. Characteristics of many different stages of the process will be seen. Within departments will be found a similar distribution of behaviors and maturity. And there will exist within an organization a central tendency toward an average behavior and maturity. That average behavior will fall within one of the five stages, and is constituted by a wide distribution of individual behaviors and maturity.

Yet probably never in the process will all elements of the organization fall into only one stage. If this concept seems contradictory consider that it seems contradictory only because our Western thought process mandates categorization in an "A/not A" manner. I will address this concept further at the end of the chapter.

Initially, there may appear to be little rationale to individual roles. A formal organizational structure does not necessarily reflect organizational function. Analysis of the true organizational system, coupled with an analysis of the formal organizational structure, often reveals contradiction. Interactions more often indicate the actual informal structure.

Before we look at the five stages of growth of the organization (see Figure 55) I will make one final synthesis. In Chapter 2 I described five stages of learning and growth. (Refer to the figure on page 11.) The five stages of quality improvement described by Glenn Hayes parallel the five steps I described as the process of learning. They are the same. This synthesis provides further understanding of the psychology of, and the actions necessary for, movement through the five stages of quality improvement.

Stage 1: Unconscious Incompetence

Stage 1 is a state of inappropriate stability, the business status quo. The traditional autocratic system of management predominates. The employee is expected to only execute specifically assigned tasks. Assignments incorporate much detail. Structure and roles are limited and task-specific. Communication goes only downward, except upon specific request.

The organization emphasizes quantity of production with an almost blatant disregard for the needs of the customer or the employee. The top management vision seems limited to "make more money." Workers are expected to pay homage to the organization because they are paid. Management's attitude is "The workers should be grateful they have a job."

Effective communication is almost nonexistent. The communication that does exist is either very formal and not customer-directed communication or is assumed. If the customer of the communication does not know it is the customer's fault. "He/she should know!"

The default concept of trust is "don't trust anyone." Everyone is out to get everything they can. Turf protection is rampant. Each person stands alone against both the outside world and the other individuals and departments of the organization.

Quality is considered to be a customer-imposed constraint. There is little, if any, understanding of meeting the needs of either internal or external customers. Again, the belief is that the customer should be satisfied that they are getting anything. The quality effort is limited to inspection of the finished product. Only accept, accept with rework, and reject decisions are made. Pressure is exerted toward the quality department not to reject product. This adversarial relationship makes the quality function a police effort.

Given the right people in the right places this organization with its inappropriate stability can and often does make money. Over the long term, the stage 1 organization is highly vulnerable, vulnerable to losing one of its key players, whether through retirement, ill-health, or job change. Often no one can step in and take over the key player's critical role. It is vulnerable to a more dynamic and innovative competitor, and vulnerable to its own market and its own work force. Emphasis on making money at the injurious expense of the customer and employee eventually erodes market position and gradually eliminates the best people from the organization.

Toward the end of stage 1, assuming an organization is moved to enter into the quality improvement process, the boat of stability starts to rock. An undercurrent of status quo dissatisfaction starts to surface.

The movement out of inappropriate stability may come from a number of sources. An upper management executive may develop a broader vision of the purpose of the business. As with the U.S. automotive industry, foreign competitive pressures may reduce the viability of the old organization and force introspective examination. Whatever the reason, the transition from stage 1 to stage 2 occurs when the glowing embers of dissatisfaction burst into flame.

Stage 2: Conscious Incompetence

Stage 2 is the most critical stage of the quality process. Stage 2 must be moved through in the fastest possible manner. The universal and predominant trait of stage 2 is confusion. Dissatisfaction shatters the organizational stability. From somewhere, usually from up above, comes an autocratic mandate for quality improvement. Old behaviors are no longer acceptable. There is little or no understanding among the majority of organization members of the nature of new roles. The old inappropriate vision is dead or terminally dying, but no new vision has emerged as a shared vision. People develop an intuitive sense that they must behave differently. They panic and sense crisis. They react to the directive of "improve quality" but without understanding the process of quality improvement. They react, but in many different ways and directions.

The turmoil and confusion incite conflict. More open individuals change willingly to new behaviors. Those individuals more resistant to change dig in and try to maintain old behaviors. They suffer. The more they dig in the more inappropriate their behavior becomes.

The confusion, conflict, and inappropriate roles of stage 2 yield a high turnover rate and seemingly continual role changing. Some of the turnover is good for the organization. Those individuals lacking vision, flexibility, and skills, feel the greatest dissatisfaction. They either leave the organization or are highly visible for corrective coaching, re-assignment, or out-placement. The organization must plan to devote resources to retraining and coaching. Both the old employees with inappropriate behaviors and new employees hired to fill vacated positions will need training.

In stage 2 the quality department enters into a state of turmoil and confusion. More resources are quickly devoted to inspecting quality. This effort adds to the overall organizational conflict, increases the cost of quality, and, in general, is not effective. Quality department employees unjustly bear the brunt of criticism for the poor quality yet have no means for quality improvement. Eventually it becomes evident that if quality is to improve action must be taken to improve the processes of production. Again, the department that has historically held a policing function has no means for implementation. Neither the department nor its technology is viewed as integral to the production process. Without good interaction behaviors, deep departmental foxholes develop.

The initial movement from lot acceptance to SPC occurs in stage 2. These two schools of thought can dig foxholes within the quality department. Advocates of each school group together to support their technology and definition of role. Again, changes in roles and technology are paramount for movement through the stage and the process. These changes mandate Adult reconciliation of differences and openness.

As the organization moves through stage 2, two modes of quality improvement emerge. The lot acceptance system continues to be the main method of insuring quality to the customer. At the same time statistical process control techniques improve the quality of process and product. SPC remains a tool of the quality department until the last part of stage 2. Production departments do not take ownership or effectively use SPC except under the close direction of the quality department. Even this limited use of SPC usually only occurs after it has been used to solve problems significant to the production department.

Along with the organizational wide confusion comes an honest perception of all that must be done. When all that must be done is actually perceived, the realization sends shock waves through the organization. Tasks far outnumber the available resources. These tasks are the correction of *root causes* of poor quality predominant during stage 1. These *root causes* encompass all three behavior bases: people, information, and things. Correction of the *root causes* requires more and improved training of people. It involves new improved information systems and behaviors. It involves upgrading previously neglected equipment and processes. All these corrections stretch organizational resources, thus prioritization becomes extremely important. The organization wants to gain the most productive change in the shortest time with available resources.

The cost of quality trend of stage 2 is opposite long-term expectation and what might be expected by the individual not cognizant of the process. Cost of quality starts to rise at the beginning of stage 2 and continues to rise throughout the stage. At the end of the stage the cost of quality has flattened out at a higher level. A trend of real reduction in the cost of quality indicates the end of stage 2.

This rise in the cost of quality is probably the greatest hurdle to quality improvement. Without an understanding of the process the snapshot perception is that the actions are producing negative results. The temptation is to abandon the process and return to the old familiar systems of managing. This reaction is typical of the conscious incompetent stage of growth. Now vision, effective coaching, and a constancy of purpose and action are of extreme importance.

The effective leadership pattern for stage 2 is the wise autocrat. I use the word autocrat meaning a predominance of "telling" behavior in the Hersey model sense. Telling behavior is not dogmatic demeanor but firm, fair, effective, and detailed instruction. Telling is the leadership style of choice, not default. The wise autocrat leader realizes that the telling behavior is most familiar to those being led and will be most effective in driving the process. At this time selling and participating leadership will not be as effective. At the same time the wise autocrat realizes that to traverse the process those being led must grow to selling behavior, then participative behavior, and eventually, where appropriate, to delegating behavior. Micro leadership of stage 2 is effective telling behavior. The macro mode of leadership is driving the growth in organizational leadership through the maturity stages.

Stage 3: Conscious Competence

Stage 3 starts with the downward turn in the cost of quality. Also appearing at the start of stage 3 is initial re-stabilization, initial development of a shared vision by both management and workers, an awareness of the inter-relatedness of systems, establishment of quality as an organizational objective, emphasis on in-process quality, establishment of roles in line with skills and behaviors, training to provide the full complement of skills necessary for achievement, a focus on defining the needs of the customer, a focus on preventative maintenance, and continued upgrade of equipment and processes.

Stage 3 can be characterized as the first concerted organizational movement toward the vision. Stage 3 is an exciting time for those with vision of the macro process. Formal organizations move away from over-control as a management technique. Archaic systems fall like raindrops. The "can't do" approach diminishes. The confusion and dejection of stage 2 shifts to enthusiasm and a "can do" attitude. The organization becomes consciously competent in the tools of quality improvement. Team interaction becomes reality. People step out of their foxholes. Many ancient chronic problems are resolved. People do tasks that were previously thought impossible. As improvement continues through the stage, a larger group of people at all levels "buy-in" to the role of statistical process control technology as a business strategy. Statistical techniques become an organization tool and value. The languages of SPC and team management become part of the business language.

Training continues to be one of the major focuses of stage 3. As more and more individuals buy in, the demands for behavior improvement mushroom. Training covers all three major categories of behaviors. Emerging teams highlight the need for improved people behavior.

The metamorphosis of the organizational information systems during stage 3 are dramatic and an outstanding characteristic. Entering stage 3, the information system may be either overly formal or nonexistent. Neither provide the customer with the information necessary to function effectively. In stage 3 the information system moves toward directness, conciseness, and customer orientation.

As the organization moves through stage 3, the rate of reduction of quality costs accelerates. Stage 3 ends by definition when the cost of quality goes below the historic level. At this point the success of the program makes the process broadly driven internally. The process has reached "Critical Mass." Now only crisis can change the trends of the process.

Stage 4: Unconscious Competence

Stage 4 starts with continuing rapid reduction in the cost of quality. All the systems of stage 3 have grown toward maturity.

The vision of excellence is well-communicated throughout the organization. Organizational and individual needs and behaviors are synchronized. Team management becomes a reality. Communications are open and frank horizontally and vertically. The rapidity of task accomplishment is astonishing.

A customer orientation and systems approach permeate stage 4. The concept of the internal customer is well understood. The focus is on synthesis of meeting customer, employee, and stockholder needs. Dynamic systems simplify the once-thought complex tasks. These systems are not overly burdened with detail. Static situations that are out of the control of the system customer are eliminated. The controllable significant 20 percent of possible control parameters are well-defined and communicated. Teams continuously review and verify continued significance of control systems. Changes are made as required by the dynamic nature of equipment and processes.

In stage 4 change becomes the norm. It is expected and continuously desired. This mentality is supported by growth in the maturity of the existing employees and leadership. An open attitude toward change is prerequisite for hiring.

Hiring becomes extremely selective. Candidates are evaluated and assigned based on effective behavior. They are fully oriented to organizational vision, information systems, statistical techniques and language, and team interaction before taking on responsibility for their assignment. Their role is well-communicated and understanding of role is verified prior to active assignment. They are partnered into actual operations by another individual in a parallel position. Because of this orientation and the synchronization of the needs of the individual and the organization, and because the role of the individual is well-defined and matched to gratifying behavior, the turnover rate drops drastically.

In stage 4, in-process acceptance systems replace audit methods as the prime method of quality verification. Audit methods are used only as verification of in-process procedures. The quality function becomes deployed to the teams responsible for the sub-processes. The after-the-fact quality department shrinks in size. The remaining organization focuses on mentoring in the systems of in-process quality with a small contingent involved with the audit function.

In this stage the quality focus is on obtaining maximum quality from existing systems. About halfway through the stage, diminishing returns on investment and effort become evident. Cost of quality continues to drop but at an increasingly slower rate.

Concern may develop toward the end of the stage that there is not much to be gained through continued effort toward quality improvement. If the organization is the industry leader and enjoys a true competitive advantage a false sense of security may creep in. The organization that fully understands the process will not let this happen, and neither will the organization that does not enjoy the leadership position. Either vision or competitive pressure will drive the organization in late stage 4 to examine again the societal impact of quality improvement. They will find that even though processes are controlled and appear to meet requirements there is a competitive advantage to assessing the cost of quality of the remaining variation in the processes. The consumer will select a product or service based on long-term ability of the product or service to meet needs. The competitive advantage becomes the ability to meet those needs over an extended period and the ability to do this with the least drain on the resources of society. This is the basis of the Taguchi approach. This pattern of thinking signals transition into stage 5.

Stage 5: Integrated Competence

Stage 5 is a state of continuous improvement in a constantly changing environment. Now the shared vision and the process for achievement are fully understood throughout the organization. The quality process is a common denominator throughout the organization. Morale is high. Organizational wide innovation is paramount because what must be done to further improve quality and competitive position has not been done before. There is a strong disdain for limiting rubrics. The vision of what can be and the successes of the past drive toward further excellence.

The focus of the quality effort is no longer on controlling existing processes. This is a given. The focus is on the innovative design of the product and the process to reduce normal variation and minimize the range of process capability.

Further Comments on the Process

The five stages of the process are summarized in the graph on the following page. I find that I continue to add characteristics of the stages to the figure as they become evident to me in examining organizational movement. I urge the reader to do likewise. Ideally the reader, with a different basis for perception, will be able to identify characteristics highly relevant to him/her and others that have eluded me.

I also want to comment further on categorizing the stage of an organization. It would be deceptive to state that even the mature organization falls

Figure 55

The Excellence Process

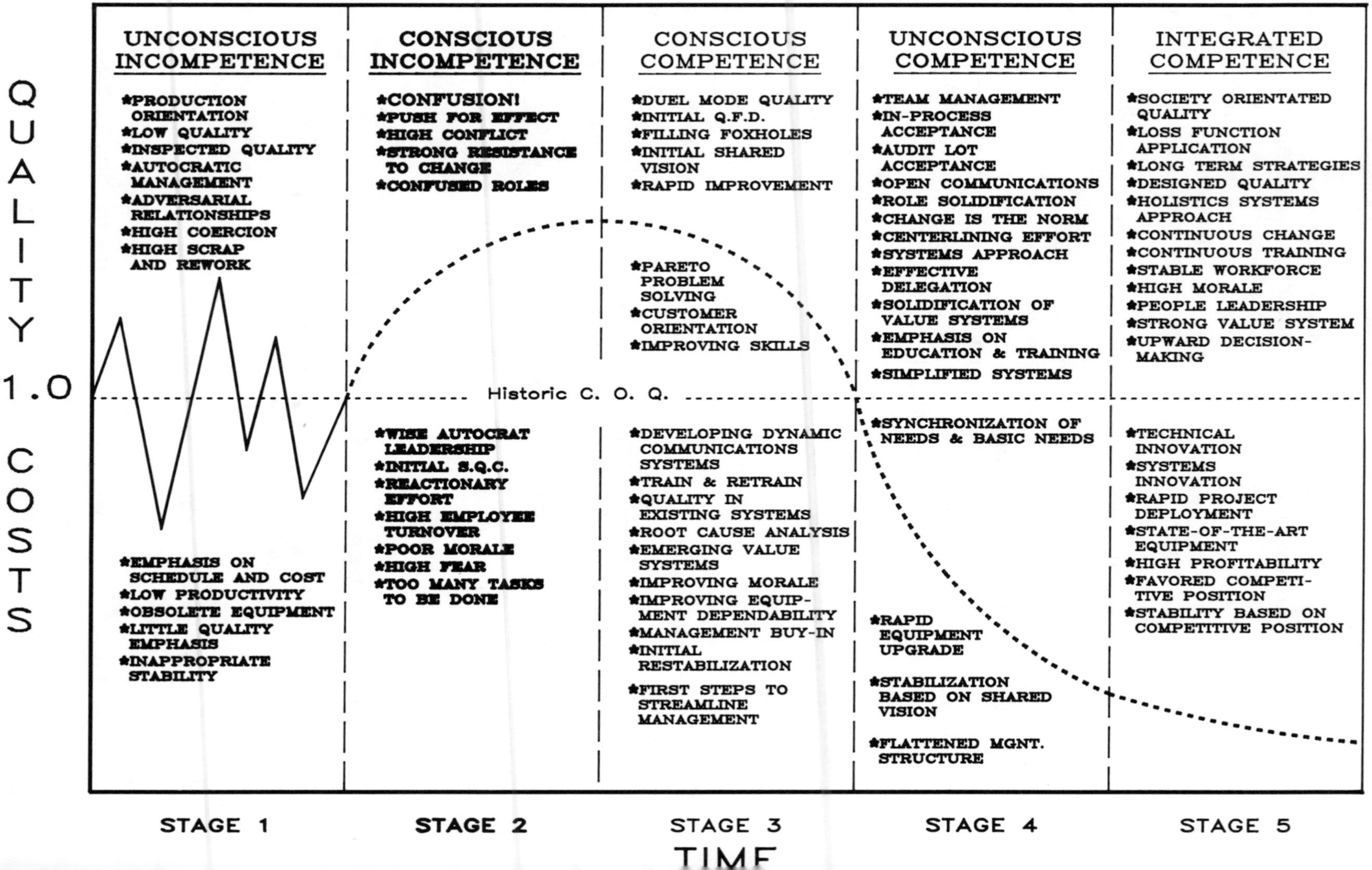
QUALITY
1.0
COSTS
UNCONSCIOUS INCOMPETENCE
*PRODUCTION ORIENTATION
*LOW QUALITY
*INSPECTED QUALITY
*AUTOCRATIC MANAGEMENT
*ADVERSARIAL RELATIONSHIPS
*HIGH COERCION
*HIGH SCRAP AND REWORK
*EMPHASIS ON SCHEDULE AND COST
*LOW PRODUCTIVITY
*OBSOLETE EQUIPMENT
*LITTLE QUALITY EMPHASIS
*INAPPROPRIATE STABILITY
CONSCIOUS INCOMPETENCE
*CONFUSION!
*PUSH FOR EFFECT
*HIGH CONFLICT
*STRONG RESISTANCE TO CHANGE
*CONFUSED ROLES
*WISE AUTOCRAT LEADERSHIP
*INITIAL S.Q.C.
*REACTIONARY EFFORT
*HIGH EMPLOYEE TURNOVER
*POOR MORALE
*HIGH FEAR
*TOO MANY TASKS TO BE DONE
CONSCIOUS COMPETENCE
*DUEL MODE QUALITY
*INITIAL Q.F.D.
*FILLING FOXHOLES
*INITIAL SHARED VISION
*RAPID IMPROVEMENT
*PARETO PROBLEM SOLVING
*CUSTOMER ORIENTATION
*IMPROVING SKILLS
*DEVELOPING DYNAMIC COMMUNICATIONS SYSTEMS
*TRAIN & RETRAIN
*QUALITY IN EXISTING SYSTEMS
*ROOT CAUSE ANALYSIS
*EMERGING VALUE SYSTEMS
*IMPROVING MORALE
*IMPROVING EQUIPMENT DEPENDABILITY
*MANAGEMENT BUY-IN
*INITIAL RESTABILIZATION
*FIRST STEPS TO STREAMLINE MANAGEMENT
UNCONSCIOUS COMPETENCE
*TEAM MANAGEMENT
*IN-PROCESS ACCEPTANCE
*AUDIT LOT ACCEPTANCE
*OPEN COMMUNICATIONS
*ROLE SOLIDIFICATION
*CHANGE IS THE NORM
*CENTERLINING EFFORT
*SYSTEMS APPROACH
*EFFECTIVE DELEGATION
*SOLIDIFICATION OF VALUE SYSTEMS
*EMPHASIS ON EDUCATION & TRAINING
*SIMPLIFIED SYSTEMS
*SYNCHRONIZATION OF NEEDS & BASIC NEEDS
*RAPID EQUIPMENT UPGRADE
*STABILIZATION BASED ON SHARED VISION
*FLATTENED MGNT. STRUCTURE
INTEGRATED COMPETENCE
*SOCIETY ORIENTATED QUALITY
*LOSS FUNCTION APPLICATION
*LONG TERM STRATEGIES
*DESIGNED QUALITY
*HOLISTICS SYSTEMS APPROACH
*CONTINUOUS CHANGE
*CONTINUOUS TRAINING
*STABLE WORKFORCE
*HIGH MORALE
*PEOPLE LEADERSHIP
*STRONG VALUE SYSTEM
*UPWARD DECISION-MAKING
*TECHNICAL INNOVATION
*SYSTEMS INNOVATION
*RAPID PROJECT DEPLOYMENT
*STATE-OF-THE-ART EQUIPMENT
*HIGH PROFITABILITY
*FAVORED COMPETITIVE POSITION
*STABILITY BASED ON COMPETITIVE POSITION
Historic C. O. Q.
STAGE 1
STAGE 2
STAGE 3
STAGE 4
STAGE 5
TIME

fully within one category. Our Western minds would like to simplify the system in this Aristotelian manner but reality does not fit such categorization.

Think of the macro quality process as being composed of a multitude of micro processes with the same characteristics and stages. Each individual, each department, each plant, each team, is involved in their own micro quality process. As the maturity of the individual grows, so grows the micro process and so grows the macro process. We can look at the macro process and attempt to define a mean stage of all the micro processes. Some action plans for growth can be addressed at the mean stage effectively. Some action plans must be addressed at a specific micro process. The requirements for growth through each micro process vary. Sometimes a growth requirement is broad enough to warrant action addressing one growth need for much of the organization. Other times the growth need critical to growth of the organization is limited to one individual or team.

Getting even more specific, think of the task of the school teacher charged with maximizing the reading skills of a class of 30 students. The effectiveness of the program is based on a maximum group skill increase. The students' skill levels are widely varied. The teacher must be cognizant of the mean skill level of the group and design some activities for the whole group. Other separate activities are needed to address specific needs of slow learners. Again, different activities effectively challenge the gifted. Often activities specific to one group are not applicable to the other group.

How big is a group? Abilities exist across a continuum. Similarity, practicality, and resources define the effective definition of a group. Practical maximization of growth, with a perception of reality, demands the micro learning processes of each group be addressed specifically. To address the mean level of the continuum denies reality and limits effectiveness.

When we attempt to address quality growth through only generic classes in statistics, interaction, or technology we address only what we perceive to be the mean stage of development. Analyzing the current stages of development and defining the critical and necessary actions at each stage of the macro and micro processes is much of the role of the mentor of excellence.

Promoting Continued Synthesis 21

If you disagree with all that you have read I have failed in achieving one of my major purposes. I return you to your world of rubrics. If you *agree* with all that I have said again I have failed. You are a slave of the thoughts of others. I have not well-communicated a process for continuous quality improvement. I have not developed a dissatisfaction with the status quo, nor have I motivated the reader to think for himself/herself. I apologize and hope time, events, and others will be more successful.

The world you experience and your perceptions are not the same as mine. If you find some truth in what you have read but question, ponder, and even doubt some of it, then I am well on the way to accomplishing my purposes. As important as defining a process for quality improvement and achieving excellence is conveying the fundamental concepts of thinking and stimulating further original thought and synthesis. I hope the reader will continue to struggle with the processes of individual growth, organizational growth, societal growth, and the quest for quality. It is only through struggle that we reach new syntheses.

The quest for growth requires willingness to occasionally step out of a prescribed role and pose the original thought. It takes a willingness to not look at others for what they do but for how they think. It takes a willingness to sometimes stand alone. Abraham Maslow struggled with graduate programs in institutions of higher learning, programs that mandated that progressive thought presented in dissertations required references. His conclusion and the root of his struggle: there are no references for truly original thought.

Much of what I have presented is based upon the thoughts and works of others and a synthesis of their thinking. I believe a very small amount of this book represents original thought. In developing the overall synthesis I found gaps—areas where I could find no previous explanations or theories. The gaps I saw were based on my experiences and perceptions. I do not submit that this work is complete. Other people will see other gaps and omissions.

I hope I have stimulated the reader to be open minded, open to new perceptions, new thoughts, new relationships, and new technology. When minds become rutted, mental death begins. What we will perceive tomorrow is not what we perceived yesterday or today. If we believe tomorrow's perceptions will be identical then our receptiveness has been limited. If we believe an individual is just like someone else our perception is limited. If we believe one process is just like another then our perception is limited. We have allowed our minds to be selective. We chose only to see patterns and traits we wanted to see. We have chosen to not see the differences.

When we keep our perception open and keep an open mind, many divergent and seemingly inconsistent observations enter our minds. Our tendency is to judge based on these perceptions immediately and file them away as either valid or invalid. Again, we are locked into an "A/not A" thought process. We have made a judgment of truth or non-truth. In reality the degree of truth in perceptions is often a continuum. There is a level of validity in each observation.

Synthesis occurs when we do not prejudge our perceptions but hold them on file. As we gain more information through perception the valid elements of all the perceptions synthesize together to form a concept perhaps totally different from each of the individual perceptions. The synthesis incorporates the valid points of the individual perceptions. If the synthesis does not pull together, the wise judgment is a synthesis has not been achieved. Lack of synthesis does not connote lack of validity. At this point the valid conclusion is "I don't know!" When the parts do not fit together we cannot logically say that the individual parts are invalid. Such a conclusion is a trap of rubricized judgment.

There probably is a stage 6, and a stage 7, and even more stages, to the quality process. We just have not defined the nature of these stages. To say that the process ends at stage 5 is to deny the continuous growth of mankind toward excellence. Empirical observation leads to the conclusion that throughout recorded history mankind has continuously moved toward further refinement. Small new innovations lead to major shifts in societies. What basis is there for saying that stage 5 is the termination of the quality process? Termination denies the continuous nature of quality improvement and the quest for excellence. It establishes a termination point only because we look for a finite conclusion. Given the rate of change and growth of society we can only associate an end to the growth process with an end to civilizations.

There will be new approaches to quality improvement. There will be new technology. Some of it may be built upon the works of the past. Some of it may be radical departure from tradition. As I said in the introduction, the rate of change in our society is accelerating so fast that within a lifetime we can expect to see many radical shifts in technology and in thinking. We can no longer afford to implement new thought and new technology by exporting to a developing society. We must gain the wisdom and flexibility to integrate the radical new development into existing society without great disturbance, and certainly without the death of the society. Continuous change will be the new norm.

Change in society starts with the individuals. Society is the composite personality of the individuals. For change to be palatable each individual must cease to base self-value on tangibles. Today's external tangibles of self-worth will not be there tomorrow. The new basis of self-worth is individual growth—growth to achieve internal self-value. Such a movement can only happen if we seek continuous growth for ourselves and for others; only if we mentor for an open, inquisitive mind.

I once had a teacher who said that we never learn when we are speaking. We only learn when we listen and are otherwise open to converting sensory observations into perceptions. I believe this concept is one of the wisest and most valid concepts of my education.

As I conclude this book and my dissertation I again will return to listening. I am sure that a year from now, through listening, I will have modified many of my concepts. I hope I, and others, will have reached an even higher synthesis.

My hope for my children and their children and for mankind is that a synthesized global society will emerge to continue the battle against entropy. The global society will continue to refine and develop the quality of living for mankind. In actuality society can do nothing, for any society is only a composite of the constituting individuals. No one can be a mentor to society. A mentor must guide individuals either individually or collectively. Learning and growth are processes of each individual. The growth of society will only happen through growth of the individuals that compose society. Each of us is responsible, at least, for the continuing growth of one individual—ourself.

Albrecht, Karl. *Brain Power: Learning to Improve Your Thinking Skills.* New York: Prentice Hall Press, 1987.

ASQC Statistics Division. *Glossary and Tables for Statistical Quality Control,* 2d ed. Milwaukee: American Society for Quality Control, 1983.

AT&T. *Statistical Quality Control Handbook,* 2d ed. Indianapolis: Western Electric Company, 1958.

Bell, Gerald. Author's personal class notes. Chapel Hill, N.C.: Graduate School of Business Administration, University of North Carolina, 1971.

Bell, Gerald. *The Achievers.* Chapel Hill, N.C.: Preston-Hill, Inc., 1973.

Bennis, Warren. "You can learn to be a leader." *For Members Only,* American Express, September 1985.

Berne, Eric. *Games People Play.* New York: Random House, 1962.

Blake, Robert R. and Jane S. Mouton. *The Managerial Grid.* Houston: Gulf Publishing Co., 1985.

Blanchard, Kenneth, and Spencer Johnson. *The One Minute Manager.* New York: William Morrow and Company, Inc., 1982.

Bolles, Richard N. *What Color Is Your Parachute?* Berkeley: Ten Speed Press, 1981.

Burke, James. *Connections.* Boston: Little, Brown and Company, 1978.

Byrne, Diane M., and Shin Taguchi. "The Taguchi approach to parameter design." *Quality Progress,* December 1987: 19.

Continuing Process Control and Process Capability Improvement. Statistical Methods Office, Operations Support Staff, Detroit: Ford Motor Company, December 1984.

Control Chart Method of Controlling Quality During Production. New York: American Standards Association, 1942.

Deming, W. Edwards. *Quality, Productivity, and Competitive Position.* Cambridge: Massachusetts Institute of Technology Center for Advanced Engineering, 1982.

Durand, Will. "Immanuel Kant and German idealism." In *The Story of Philosophy.* New York: Pocket Books, 1961.

Flory, C.D. (ed.), and the staff of Rorher, Hibler, & Replogle. *Managers for Tomorrow,* 3d ed. New York: The New American Library, Inc., 1967.

Freese, Frank. *Elementary Forest Sampling.* Washington, D.C.: U.S. Department of Agriculture, Forest Service; Agriculture Handbook No. 232. U.S. Government Printing Office, 1962.

Gelman, David, Nikkifinke Greenberg, and Jeff Copeland. "The megatrends man." *Newsweek,* September 23, 1985: 58.

Grant, Eugene L., and Richard S. Leavenworth. *Statistical Quality Control,* 5th ed. New York: McGraw-Hill Book Company, 1980.

Guaspari, John. *I Know It When I See It: A Modern Fable About Quality.* New York: Anacom, a division of American Management Association, 1985.

Harris. Thomas A. *I'm OK—You're OK, a Practical Guide to Transactional Analysis.* New York: Harper & Row, 1969.

Hayes, Glenn E. "5 quality and productivity challenges for management." *Quality Progress,* October 1985: 42–46.

Hersey, Paul. *The Situational Leader—The Other 59 Minutes* (audio cassettes). Chicago: Nightingale-Conant Corp., 1985.

Ishikawa, Kaoru. *What Is Total Quality Control? The Japanese Way.* Englewood Cliffs, N.J.: Prentice-Hall, Inc., 1985.

Jensen, Christian. *Supervisory Training Workshop Handbook.* Ridgefield, Conn.: The Dan Group, 1986.

Juran, J.M., Frank M. Gryna, and R.S. Bingham Jr. *Quality Control Handbook,* 3d ed. New York: McGraw-Hill Book Company, 1974.

Kackar, Raghu N. "Off-line quality control, parameter design, and the Taguchi method." *Journal of Quality Technology.* October 1985: 176.

Kohn, Alfie. "It's hard to get left out of a pair." *Psychology Today,* October 1987: 53.

Krech, David, and Richard S. Crutchfield. *Elements of Psychology.* New York: Alfred A. Knopf, 1958.

Likert, Rensis. *The Human Organization.* New York: McGraw-Hill Book Company, 1967.

Lydall Executive Leadership Workshop (a seminar textbook). Ridgefield, Conn.: The Dan Group, 1985.

Maslow, Abraham H. *Motivitation and Personality.* New York: Harper and Row, 1954.

McGregor, Douglas. *The Human Side of Enterprise.* New York: McGraw-Hill, 1960.

Naisbitt, John. *Megatrends.* New York: Warner Books, 1984.

Naisbitt, John and P. Aburdene. *Re-inventing the Corporation.* New York: Warner Books, 1985.

Ortega y Gasset, Jose. *The Revolt of the Masses*. New York: W.W. Norton & Company, Inc., 1960.

Peters, Thomas J., and Robert H. Waterman. *In Search of Excellence— Lessons from America's Best-Run Companies*. New York: Harper & Row, 1982.

Pujol, John. "How does Johnny learn to use new technology." *Southern Pulp & Paper,* May 1986: 23.

Shainin, Dorian. *How to Solve Tough Quality Problems* (seminar text and notes). Covington, Tenn.: Dorian Shainin, 1983.

Sheehy, Gail. *Passages: Predictable Crises in Adult Life*. New York: E.P. Dutton & Co., 1976.

Sullivan, L.P. "The seven stages in company-wide quality control." *Quality Progress,* May 1986: 77.

Taguchi, Genichi. *Introduction to Quality Engineering, Designing Quality into Products and Processes*. Hong Kong: Asian Productivity Organization, 1986.

Trotter, Robert J. "The mystery of mastery." *Psychology Today,* July 1986: 32.

Index

Stockholder, 43, fig. 13, 42
Structure, 180
Sub-routine, 106
Sullivan, L. P., 3
Superior-subordinate pattern. See Vertical
    pattern
Supervising, 76, fig. 18, 75
Supplier
    definition, 6
    partnering, 173
Synthesized solutions, 187
Synthesizing, 77, fig. 19, 77
    promotion, 207
System, 73
System Process Flow, fig. 25, 109

TA. See Transactional Analysis
Taguchi, Genichi, 158
    product and process design, 172
Taguchi loss function, 158, fig. 47, 159
    curve, 140, fig. 44, 140
Taking instructions, 76, fig. 18, 75
Taoism, 14
Target, 138
Task
    education and training, 87
    quality, 149, 151, fig. 46, 153
Task behavior, 77, fig. 20, 78
    assessment, 82, fig. 23, 83
Taylor, Frederick, 70
Team
    contributors, 84
    interaction, 29
    organization, 182, fig. 50, 183
    roles, 192
Technology, 88
    quality, 149
    specialization and pocketing, 151
Telling, 43, 79, figs. 14, 44; 21, 79
    conscious incompetence, 200
Tending, 78, fig. 20, 78
Termination, 208
Test, 130
Thing behavior, 77, fig. 20, 78
    assessment, 82, fig. 23, 83
    quality, 149, 150
    system, 73
Things, 29, fig. 7, 30
    people and positions, 73
    quality, 149
Third dimension, 38, fig. 12, 39
Third Way, 70
Third World, 179
Threat, 71
3-Dimensional Behavior Model, fig. 12, 39
Three Management Styles, fig. 10, 35
Time, 129
    factor, 132
Tolman, E. C.
    introduction, xxiii
Tone-of-voice, 59
Total population, 127
Tracking, 54
Training, 87
    conscious incompetence, 199

cost of quality, 157
    specifics, 91
Transaction, 52, fig. 16, 53
Transactional Analysis, or TA
    conflict, 70
    organization, 177
    psychological system, 49, fig. 15, 51
Transmitter, 96
Trial close, 98
Trust
    delegation, 46
    partnering, 173
    policy, 166
    unconscious incompetence, 198
Truth
    macro process, 7, fig. 2, 7
    policy, 166
    vision, 16
Turnover rate, 202
Two Measures of Any Variable Data, fig.
    40, 134

U chart, 118
Unconscious competent, 202, fig. 55, 204
    definition, 10, fig. 3, 11
Unconscious incompetent, 198, fig. 55, 204
    definition, 10, fig. 3, 11
    reflecting, 59
    training, 92
Underground information sources, 101
Understanding, 49
United States, 3

Values, 46
    discipline, 170
    policy, 174
    purpose, 191, fig. 54, 195
Value systems, 60
    policy, 166
Valuing, 61
    conflict, 70
Variation, 125
    sources, 126
    X-Y chart, 116
Variety, 182
Vertical pattern, or superior subordinate
    pattern
    quality, 27
Vision, 16
    conscious competence, 201
    definition, 9
    discipline, 170
    organizations, 183
    policy, 165
    purpose, 192, fig. 54, 195
Visual perception, 98

West, Gerald
    acknowledgment, xxii
    organizations, 187
What, 58